COMPUTER SYSTEM ARCHITECTURE

COMPUTER SYSTEM ARCHITECTURE

Rajneesh Narayan

CENTRUM PRESS
NEW DELHI-110002 (INDIA)

CENTRUM PRESS
H.O.: 4360/4, Ansari Road, Daryaganj,
New Delhi-110002 (India)
Tel: 23278000, 23261597, 23255577, 23286875
B.O.: No. 1015, Ist Main Road, BSK IIIrd Stage,
IIIrd Phase, IIIrd Block, Bangalore-560085 (INDIA)
Tel: 080-41723429
Email: centrumpress@gmail.com
Visit us at: www.centrumpress.com

Computer System Architecture

First Edition, 2010

ISBN 978-93-80540-51-1

PRINTED IN INDIA

Printed at Balaji Offset, Delhi.

Contents

Preface

In computer science, computer architecture is the conceptual design and fundamental operational structure of a computer system. It is a blueprint and functional description of requirements and design implementations for the various parts of a computer, focusing largely on the way by which the central processing unit (CPU) performs internally and accesses addresses in memory. It may also be defined as the science and art of selecting and interconnecting hardware components to create computers that meet functional, performance and cost goals.

The term "architecture" in computer literature can be traced to the work of Lyle R. Johnson and Frederick P. Brooks, Jr., members in 1959 of the Machine Organization department in IBM's main research center. Johnson had the opportunity to write a proprietary research communication about Stretch, an IBM-developed supercomputer for Los Alamos Scientific Laboratory. In attempting to characterize his chosen level of detail for discussing the luxuriously embellished computer, he noted that his description of formats, instruction types, hardware parameters, and speed enhancements was at the level of "system architecture" – a term that seemed more useful than "machine organization." Subsequently, Brooks, one of the Stretch designers, started Chapter 2 of a book (Planning a Computer System: Project Stretch, ed. W. Buchholz, 1962) by writing, "Computer architecture, like other architecture, is the art of determining the needs of the user of a structure and then designing to meet those needs as effectively as possible within economic and technological constraints." Brooks went on to play a major role in the development of the IBM System/360 line of computers, where "architecture" gained currency as a noun with the definition "what the user needs to know." Later the computer world would employ the term in many less-explicit ways.

The first mention of the term *architecture* in the referred computer literature is in a 1964 article describing the IBM System/360. The article defines architecture as the set of "attributes of a system as seen by the programmer, i.e., the conceptual structure and functional behaviour, as distinct from the organization of the data flow and controls, the logical design, and the physical implementation." In the definition, the *programmer* perspective of the computer's functional behaviour is key. The conceptual structure part of an architecture description makes the functional behaviour comprehensible, and extrapolatable to a range of Use cases. Only later on did 'internals' such as "the way by which the CPU performs internally and accesses addresses in memory," mentioned above, slip into the definition of computer architecture.

Objective is writing this book is to explain the Computer Architecture's concepts in an easy-to-understand language. It is observed that most of the books available in the market do not cover the complete contents of the topic in detail.

— *Rajneesh Narayan*

1

Introduction

Computer Systems Architecture

The discipline that defines the conceptual structure and functional behaviour of a computer system. It is analogous to the architecture of a building, determining the overall organization, the attributes of the component parts, and how these parts are combined. It is related to, but different from, computer implementation. Architecture consists of those characteristics which affect the design and development of software programs, whereas implementation focuses on those characteristics which determine the relative cost and performance of the system. The architect's main goal has long been to produce a computer that is as fast as possible, within a given set of cost constraints. Over the years, other goals have been added, such as making it easier to run multiple programs concurrently or improving the performance of programs written in higher-level languages.

A computer system consists of four major components: storage, processor, peripherals, and input/output (communication). The storage system is used to keep data and programs; the processor is the unit that controls the operation of the system and carries out various computations; the peripheral devices are used to communicate with the outside world; and the input/output system allows the previous components to communicate with one another.

Storage

The storage or memory of a computer system holds the data that the computer will process and the instructions that indicate what processing is to be done. In a digital computer, these are stored in a form known as binary, which means that each datum or instruction is represented by a series of bits. Bits are conceptually combined into larger units called bytes (usually 8 bits each) and words (usually 8 to 64 bits each). A computer will generally have several different kinds of storage devices, each organized to hold one or more words of data. These types include registers, main memory, and secondary or auxiliary storage.

Registers are the fastest and most costly storage units in a computer. Normally contained within the processing unit, registers hold data that are involved with the computation currently being performed.

Main memory holds the data to be processed and the instructions that specify what processing is to be done. A major goal of the computer architect is to increase the effective speed and size of a memory system without incurring a large cost penalty. Two prevalent techniques for increasing effective speed are interleaving and caching, while virtual memory is a popular way to increase the effective size. Interleaving involves the use of two or more independent memory systems, combined in a way that makes them appear to be a single, faster system. With caching, a small, fast memory system contains the most frequently used words from a slower, larger main memory.

Virtual memory is a technique whereby the programmer is given the illusion of a very large main memory, when in fact it has only a modest size. This is achieved by placing the contents of the large, "virtual" memory on a large but slow auxiliary storage device, and bringing portions of it into main memory, as required by the programs, in a way that is transparent to the programmer.

Auxiliary memory (sometimes called secondary storage) is the slowest, lowest-cost, and highest-capacity computer storage area. Programs and data are kept in auxiliary memory when not in immediate use, so that auxiliary memory is essentially a long-term storage medium. There are two basic types of secondary storage: sequential and direct-access. Sequential-access secondary storage devices, of which magnetic tape is the most common, permit data to be accessed in a linear sequence. A direct-access device is one whose data may be accessed in any order. Disks and drums are the most commonly encountered devices of this type.

Memory mapping is one of the most important aspects of modern computer memory designs. In order to understand its function, the concept of an address space must be considered. When a program resides in a computer's main memory, there is a set of memory cells assigned to the program and its data. This is known as the program's logical address space. The computer's physical address space is the set of memory cells actually contained in the main memory. Memory mapping is simply the method by which the computer translates between the computer's logical and physical address spaces. The most straightforward mapping scheme involves use of a bias register. Assignment of a different bias value to each program in memory enables the programs to coexist without interference.

Another strategy for mapping is known as paging. This technique involves dividing both logical and physical address spaces into equal-sized blocks called pages. Mapping is achieved by means of a page map, which can be thought of as a series of bias registers.

Processing

A computer's processor (processing unit) consists of a control unit, which directs the operation of the system, and an arithmetic and logic unit, which performs computational operations. The design of a processing unit involves selection of a register set, communication paths between these registers, and a means of directing and controlling how these operate. Normally, a processor is directed by a program, which consists of a series of instructions that are kept in main memory.

Although the process of decoding and executing instructions is often carried out by logic circuitry, the complexity of instruction sets can lead to very large and cumbersome circuits for this purpose. To alleviate this problem, a technique known as microprogramming was developed. With microprogramming, each instruction is actually a macrocommand that is carried out by a microprogram, written in a microinstruction language. The microinstructions are very simple, directing data to flow between registers, memories, and arithmetic units.

It should be noted that microprogramming has nothing to do with microprocessors. A microprocessor is a processor implemented through a single, highly integrated circuit.

Peripherals and Communication

A typical computer system includes a variety of peripheral devices such as printers, keyboards, and displays. These devices translate electronic signals into mechanical motion or light (or vice versa) so as to communicate with people.

There are two common approaches for connecting peripherals and secondary storage devices to the rest of the computer: The channel and the bus. A channel is essentially a wire or group of wires between a peripheral device and a memory device. A multiplexed channel allows several devices to be connected to the same wire. A bus is a form of multiplexed channel that can be shared by a large number of devices. The overhead of sharing many devices means that the bus has lower peak performance than a channel; but for a system with many peripherals, the bus is more economical than a large number of channels.

A computer controls the flow of data across buses or channels by means of special instructions and other mechanisms. The simplest scheme is known as program-controlled input/output (I/O). Direct memory access I/O is a technique by which the computer signals the device to transmit a block of data, and the data are transmitted directly to memory, without the processor needing to wait.

Interrupts are a form of signal by which a peripheral device notifies a processor that it has completed transmitting data. This is very helpful in a direct memory access scheme, for the processor cannot always predict in advance how long it will take to transmit a block of data. Architects often design elaborate interrupt schemes to simplify the situation where several peripherals are active simultaneously.

Digital Computer

A device that processes numerical information; more generally, any device that manipulates symbolic information according to specified computational procedures. The term digital computer—or simply, computer—embraces calculators, computer workstations, control computers (controllers) for applications such as domestic appliances and industrial processes, data-processing systems, microcomputers, microcontrollers, multiprocessors, parallel computers, personal computers, network servers, and supercomputers.

A digital computer is an electronic computing machine that uses the binary digits (bits) 0 and 1 to represent all forms of information internally in digital form. Every computer has a set of instructions that define the basic functions it can perform. Sequences of these instructions constitute machine-language programs that can be stored in the computer and used to tailor it to an essentially unlimited number of specialized applications. Calculators are small computers specialized for mathematical computations. General-purpose computers range from pocket-sized personal digital assistants (notepad computers), to medium-sized desktop computers (personal computers and workstations), to large, powerful computers that are shared by many users via a computer network. The vast majority of digital computers now in use are inexpensive, special-purpose microcontrollers that are embedded, often invisibly, in such devices as toys, consumer electronic equipment, and automobiles.

The main data-processing elements of a computer reside in a small number of electronic integrated circuits (ICs) that form a microprocessor or central processing unit (CPU). Electronic technology allows a basic instruction such as "add two numbers" to be executed many millions of times per second. Other electronic devices are used for program and data storage (memory circuits) and for communication with external devices and human users (input-output circuits). Nonelectronic (magnetic, optical, and mechanical) devices also appear in computers. They are used to construct input-output devices such as keyboards, monitors (video screens), secondary memories, printers, sensors, and mechanical actuators.

Information is stored and processed by computers in fixed-sized units called words. Common word sizes are 8, 16, 32, and 64 bits. Four-bit words can be used to encode the first 16 integers. By increasing the word size, the number of different items that can be represented and their precision can be made as large as desired. A common word size in personal computers is 32 bits, which allows 2^{32} = 4,294,967,296 distinct numbers to be represented.

Computer words can represent many different forms of information, not just numbers. For example, 8-bit words called characters or bytes are used to encode text symbols (the 10 decimal digits, the 52 upper- and lowercase letters of the English alphabet, and punctuation marks). A widely used code of this type is ASCII (American Standard Code for Information Interchange). Visual information can be reduced to black and white dots (pixels) corresponding to 0's and 1's. Audio information can be digitized by mapping a small element of sound into a binary word; for example, a compact disk (CD) uses several million 16-bit words to store an audio recording. Logical quantities encountered in reasoning or decision making can be captured by associating 1 with true and 0 with false. Hence, most forms of information are readily reduced to a common, numberlike binary format suitable for processing by computer.

Logic Components

The operation of a digital computer can be viewed at various levels of abstraction, which are characterized by components of different complexity. These levels range from the low, transistor level seen by an electronic circuit designer to the high, system level seen by a computer user. A useful intermediate level is the logic level, where the basic components process individual bits. By using other basic components called gates, logic circuits can be constructed to perform many useful operations.

System Organization

An accumulator is a digital system that constitutes a simple processor capable of executing a few instructions. By introducing more data-processing circuits and registers, as well as control circuits for a larger set of instructions, a practical, general-purpose processor can be constructed. Such a processor forms the "brain" of every computer, and is referred to as its central processing unit. A CPU implemented on a single integrated-circuit chip is called a microprocessor.

A typical computer program is too large to store in the CPU, so another component called the main memory is used to store a program's instructions and associated data while they are being executed (Fig. 1). Main memory consists of high-speed integrated circuits designed to allow storage and retrieval of information one word at a time. All words in main memory can be accessed with equal ease; hence this is also called a random-access memory (RAM).

A computer program is processed by loading it into main memory and then transferring its instructions and data one word (or a few words) at a time to the CPU for processing. Hence, there is a continual flow of instructions and data words between the CPU and its main memory. As millions of words must be transferred per second, a high-speed communication link is needed between the CPU and main memory. The system bus fills this role.

A computer has input-output (I/O) control circuits and buses to connect it to external input-output devices (also called peripherals). Typical input-output devices are a keyboard, which is an input device, and a printer, which is an output device. Because most computers need more storage space than main memory can supply, they also employ secondary memory units which form part of the computer's input-output subsystem. Common secondary memory devices are hard disk drives, flexible (floppy) disk drives, and magnetic tape units. Compared to main memory, secondary memories employ storage media (magnetic disks and tapes) that have higher capacity and lower cost. However, secondary memories are also significantly slower than main memory.

No explicit instructions are needed for input-output operations if input-output devices share with main memory the available memory addresses. This is known as memory-mapped input-output, and allows load and store instructions to be used to transfer data between the CPU and input-output devices. In general, a computer's instruction set should include a selection of instructions of the following three types: (1) Data-transfer instructions that move data unchanged between the CPU, main memory, and input-output devices. (2) Data-processing instructions that perform numerical operations such as add, subtract, multiply, and divide, as well as nonnumerical (logical) operations, such as NOT, AND, EXCLUSIVE-OR, and SHIFT. (3) Program-control instructions that can change the order in which instructions are executed, for example branch, branch-on-zero, call procedure, and return from procedure.

The instruction unit (I unit) of a CPU, also called the program control unit, is responsible for fetching instructions from main memory, using the program counter as the instruction address register. The opcode of a newly fetched instruction I is placed in the instruction register. The opcode is then decoded to determine the sequence of actions required to execute I. These may include the loading or storing of data assigned to main memory, in which case the I unit computes all needed addresses and issues all needed control signals to the CPU and the system bus. Data are processed in the CPU's execution unit (E unit), also called the datapath, which contains a set of registers used for temporary storage of data operands, and an arithmetic logic unit (ALU), which contains the main data-processing circuits.

Internal Organization of a CPU

Performance Measures

A simple indicator of a CPU's performance is the frequency f of its central timing signal (clock), measured in millions of clock signals issued per second or megahertz (MHz). The clock frequency depends on the integrated-circuit technology used; frequencies of several hundred megahertz are achievable with current technology. Each clock signal triggers execution of a basic instruction such as a fixed-point addition; hence, the time required to execute such an instruction (the clock cycle time) is $1/f$ microseconds. Complex instructions like multiplication or operations on floating-point numbers require several clock cycles to complete their execution. Another measure of CPU performance is the (average) instruction execution rate, measured in millions of instructions per second (MIPS).

Instruction execution time is strongly affected by the time to move instructions or data between the CPU and main memory. The time required by the CPU to access a word in main memory is typically about five times longer than the CPU's clock cycle time. This disparity in speed has existed since the earliest computers despite efforts to develop memory circuits that would be fast enough to keep up with the fastest CPUs. Maximum performance requires the CPU to be supplied with a steady flow of instructions that need to be executed. This flow is disrupted by branch instructions, which account for 20% or more of the instructions in a typical program.

To deal with the foregoing issues, various performance-enhancing features have been incorporated into the design of computers. The communication bottleneck between the CPU and main memory is reduced by means of a cache, which is a special memory unit inserted between the two units. The cache is smaller than main memory but can be accessed more rapidly, and is often placed on the same integrated-circuit chip as the CPU. Its effect is to reduce the average time required by the CPU to send information to or receive information from the memory subsystem. Special logic circuits support the complex flow of information among main memory, the cache, and the registers of the CPU. However, the cache is largely invisible to the programs being executed.

The instruction execution rate can be increased by executing several instructions concurrently. One approach is to employ several E units that are tailored to different instruction types. Examples are an integer unit designed to execute fixed-point instructions and a floating-point unit designed for floating-point instructions. The CPU can then execute a fixed-point instruction and a floating-point instruction at the same time. Processors that execute several instructions in parallel in this way are called superscalar.

Another speedup technique called pipelining allows several instructions to be processed simultaneously in special circuits called pipelines. Execution of an instruction is broken into several consecutive steps, each of which can be assigned to a separate stage of the pipeline. This makes it possible for an *n*-stage E unit to overlap the execution of up to *n* different instructions. A pipeline processing circuit resembles an assembly line on which many products are in various stages of manufacture at the same time. The ability of a CPU to execute several instructions at the same time by using multiple or pipelined E units is highly dependent on the availability of instructions of the right type at the right time in the program being executed. A useful measure of the performance of a CPU that employs internal parallelism is the average number of clock cycles per instruction (CPI) needed to execute a representative set of programs.

CISCs and RISCs

A software implementation of a complex operation like multiply is slower than the corresponding hardware implementation. Consequently, as advances in IC technology lowered the cost of hardware circuits, instruction sets tended to increase in size and complexity. By the mid-1980s, many microprocessors had instructions of several hundred different types, characterized by diverse formats, memory addressing modes, and execution times. The heterogeneous instruction sets of these complex instruction set computers (CISCs) have some disadvantages. Complex instructions require more processing circuits, which tend to make CISCs large and expensive. Moreover, the decoding and execution of complex instruction can slow down the processing of simple instructions.

To address the defects of CISCs, a new class of fast computers referred to as reduced instruction set computers (RISCs) was introduced. RISCs are characterized by fast, efficient—but not necessarily small—instruction sets. The following features are common to most RISCs: (1) All instructions are of fixed length and have just a few opcode formats and addressing modes. (2) The only instructions that address memory are load and store instructions; all other instructions require their operands to be placed in CPU registers. (3) The fetching and processing of most instructions is overlapped in pipelined fashion. In computer engineering, computer architecture is the conceptual design and fundamental operational structure of a computer system.

It is a blueprint and functional description of requirements and design implementations for the various parts of a computer, focusing largely on the way by which the central processing unit (CPU) performs internally and accesses addresses in memory.

It may also be defined as the science and art of selecting and interconnecting hardware components to create computers that meet functional, performance and cost goals.

Computer Architecture Comprises at least three main Subcategories

- *Instruction set architecture*, or ISA, is the abstract image of a computing system that is seen by a machine language (or assembly language) programmer, including the instruction set, word size, memory address modes, processor registers, and address and data formats.
- *Microarchitecture*, also known as *Computer organization* is a lower level, more concrete and detailed, description of the system that involves how the constituent parts of the system are interconnected and how they interoperate in order to implement the ISA. The size of a computer's cache for instance, is an organizational issue that generally has nothing to do with the ISA.
- *System Design* which includes all of the other hardware components within a computing system such as:
  1. system interconnects such as computer buses and switches
  2. memory controllers and hierarchies
  3. CPU off-load mechanisms such as direct memory access
  4. issues like multi-processing.

Once both ISA and microarchitecture have been specified, the actual device needs to be designed into hardware.

This design process is called *implementation*. Implementation is usually not considered architectural definition, but rather hardware design engineering.

Implementation can be Further Broken Down into Three (not Fully Distinct) Pieces

- Logic Implementation-design of blocks defined in the microarchitecture at (primarily) the register-transfer and gate levels.
- Circuit Implementation-transistor-level design of basic elements (gates, multiplexers, latches etc) as well as of some larger blocks (ALUs, caches etc) that may be implemented at this level, or even (partly) at the physical level, for performance reasons.
- Physical Implementation-physical circuits are drawn out, the different circuit components are placed in a chip floor-plan or on a board and the wires connecting them are routed.

For CPUs, the entire implementation process is often called CPU design.

More specific usages of the term include more general wider-scale hardware architectures, such as cluster computing and Non-Uniform Memory Access (NUMA) architectures.

History

The term "architecture" in computer literature can be traced to the work of Lyle R. Johnson and Frederick P. Brooks, Jr., members in 1959 of the Machine Organization department in IBM's main research centre. Johnson had the opportunity to write a proprietary research communication about Stretch, an IBM-developed supercomputer for Los Alamos Scientific Laboratory. In attempting to characterize his chosen level of detail for discussing the luxuriously embellished computer, he noted that his description of formats, instruction types, hardware parameters, and speed enhancements was at the level of "system architecture" – a term that seemed more useful than "machine organization." Subsequently, Brooks, one of the Stretch designers by writing, "Computer architecture, like other architecture, is the art of determining the needs of the user of a structure and then designing to meet those needs as effectively as possible within economic and technological constraints." Brooks went on to play a major role in the development of the IBM System/360 line of computers, where "architecture" gained currency as a noun with the definition "what the user needs to know." Later the computer world would employ the term in many less-explicit ways.

The first mention of the term *architecture* in the referred computer literature is in a 1964 article describing the IBM System/360. The article defines architecture as the set of "attributes of a system as seen by the programmer, i.e., the conceptual structure and functional behaviour, as distinct from the organization of the data flow and controls, the logical design, and the physical implementation." In the definition, the *programmer* perspective of the computer's functional behaviour is key. The conceptual structure part of an architecture description makes the functional behaviour comprehensible, and extrapolatable to a range of Use cases. Only later on did 'internals' such as "the way by which the CPU performs internally and accesses addresses in memory," mentioned above, slip into the definition of computer architecture.

Computer Architecture Topics

Sub-Definitions

Some practitioners of computer architecture at companies such as Intel and AMD use more fine distinctions:

- Macroarchitecture-architectural layers that are more abstract than microarchitecture, e.g. ISA
- ISA (Instruction Set Architecture)-as defined above
- Assembly ISA-a smart assembler may convert an abstract assembly language common to a group of machines into slightly different machine language for different implementations
- Programmer Visible Macroarchitecture-higher level language tools such as compilers may define a consistent interface or contract to programmers using them, abstracting differences between underlying ISA, UISA, and microarchitectures. E.g. the C, C++, or Java standards define different Programmer Visible Macroarchitecture-although in practice the C microarchitecture for a particular computer includes.
- UISA (Microcode Instruction Set Architecture)-a family of machines with different hardware level microarchitectures may share a common microcode architecture, and hence a UISA.
- Pin Architecture-the set of functions that a microprocessor is expected to provide, from the point of view of a hardware platform. E.g. the x86 A20M, FERR/IGNNE or FLUSH pins, and the messages that the processor is expected to emit after

completing a cache invalidation so that external caches can be invalidated. Pin architecture functions are more flexible than ISA functions-external hardware can adapt to changing encodings, or changing from a pin to a message-but the functions are expected to be provided in successive implementations even if the manner of encoding them changes.

Design Goals

The exact form of a computer system depends on the constraints and goals for which it was optimized. Computer architectures usually trade off standards, cost, memory capacity, latency and throughput. Sometimes other considerations, such as features, size, weight, reliability, expandability and power consumption are factors as well.

The most common scheme carefully chooses the bottleneck that most reduces the computer's speed. Ideally, the cost is allocated proportionally to assure that the data rate is nearly the same for all parts of the computer, with the most costly part being the slowest. This is how skillful commercial integrators optimize personal computers.

Performance

Computer performance is often described in terms of clock speed (usually in MHz or GHz). This refers to the cycles per second of the main clock of the CPU. However, this metric is somewhat misleading, as a machine with a higher clock rate may not necessarily have higher performance. As a result manufacturers have moved away from clock speed as a measure of performance.

Computer performance can also be measured with the amount of cache a processor has. If the speed, MHz or GHz, were to be a car then the cache is like the gas tank. No matter how fast the car goes, it will still need to get gas. The higher the speed, and the greater the cache, the faster a processor runs.

Modern CPUs can execute multiple instructions per clock cycle, which dramatically speeds up a program. Other factors influence speed, such as the mix of functional units, bus speeds, available memory, and the type and order of instructions in the programs being run.

There are two main types of speed, latency and throughput. Latency is the time between the start of a process and its completion. Throughput is the amount of work done per unit time. Interrupt latency is the guaranteed maximum response time of the system to an electronic event (*e.g.* when the disk drive finishes moving some data). Performance is affected by a very wide range of design choices — for example, pipelining a processor usually makes latency worse (slower) but makes throughput better. Computers that control machinery usually need low interrupt latencies. These computers operate in a real-time environment and fail if an operation is not completed in a specified amount of time. For example, computer-controlled anti-lock brakes must begin braking almost immediately after they have been instructed to brake.

The performance of a computer can be measured using other metrics, depending upon its application domain. A system may be CPU bound (as in numerical calculation), I/O bound (as in a webserving application) or memory bound (as in video editing). Power consumption has become important in servers and portable devices like laptops.

Benchmarking tries to take all these factors into account by measuring the time a computer takes to run through a series of test programs. Although benchmarking shows strengths, it may not help one to choose a computer. Often the measured machines split on different measures. For example, one system might handle scientific applications quickly, while another might play popular video games more smoothly. Furthermore, designers have been known to add special features to their products, whether in hardware or software, which permit a specific benchmark to execute quickly but which do not offer similar advantages to other, more general tasks.

Power Consumption

Power consumption is another design criterion that factors in the design of modern computers. Power efficiency can often be traded for performance or cost benefits. With the increasing power density of modern circuits as the number of transistors per chip scales (Moore's Law), power efficiency has increased in importance. Recent processor designs such as the Intel Core 2 put more emphasis on increasing power efficiency. Also, in the world of embedded computing, power efficiency has long been and remains the primary design goal next to performance.

Digital Logic Circuit

Digital Electronics

Digital electronics are systems that represent signals as discrete levels, rather than as a continuous range. In most cases the number of states is two, and these states are represented by two voltage levels: one near to zero volts and one at a higher level depending on the supply voltage in use. These two levels are often represented as "Low" and "High."

The fundamental advantage of digital techniques stem from the fact it is easier to get an electronic device to switch into one of a number of known states than to accurately reproduce a continuous range of values.

Digital electronics are usually made from large assemblies of logic gates, simple electronic representations of Boolean logic functions.

Advantages

One advantage of digital circuits when compared to analog circuits is that signals represented digitally can be transmitted without degradation due to noise. For example, a continuous audio signal, transmitted as a sequence of 1s and 0s, can be reconstructed without error provided the noise picked up in transmission is not enough to prevent identification of the 1s and 0s. An hour of music can be stored on a compact disc as about 6 billion binary digits.

In a digital system, a more precise representation of a signal can be obtained by using more binary digits to represent it. While this requires more digital circuits to process the signals, each digit is handled by the same kind of hardware. In an analog system, additional resolution requires fundamental improvements in the linearity and noise charactersitics of each step of the signal chain.

Computer-controlled digital systems can be controlled by software, allowing new functions to be added without changing hardware. Often this can be done outside of the factory by updating the product's software. So, the product's design errors can be corrected after the product is in a customer's hands.

Information storage can be easier in digital systems than in analog ones. The noise-immunity of digital systems permits data to be stored and retrieved without degradation. In an analog system, noise from aging and wear degrade the information stored. In a digital system, as long as the total noise is below a certain level, the information can be recovered perfectly.

Disadvantages

In some cases, digital circuits use more energy than analog circuits to accomplish the same tasks, thus producing more heat. In portable or battery-powered systems this can limit use of digital systems.

For example, battery-powered cellular telephones often use a low-power analog front-end to amplify and tune in the radio signals from the base station. However, a base station has grid power and can use power-hungry, but very flexible software radios. Such base stations can be easily reprogrammed to process the signals used in new cellular standards.

Digital circuits are sometimes more expensive, especially in small quantities.

The sensed world is analog, and signals from this world are analog quantities. For example, light, temperature, sound, electrical conductivity, electric and magnetic fields are analog. Most useful digital systems must translate from continuous analog signals to discrete digital signals. This causes quantization errors.

Quantization error can be reduced if the system stores enough digital data to represent the signal to the desired degree of fidelity. The Nyquist-Shannon sampling theorem provides an important guideline as to how much digital data is needed to accurately portray a given analog signal.

In some systems, if a single piece of digital data is lost or misinterpreted, the meaning of large blocks of related data can completely change. Because of the cliff effect, it can be difficult for users to tell if a particular system is right on the edge of failure, or if it can tolerate much more noise before failing.

Digital fragility can be reduced by designing a digital system for robustness. For example, a parity bit or other error management method can be inserted into the signal path. These schemes help the system detect errors, and then either correct the errors, or at least ask for a new copy of the data. In a state-machine, the state transition logic can be designed to catch unused states and trigger a reset sequence or other error recovery routine.

Embedded software designs that employ Immunity Aware Programming, such as the practice of filling unused program memory with interrupt instructions that point to an error recovery routine. This helps guard against failures that corrupt the microcontroller's instruction pointer which could otherwise cause random code to be executed.

Digital memory and transmission systems can use techniques such as error detection and correction to use additional data to correct any errors in transmission and storage.

On the other hand, some techniques used in digital systems make those systems more vulnerable to single-bit errors. These techniques are acceptable when the underlying bits are reliable enough that such errors are highly unlikely.

A single-bit error in audio data stored directly as linear pulse code modulation (such as on a CD-ROM) causes, at worst, a single click. Instead, many people use audio compression to save storage space and download time, even though a single-bit error may corrupt the entire song.

Analog Issues in Digital Circuits

Digital circuits are made from analog components. The design must assure that the analog nature of the components doesn't dominate the desired digital behaviour. Digital systems must manage noise and timing margins, parasitic inductances and capacitances, and filter power connections.

Bad designs have intermittent problems such as "glitches", vanishingly-fast pulses that may trigger some logic but not others, "runt pulses" that do not reach valid "threshold" voltages, or unexpected ("undecoded") combinations of logic states.

Since digital circuits are made from analog components, digital circuits calculate more slowly than low-precision analog circuits that use a similar amount of space and power. However, the digital circuit will calculate more repeatably, because of its high noise immunity. On the other hand, in the high-precision domain (for example, where 14 or more bits of precision are needed), analog circuits require much more power and area than digital equivalents.

Construction

A digital circuit is often constructed from small electronic circuits called logic gates. Each logic gate represents a function of boolean logic. A logic gate is an arrangement of electrically controlled switches.

The output of a logic gate is an electrical flow or voltage, that can, in turn, control more logic gates. Logic gates often use the fewest number of transistors in order to reduce their size, power consumption and cost, and increase their reliability.

Integrated circuits are the least expensive way to make logic gates in large volumes. Integrated circuits are usually designed by engineers using electronic design automation software.

Another form of digital circuit is constructed from lookup tables, (many sold as "programmable logic devices", though other kinds of PLDs exist). Lookup tables can perform the same functions as machines based on logic gates, but can be easily reprogrammed without changing the wiring. This means that a designer can often repair design errors without changing the arrangement of wires. Therefore, in small volume products, programmable logic devices are often the preferred solution. They are usually designed by engineers using electronic design automation software.

When the volumes are medium to large, and the logic can be slow, or involves complex algorithms or sequences, often a small microcontroller is programmed to make an embedded system. These are usually programmed by software engineers.

When only one digital circuit is needed, and its design is totally customized, as for a factory production line controller, the conventional solution is a programmable logic controller, or PLC. These are usually programmed by electricians, using ladder logic.

Structure of Digital Systems

Engineers use many methods to minimize logic functions, in order to reduce the circuit's complexity. When the complexity is less, the circuit also has fewer errors and less electronics, and is therefore less expensive.

The most widely used simplification is a minimization algorithm like the Espresso heuristic logic minimizer within a CAD system, although historically, binary decision diagrams, an automated Quine–McCluskey algorithm, truth tables, Karnaugh Maps, and Boolean algebra have been used.

Representations are crucial to an engineer's design of digital circuits. Some analysis methods only work with particular representations.

The classical way to represent a digital circuit is with an equivalent set of logic gates. Another way, often with the least electronics, is to construct an equivalent system of electronic switches (usually transistors). One of the easiest ways is to simply have a memory containing a truth table. The inputs are fed into the address of the memory, and the data outputs of the memory become the outputs.

For automated analysis, these representations have digital file formats that can be processed by computer programs. Most digital engineers are very careful to select computer programs ("tools") with compatible file formats.

To choose representations, engineers consider types of digital systems. Most digital systems divide into "combinational systems" and "sequential systems." A combinational system always presents the same output when given the same inputs. It is basically a representation of a set of logic functions, as already discussed.

A sequential system is a combinational system with some of the outputs fed back as inputs. This makes the digital machine perform a "sequence" of operations. The simplest sequential system is probably a flip flop, a mechanism that represents a binary digit or "bit".

Sequential systems are often designed as state machines. In this way, engineers can design a system's gross behaviour, and even test it in a simulation, without considering all the details of the logic functions.

Sequential systems divide into two further subcategories. "Synchronous" sequential systems change state all at once, when a "clock" signal changes state. "Asynchronous" sequential systems propagate changes whenever inputs change. Synchronous sequential systems are made of well-characterized asynchronous circuits such as flip-flops, that change only when the clock changes, and which have carefully designed timing margins.

The usual way to implement a synchronous sequential state machine is divide it into a piece of combinational logic and a set of flip flops called a "state register." Each time a clock signal ticks, the state register captures the feedback generated from the previous state of the combinational logic, and feeds it back as an unchanging input to the combinational part of the state machine. The fastest rate of the clock is set by the most time-consuming logic calculation in the combinational logic.

The state register is just a representation of a binary number. If the states in the state machine are numbered (easy to arrange), the logic function is some combinational logic that produces the number of the next state.

In comparison, asynchronous systems are very hard to design because all possible states, in all possible timings must be considered. The usual method is to construct a table of the minimum and maximum time that each such state can exist, and then adjust the circuit to minimize the number of such states, and force the circuit to periodically wait for all of its parts to enter a compatible state. (This is called "self-resynchronization.") Without such careful design, it is easy to accidentally produce asynchronous logic that is "unstable", that is, real electronics will have unpredictable results because of the cumulative delays caused by small variations in the values of the electronic components. Certain circuits (such as the synchronizer flip-flops, switch debouncers, and the like which allow external unsynchronized signals to enter synchronous logic circuits) are inherently asynchronous in their design and must be analyzed as such.

As of 2005, almost all digital machines are synchronous designs because it is much easier to create and verify a synchronous design—the software currently used to simulate digital machines does not yet handle asynchronous designs. However, asynchronous logic is thought to be superior, if it can be made to work, because its speed is not constrained by an arbitrary clock; instead, it simply runs at the maximum speed permitted by the propagation rates of the logic gates from which it is constructed. Building an asynchronous circuit using faster parts implicitly makes the circuit "go" faster.

More generally, many digital systems are data flow machines. These are usually designed using synchronous register transfer logic, using hardware description languages such as VHDL or Verilog.

In register transfer logic, binary numbers are stored in groups of flip flops called registers. The outputs of each register are a bundle of wires called a "bus" that carries that number to other calculations. A calculation is simply a piece of combinational logic. Each calculation also has an output bus, and these may be connected to the inputs of several registers. Sometimes a register will have a multiplexer on its input, so that it can store a number from any one of several buses. Alternatively, the outputs of several items may be connected to a bus through buffers that can turn off the output of all of the devices except one. A sequential state machine controls when each register accepts new data from its input.

In the 1980s, some researchers discovered that almost all synchronous register-transfer machines could be converted to asynchronous designs by using first-in-first-out synchronization logic. In this scheme, the digital machine is characterized as a set of data flows. In each step of the flow, an asynchronous "synchronization circuit" determines when the outputs of that step are valid, and presents a signal that says, "grab the data" to the stages that use that stage's inputs. It turns out that just a few relatively simple synchronization circuits are needed.

The most general-purpose register-transfer logic machine is a computer. This is basically an automatic binary abacus. The control unit of a computer is usually designed as a microprogram run by a microsequencer. A microprogram is much like a player-piano roll. Each table entry or "word" of the microprogram commands the state of every bit that controls the computer. The sequencer then counts, and the count addresses the memory or combinational logic machine that contains the microprogram. The bits from the microprogram control the arithmetic logic unit, memory and other parts of the computer, including the microsequencer itself.

In this way, the complex task of designing the controls of a computer is reduced to a simpler task of programming a relatively independent collection of much simpler logic machines.

Computer architecture is a specialized engineering activity that tries to arrange the registers, calculation logic, buses and other parts of the computer in the best way for some purpose. Computer architects have applied large amounts of ingenuity to computer design to reduce the cost and increase the speed and immunity to programming errors of computers. An increasingly common goal is to reduce the power used in a battery-powered computer system, such as a cell-phone. Many computer architects serve an extended apprenticeship as microprogrammers.

"Specialized computers" are usually a conventional computer with a special-purpose microprogram.

Automated Design Tools

To save costly engineering effort, much of the effort of designing large logic machines has been automated. The computer programs are called "electronic design automation tools" or just "EDA." Simple truth table-style descriptions of logic are often optimized with EDA that automatically produces reduced systems of logic gates or smaller lookup tables that still produce the desired outputs. The most common example of this kind of software is the Espresso heuristic logic minimizer.

Most practical algorithms for optimizing large logic systems use algebraic manipulations or binary decision diagrams, and there are promising experiments with genetic algorithms and annealing optimizations.

To automate costly engineering processes, some EDA can take state tables that describe state machines and automatically produce a truth table or a function table for the combinatorial part of a state machine. The state table is a piece of text that lists each state, together with the conditions controlling the transitions between them and the belonging output signals.

It is common for the function tables of such computer-generated state-machines to be optimized with logic-minimization software such as Minilog.

Often, real logic systems are designed as a series of sub-projects, which are combined using a "tool flow." The tool flow is usually a "script," a simplified computer language that can invoke the software design tools in the right order.

Tool flows for large logic systems such as microprocessors can be thousands of commands long, and combine the work of hundreds of engineers.

Writing and debugging tool flows is an established engineering speciality in companies that produce digital designs. The tool flow usually terminates in a detailed computer file or set of files that describe how to physically construct the logic. Often it consists of instructions to draw the transistors and wires on an integrated circuit or a printed circuit board.

Parts of tool flows are "debugged" by verifying the outputs of simulated logic against expected inputs. The test tools take computer files with sets of inputs and outputs, and highlight discrepancies between the simulated behaviour and the expected behaviour.

Once the input data is believed correct, the design itself must still be verified for correctness. Some tool flows verify designs by first producing a design, and then scanning the design to produce compatible input data for the tool flow. If the scanned data matches the input data, then the tool flow has probably not introduced errors.

The functional verification data are usually called "test vectors." The functional test vectors may be preserved and used in the factory to test that newly constructed logic works correctly. However, functional test patterns don't discover common fabrication faults. Production tests are often designed by software tools called "test pattern generators." These generate test vectors by examining the structure of the logic and systematically generating tests for particular faults. This way the fault coverage can closely approach 100%, provided the design is properly made testable.

Once a design exists, and is verified and testable, it often needs to be processed to be manufacturable as well. Modern integrated circuits have features smaller than the wavelength of the light used to expose the photoresist. Manufacturability software adds interference patterns to the exposure masks to eliminate open-circuits, and enhance the masks' resolution and contrast.

Design for Testability

A large logic machine (say,. with more than a hundred logical variables) can have an astronomical number of possible states. Obviously, in the factory, testing every state is impractical if testing each state takes a microsecond, and there are more states than the number of microseconds since the universe began. Unfortunately, this ridiculous-sounding case is typical.

Fortunately, large logic machines are almost always designed as assemblies of smaller logic machines. To save time, the smaller sub-machines are isolated by permanently-installed "design for test" circuitry, and are tested independently.

One common test scheme known as "scan design" moves test bits serially (one after another) from external test equipment through one or more serial shift registers known as "scan chains". Serial scans have only one or two wires to carry the data, and minimize the physical size and expense of the infrequently-used test logic.

After all the test data bits are in place, the design is reconfigured to be in "normal mode" and one or more clock pulses are applied, to test for faults (e.g. stuck-at low or stuck-at high) and capture the test result into flip-flops and/or latches in the scan shift register(s). Finally, the result of the test is shifted out to the block boundary and compared against the predicted "good machine" result.

In a board-test environment, serial to parallel testing has been formalized with a standard called "JTAG" (named after the "Joint Test Action Group" that proposed it).

Another common testing scheme provides a test mode that forces some part of the logic machine to enter a "test cycle." The test cycle usually exercises large independent parts of the machine.

Trade-offs

Several numbers determine the practicality of a system of digital logic. Engineers explored numerous electronic devices to get an ideal combination of fanout, speed, low cost and reliability.

The cost of a logic gate is crucial. In the 1930s, the earliest digital logic systems were constructed from telephone relays because these were inexpensive and relatively reliable. After that, engineers always used the cheapest available electronic switches that could still fulfil the requirements.

The earliest integrated circuits were a happy accident. They were constructed not to save money, but to save weight, and permit the Apollo Guidance Computer to control an inertial guidance system for a spacecraft. The first integrated circuit logic gates cost nearly $50 (in 1960 dollars, when an engineer earned $10,000/year). To everyone's surprise, by the time the circuits were mass-produced, they had become the least-expensive method of constructing digital logic. Improvements in this technology have driven all subsequent improvements in cost.

With the rise of integrated circuits, reducing the absolute number of chips used represented another way to save costs. The goal of a designer is not just to make the simplest circuit, but to keep the component count down. Sometimes this results in slightly more complicated designs with respect to the underlying digital logic but nevertheless reduces the number of components, board size, and even power consumption.

For example, in some logic families, NAND gates are the simplest digital gate to build. All other logical operations can be implemented by NAND gates. If a circuit already required a single NAND gate, and a single chip normally carried four NAND gates, then the remaining gates could be used to implement other logical operations like logical and. This could eliminate the need for a separate chip containing those different types of gates.

The "reliability" of a logic gate describes its mean time between failure (MTBF). Digital machines often have millions of logic gates. Also, most digital machines are "optimized" to reduce their cost. The result is that often, the failure of a single logic gate will cause a digital machine to stop working.

Digital machines first became useful when the MTBF for a switch got above a few hundred hours. Even so, many of these machines had complex, well-rehearsed repair procedures, and would be nonfunctional for hours because a tube burned-out, or a moth got stuck in a relay. Modern transistorized integrated circuit logic gates have MTBFs of nearly a trillion (1×10^{12}) hours, and need them because they have so many logic gates.

Fanout describes how many logic inputs can be controlled by a single logic output. The minimum practical fanout is about five. Modern electronic logic using CMOS transistors for switches have fanouts near fifty, and can sometimes go much higher.

The "switching speed" describes how many times per second an inverter (an electronic representation of a "logical not" function) can change from true to false and back. Faster logic can accomplish more operations in less time. Digital logic first became useful when switching speeds got above fifty hertz, because that was faster than a team of humans operating mechanical calculators. Modern electronic digital logic routinely switches at five gigahertz (5×10^{9} hertz), and some laboratory systems switch at more than a terahertz (1×10^{12} hertz).

Logic Families

Design started with relays. Relay logic was relatively inexpensive and reliable, but slow. Occasionally a mechanical failure would occur. Fanouts were typically about ten, limited by the resistance of the coils and arcing on the contacts from high voltages.

Later, vacuum tubes were used. These were very fast, but generated heat, and were unreliable because the filaments would burn out. Fanouts were typically five to seven, limited by the heating from the tubes' current. In the 1950s, special "computer tubes" were developed with filaments that omitted volatile elements like silicon. These ran for hundreds of thousands of hours.

The first semiconductor logic family was Resistor-transistor logic. This was a thousand times more reliable than tubes, ran cooler, and used less power, but had a very low fan-in of three. Diode-transistor logic improved the fanout up to about seven, and reduced the power. Some DTL designs used two power-supplies with alternating layers of NPN and PNP transistors to increase the fanout.

Transistor logic (TTL) was a great improvement over these. In early devices, fanout improved to ten, and later variations reliably achieved twenty. TTL was also fast, with some variations achieving switching times as low as twenty nanoseconds. TTL is still used in some designs.

Another contender was emitter coupled logic. This is very fast but uses a lot of power. It's now used mostly in radio-frequency circuits.

Modern integrated circuits mostly use variations of CMOS, which is acceptably fast, very small and uses very little power. Fanouts of forty or more are possible, with some speed penalty.

Non-Electronic Logic

It is possible to construct non-electronic digital mechanisms. In principle, any technology capable of representing discrete states and representing logic operations could be used to build mechanical logic. MIT students Erlyne Gee, Edward Hardebeck, Danny Hillis (co-author of The Connection Machine), Margaret Minsky and brothers Barry and Brian Silverman, built two working computers from Tinker toys, string, a brick, and a sharpened pencil. The Tinkertoy computer is supposed to be in the Houston Museum of Natural Science.

Hydraulic, pneumatic and mechanical versions of logic gates exist and are used in situations where electricity cannot be used. The first two types are considered under the heading of fluidics. One application of fluidic logic is in military hardware that is likely to be exposed to a nuclear electromagnetic pulse (nuclear EMP, or NEMP) that would destroy electrical circuits.

Mechanical logic is frequently used in inexpensive controllers, such as those in washing machines. Famously, the first computer design, by Charles Babbage, was designed to use mechanical logic. Mechanical logic might also be used in very small computers that could be built by nanotechnology.

Another example is that if two particular enzymes are required to prevent the construction of a particular protein, this is the equivalent of a biological "NAND" gate.

Recent Developments

The discovery of superconductivity has enabled the development of Rapid Single Flux Quantum (RSFQ) circuit technology, which uses Josephson junctions instead of transistors. Most recently, attempts are being made to construct purely optical computing systems capable of processing digital information using nonlinear optical elements.

Boolean Algebra (logic)

Boolean algebra (or Boolean logic) is a logical calculus of truth values, developed by George Boole in the 1990s. It resembles the algebra of real numbers, but with the numeric operations of multiplication xy, addition $x + y$, and negation "*x* replaced by the respective logical operations of conjunction *x*"'*y*, disjunction *x*("*y*, and complement $\neg x$. The Boolean operations are these and all other operations that can be built from these, such as *x*"'(*y*("*z*). These turn out to coincide with the set of all operations on the set $\{0,1\}$ that take only finitely many arguments; there are 2^{2^n} such operations when there are n arguments.

The laws of Boolean algebra can be defined axiomatically as certain equations called axioms together with their logical consequences called theorems, or semantically as those equations that are true for every possible assignment of 0 or 1 to their variables. The axiomatic approach is sound and complete in the sense that it proves respectively neither more nor fewer laws than the semantic approach.

Values

Boolean algebra is the algebra of two values. These are usually taken to be 0 and 1, as we shall do here, although F and T, false and true, etc. are also in common use. For the purpose of understanding Boolean algebra any Boolean domain of two values will do.

Regardless of nomenclature, the values are customarily thought of as essentially logical in character and are therefore referred to as truth values, in contrast to the natural numbers or the reals which are considered numerical values. On the other hand the algebra of the integers modulo 2, while ostensibly just as numeric as the integers themselves, was shown to constitute exactly Boolean algebra, originally by I.I. Zhegalkin in

1927 and rediscovered independently in the west by Marshall Stone in 1936. So in fact there is some ambiguity in the true nature of Boolean algebra: it can be viewed as either logical or numeric in character.

More generally Boolean algebra is the algebra of values from any Boolean algebra as a model of the laws of Boolean algebra. For example the bit vectors of a given length, as with say 32-bit computer words, can be combined with Boolean operations in the same way as individual bits, thereby forming a 2^{32}-element Boolean algebra under those operations. Any such combination applies the same Boolean operation to all bits simultaneously.

This passage from the Boolean algebra of 0 and 1 to these more general Boolean algebras is the Boolean counterpart of the passage from the algebra of the ring of integers to the algebra of commutative rings in general. The two-element Boolean algebra is the prototypical Boolean algebra in the same sense as the ring of integers is the prototypical commutative ring. Boolean logic as the subject matter of this article is independent of the choice of Boolean algebra (the same equations hold of every nontrivial Boolean algebra); hence, there is no need here to consider any Boolean algebra other than the two-element one. The article on Boolean algebra (structure) treats Boolean algebras themselves.

Various Representations of Boolean Operations

The symbols used in digital electronics for conjunction and disjunction; the input ports are on the left and the signals flow through to the output port on the right. Inverters negating the input signals on the way in, or the output signals on the way out, are represented as circles on the port to be inverted.

All Boolean Operations

There are infinitely many expressions that can be built from two variables using the above operations, suggesting great expressiveness. Yet a straightforward counting argument shows that only 16 distinct binary operations on two values are possible. Any given binary operation is fully determined by its output values for each possible combination of input values. The two arguments have $2 \times 2 = 4$ possible combinations of values between them, and there are $2^4 = 16$ ways of assigning an output value to each of these four input values. The choice of one of these 16 assignments then determines the operation; so all together there are only 16 distinct binary operations.

The 16 binary Boolean operations can be organized as follows:

Two constant operations, 0 and 1.

Four operations dependent on one variable, namely x, $\neg x$, y, and $\neg y$, whose truth tables amount to two juxtaposed rectangles, one containing two 1s and the other two 0s.

Two operations with a "checkerboard" truth table, namely XOR and EQV.

Four operations are obtained from disjunction with some subset of its inputs negated, namely $x \vee y$, $x \rightarrow y$, $y \rightarrow x$, and $x \lfloor y$; their truth tables contain a single 0.

The final four come from the same treatment applied to conjunction, having a single 1 in their truth tables.

10 of the 16 operations depend on both variables; all are representable schematically as an AND-gate, an OR-gate, or an XOR-gate, with one port optionally inverted. For the AND and OR gates the location of each inverter matters, for the XOR gate it does not, only whether there is an even or odd number of inverters.

Operations of other arities are possible. For example the ternary counterpart of disjunction can be obtained as $(x \vee y)$("z. In general an n-ary operation, one having n inputs, has 2^n possible valuations of those inputs. An operation has two possibilities for each of these, whence there exist 2^{2^n} n-ary Boolean operations. For example, there are 2^{32} = 4,294,967,296 operations with 5 inputs.

Although Boolean algebra confines attention to operations that return a single bit, the concept generalizes to operations that take n bits in and return m bits instead of one bit. Digital circuit designers draw such operations as suitably shaped boxes with n wires entering on the left and m wires exiting on the right.

Such multi-output operations can be understood simply as m n-ary operations. The operation count must then be raised to the m-th power, or, in the case of n inputs, $(2^{2^n})^m = 2^{m2^n}$ operations. The number of Boolean operations of this generalized kind with say 5 inputs and 5 outputs is 1.46×10^{48}. A logic gate or computer module mapping 32 bits to 32 bits could implement any of $5.47 \times 10^{41,373,247,567}$ operations, more than is obtained by squaring a googol 28 times.

Laws

Axioms

With values and operations in hand, the next aspect of Boolean algebra is that of laws or properties. As with many kinds of algebra, the principal laws take the form of equations between terms built up from variables using the operations of the algebra. Such an equation is deemed a law or identity just when both sides have the same value for all values of the variables, equivalently when the two terms denote the same operation.

Numeric algebra has laws such as commutativity of addition and multiplication, $x + y = y + x$ and $xy = yx$. Similarly, Boolean algebra has commutativity in that $x\ (\vee y = y\ (\vee x$ for disjunction and $x \wedge y = y \wedge x$ for conjunction. Not all binary operations are commutative; Boolean implication is not commutative, like subtraction and division.

Again numeric subtraction and logical implication serve as examples, this time of binary operations that are not associative. On the other hand exclusive-or, being just addition mod 2, is both commutative and associative.

Boolean algebra does not completely mirror numeric algebra however, as both conjunction and disjunction satisfy idempotence, expressed respectively as $x \vee x = x$ and $x \wedge x = x$. These laws are easily verified by considering the two valuations 0 and 1 for x. But since $2 + 2 = 2 \times 2 = 4$ in arithmetic, clearly numeric addition and multiplication are not idempotent. With arithmetic mod 2 on the other hand, multiplication is idempotent, though not addition since $1 + 1 = 0$ mod 2, reflected logically in the idempotence of conjunction but not of exclusive-or.

A more subtle difference between number and logic is with $x(x + y)$ and $x + xy$, neither of which equal x numerically. In Boolean algebra however, both $x \wedge (x \vee y)$ and $x \vee (x \wedge y)$ are equal to x, as can be verified for each of the four possible valuations for x and y. These two Boolean laws are called the laws of *absorption.* These laws (both are needed) together with the associativity, commutativity, and idempotence of conjunction and disjunction constitute the defining laws or axioms of lattice theory. (Actually idempotence can be derived from the other axioms.)

The laws of lattice theory along with these first two la

negation axiomatize the theory of complemented lattices. Including either distributivity law then axiomatizes the theory of complemented distributive lattices. The next two sections show that this theory is sufficient to axiomatize all the valid laws or identities of two-valued logic, that is, Boolean algebra. It follows that Boolean algebra as commonly defined in terms of these axioms coincides with the intuitive semantic notion of the valid identities of two-valued logic.

Derivations

While the Boolean laws enumerated are certainly highlights of Boolean algebra, they by no means exhaust the laws, of which there are infinitely many, nor do they even exhaust the highlights. As it is out of the question to proceed in the *ad hoc* way of the preceding section for ever, the question arises as to how best to present the remaining laws.

One way of establishing an equation as being a law is to verify its truth for all valuations of its variables, sometimes called the method of truth tables. This is the method we depended to justify each law as we introduced it, constituting the semantic approach to establishing laws. From a practical standpoint the method lends itself to computer implementation for 20-30 variables because the enumeration of valuations is straightforward to program and boring to carry out, making it ideal work for a computer. Because there are 2^n valuations to check the method starts to become impractical as 40 variables is approached. Beyond that the approach becomes of value mainly as the in-principle semantic definition of what constitutes an identically true or *valid* equation.

Reflexivity: $t = t$. That is, any equation whose two sides are the same term t is a law. (While arguably an axiom rather than a rule since it has no premises, we classify it as a rule because like the other three rules it is domain-independent, making no mention of specific logical, numeric, or other operations.)

Symmetry: From $s = t$ infer $t = s$. That is, the two sides of a law may be interchanged. Intuitively one attaches no importance to which side of an equation a term comes from.

Transitivity: A chain $s = t = u$ of two laws yields the law $s = u$. (This law of "cutting out the middleman" is applied four times in the above example to eliminate the intermediate terms.)

Substitution: Given two laws and a variable, each occurrence of that variable in the first law may be replaced by one or the other side of the second law. (Distinct occurrences can be replaced by distinct sides, but every occurrence must be replaced by one or the other side.)

While the first equation in the above example might seem simply a straightforward application of the associativity law, when analyzed more carefully according to the above rules it can be seen to require something more. We can justify it in terms of the reflexivity and substitution rules. Beginning with the laws $x\vee(y\vee z) = (x\vee y)\vee z$ and $w\vee x = w\vee x$, we use substitution to replace both occurrences of x by $w\vee x$ to arrive at the first equation. All five equations in the chain are accounted for along similar lines, with commutativity in place of associativity in the middle equation.

Soundness and Completeness

It can be shown that the two approaches, semantic and syntactic, to constructing all the laws of Boolean algebra lead to the same set of laws. We say that the syntactic approach is sound when it yields a subset of the semantically obtained laws, and complete when it yields a superset thereof. We can then restate this coinciding of the semantic and syntactic approaches as the soundness and completeness of the syntactic approach with respect to (or as calibrated by) the semantic approach.

Soundness follows firstly from the fact that the initial laws or axioms we started from were all identities, that is, semantically true laws. Secondly it depends on the easily verified fact that the rules preserve identities.

Completeness can be proved by first deriving a few additional useful laws and then showing how to use the axioms and rules to prove that a term with n variables, ordered alphabetically say, is equal to its n-ary normal form, namely a unique term associated with the n-ary Boolean operation realized by that term with the variables in that order. It then follows that if two terms denote the same operation (the same thing as being semantically equal), they are both provably equal to the normal form term denoting that operation, and hence by transitivity provably equal to each other.

There is more than one suitable choice of normal form, but complete disjunctive normal form will do. A literal is either a variable or a negated variable. A disjunctive normal form (DNF) term is a disjunction of conjunctions of literals. (Associativity allows a term such as $x \vee (y \vee z)$ to be viewed as the ternary disjunction $x \vee y \vee z$, likewise for longer disjunctions, and similarly for conjunction.) A DNF term is *complete* when every disjunct (conjunction) contains exactly one occurrence of each variable, independently of whether or not the variable is negated. Such a conjunction uniquely represents the operation it denotes by virtue of serving as a coding of those valuations at which the operation returns 1. Each conjunction codes the valuation setting the positively occurring variables to 1 and the negated ones to 0; the value of the conjunction at that valuation is 1, and hence so is the whole term. At valuations corresponding to omitted conjunctions, all conjunctions present in the term evaluate to 0 and hence so does the whole term.

Digital Signal Processing

Digital signal processing (DSP) is concerned with the representation of the signals by a sequence of numbers or symbols and the processing of these signals. Digital signal processing and analog signal processing are subfields of signal processing. DSP includes subfields like: audio and speech signal processing, sonar and radar signal processing, sensor array processing, spectral estimation, statistical signal processing, digital image processing, signal processing for communications, biomedical signal processing, seismic data processing, etc.

Since the goal of DSP is usually to measure or filter continuous real-world analog signals, the first step is usually to convert the signal from an analog to a digital form, by using an analog to digital converter. Often, the required output signal is another analog output signal, which requires a digital to analog converter. Even if this process is more complex than analog processing and has a discrete value range, the stability of digital signal processing thanks to error detection and correction and being less vulnerable to noise makes it advantageous over analog signal processing for many, though not all, applications.

DSP algorithms have long been run on standard computers, on specialized processors called digital signal processors (DSPs), or on purpose-built hardware such as application-specific integrated circuit (ASICs). Today there are additional technologies used for digital signal processing including more powerful general purpose microprocessors, field-programmable gate arrays (FPGAs), digital signal controllers (mostly for industrial apps such as motor control), and stream processors, among others.

DSP Domains

In DSP, engineers usually study digital signals in one of the following domains: time domain (one-dimensional signals), spatial domain (multidimensional signals), frequency domain, autocorrelation domain, and wavelet domains. They choose the domain in which to process a signal by making an informed guess (or by trying different possibilities) as to which domain best represents the essential characteristics of the signal. A sequence of samples from a measuring device produces a time or spatial domain representation, whereas a discrete Fourier transform produces the frequency domain information, that is the frequency spectrum. Autocorrelation is defined as the cross-correlation of the signal with itself over varying intervals of time or space.

Signal Sampling

With the increasing use of computers the usage of and need for digital signal processing has increased. In order to use an analog signal on a computer it must be digitized with an analog to digital converter (ADC). Sampling is usually carried out in two stages, discretization and quantization. In the discretization stage, the space of signals is partitioned into equivalence classes and quantization is carried out by replacing the signal with representative signal of the corresponding equivalence class. In the quantization stage the representative signal values are approximated by values from a finite set.

The Nyquist–Shannon sampling theorem states that a signal can be exactly reconstructed from its samples if the sampling frequency is greater than twice the highest frequency of the signal. In practice, the sampling frequency is often significantly more than twice the required bandwidth.

A digital to analog converter (DAC) is used to convert the digital signal back to analog. The use of a digital computer is a key ingredient in digital control systems.

Time and Space Domains

The most common processing approach in the time or space domain is enhancement of the input signal through a method called filtering. Filtering generally consists of some transformation of a number of surrounding samples around the current sample of the input or output signal. There are various ways to characterize filters; for example:

- A "linear" filter is a linear transformation of input samples; other filters are "non-linear." Linear filters satisfy the superposition condition, i.e. if an input is a weighted linear combination of different signals, the output is an equally weighted linear combination of the corresponding output signals.
- A "causal" filter uses only previous samples of the input or output signals; while a "non-causal" filter uses future input samples. A non-causal filter can usually be changed into a causal filter by adding a delay to it.
- A "time-invariant" filter has constant properties over time; other filters such as adaptive filters change in time.
- Some filters are "stable", others are "unstable". A stable filter produces an output that converges to a constant value with time, or remains bounded within a finite interval. An unstable filter can produce an output that grows without bounds, with bounded or even zero input.
- A "finite impulse response" (FIR) filter uses only the input signal, while an "infinite impulse response" filter (IIR) uses both the input signal and previous samples of the output signal. FIR filters are always stable, while IIR filters may be unstable.

Most filters can be described in Z-domain (a superset of the frequency domain) by their transfer functions. A filter may also be described as a difference equation, a collection of zeroes and poles or, if it is an FIR filter, an impulse response or step response. The output of an FIR filter to any given input may be calculated by convolving the input signal with the impulse response. Filters can also be represented by block diagrams which can then be used to derive a sample processing algorithm to implement the filter using hardware instructions.

Frequency Domain

Signals are converted from time or space domain to the frequency domain usually through the Fourier transform. The Fourier transform converts the signal information to a magnitude and phase component of each frequency. Often the Fourier transform is converted to the power spectrum, which is the magnitude of each frequency component squared.

The most common purpose for analysis of signals in the frequency domain is analysis of signal properties. The engineer can study the spectrum to determine which frequencies are present in the input signal and which are missing.

Filtering, particularly in non realtime work can also be achieved by converting to the frequency domain, applying the filter and then converting back to the time domain. This is a fast, O (n log n) operation, and can give essentially any filter shape including excellent approximations to brickwall filters.

There are some commonly used frequency domain transformations. For example, the cepstrum converts a signal to the frequency domain through Fourier transform, takes the logarithm, then applies another Fourier transform. This emphasizes the frequency components with smaller magnitude while retaining the order of magnitudes of frequency components.

Frequency Domain Analysis is also Called *Spectrum*-or *Spectral Analysis*

Applications

The main applications of DSP are audio signal processing, audio compression, digital image processing, video compression, speech processing, speech recognition, digital communications, RADAR, SONAR, seismology, and biomedicine. Specific examples are speech compression and transmission in digital mobile phones, room matching equalization of sound in Hifi and sound reinforcement applications, weather forecasting, economic forecasting, seismic data processing, analysis and control of industrial processes, computer-generated animations in movies, medical imaging such as CAT scans and MRI, MP3 compression, image manipulation, high fidelity loudspeaker crossovers and equalization, and audio effects for use with electric guitar amplifiers.

Implementation

Digital signal processing is often implemented using specialised microprocessors such as the DSP56000, the TMS320, or the SHARC.

These often process data using fixed-point arithmetic, although some versions are available which use floating point arithmetic and are more powerful. For faster applications FPGAs might be used. Beginning in 2007, multicore implementations of DSPs have started to emerge from companies including Freescale and Stream Processors, Inc. For faster applications with vast usage, ASICs might be designed specifically. For slow applications, a traditional slower processor such as a microcontroller may be adequate.

Techniques

- Bilinear transform
- Discrete Fourier transform
- Discrete-time Fourier transform
- Filter design
- LTI system theory
- Minimum phase
- Transfer function
- Z-transform
- Goertzel algorithm
- s-plane.

Overview

As you know, all information inside a computer is processed and stored as 0-1 bits. Here we will look at the basic building blocks used to manipulate this 0-1 information.

Combinational Logic

The term combinational logic refers to circuitry that transforms bits, as opposed to storing bits. For example, the ALU portion of a CPU transforms data, e.g. transforming two input word-sized bit strings into an output which is the sum of the two inputs.

Logic Gate

A logic gate performs a logical operation on one or more logic inputs and produces a single logic output. The logic normally performed is Boolean logic and is most commonly found in digital circuits. Logic gates are primarily implemented electronically using diodes or transistors, but can also be constructed using electromagnetic relays, fluidics, optics, molecules, or even mechanical elements. In electronic logic, a logic level is represented by a voltage or current, (which depends on the type of electronic logic in use). Each logic gate requires power so that it can source and sink currents to achieve the correct output voltage. In logic circuit diagrams the power is not shown, but in a full electronic schematic, power connections are required.

Truth Table

A truth table is a table that describes the behaviour of a logic gate. It lists the value of the output for every possible combination of the inputs and can be used to simplify the number of logic gates and level of nesting in an electronic circuit. In general the truth table does not lead to an efficient implementation; a minimization procedure, using Karnaugh maps, the Quine–McCluskey algorithm or a heuristic algorithm is required for reducing the circuit complexity.

Background

The simplest form of electronic logic is diode logic. This allows AND and OR gates to be built, but not inverters, and so is an incomplete form of logic. Further, without some kind of amplification it is not possible to have such basic logic operations cascaded as required for more complex logic functions.

To build a functionally complete logic system, relays, valves (vacuum tubes), or transistors can be used. The simplest family of logic gates using bipolar transistors is called resistor-transistor logic (RTL). Unlike diode logic gates, RTL gates can be cascaded indefinitely to produce more complex logic functions.

These gates were used in early integrated circuits. For higher speed, the resistors used in RTL were replaced by diodes, leading to diode-transistor logic (DTL). It was then discovered that one transistor could do the job of two diodes in the space of one diode even better, by more quickly switching off the following stage, so transistor-transistor logic, or TTL, was created.

In virtually every type of contemporary chip implementation of digital systems, the bipolar transistors have been replaced by complementary field-effect transistors (MOSFETs) to reduce size and power consumption still further, thereby resulting in complementary metal–oxide–semiconductor (CMOS) logic.

For small-scale logic, designers now use prefabricated logic gates from families of devices such as the TTL 7400 series by Texas Instruments and the CMOS 4000 series by RCA, and their more recent descendants. Increasingly, these fixed-function logic gates are being replaced by programmable logic devices, which allow designers to pack a large number of mixed logic gates into a single integrated circuit. The field-programmable nature of programmable logic devices such as FPGAs has removed the 'hard' property of hardware; it is now possible to change the logic design of a hardware system by reprogramming some of its components, thus allowing the features or function of a hardware implementation of a logic system to be changed.

Electronic logic gates differ significantly from their relay-and-switch equivalents. They are much faster, consume much less power, and are much smaller (all by a factor of a million or more in most cases). Also, there is a fundamental structural difference. The switch circuit creates a continuous metallic path for current to flow (in either direction) between its input and its output. The semiconductor logic gate, on the other hand, acts as a high-gain voltage amplifier, which sinks a tiny current at its input and produces a low-impedance voltage at its output. It is not possible for current to flow between the output and the input of a semiconductor logic gate.

Another important advantage of standardised integrated circuit logic families, such as the 7400 and 4000 families, is that they can be cascaded. This means that the output of one gate can be wired to the inputs of one or several other gates, and so on. Systems with varying degrees of complexity can be built without great concern of the designer for the internal workings of the gates, provided the limitations of each integrated circuit are considered.

The output of one gate can only drive a finite number of inputs to other gates, a number called the 'fanout limit'. Also, there is always a delay, called the 'propagation delay', from a change in input of a gate to the corresponding change in its output. When gates are cascaded, the total propagation delay is approximately the sum of the individual delays, an effect which can become a problem in high-speed circuits. Additional delay can be caused when a large number of inputs are connected to an output, due to the distributed capacitance of all the inputs and wiring and the finite amount of current that each output can provide.

Logic Gates

NAND and NOR logic gates are the two pillars of logic, in that all other types of Boolean logic gates (i.e., AND, OR, NOT, XOR, XNOR) can be created from a suitable network of just NAND or just NOR gate(s). They can be built from relays or transistors, or any other technology that can create an inverter and a two-input AND or OR gate. Hence the NAND and NOR gates are called the universal gates.

For an input of 2 variables, there are 16 possible boolean algebraic functions. These 16 functions are enumerated below, together with their outputs for each combination of inputs variables.

INPUT A	0	0	1	1	Meaning
B	0	1	0	1	
OUTPUT FALSE	0	0	0	0	Whatever *A* and *B*, the output is false. Contradiction.
A AND B	0	0	0	1	Output is true if and only if (iff) both *A* and *B* are true.
A B	0	0	1	0	*A* doesn't imply *B*. True iff *A* but not *B*.
A	0	0	1	1	True whenever *A* is true.
A B	0	1	0	0	*A* is not implied by *B*. True iff not *A* but *B*.
B	0	1	0	1	True whenever *B* is true.
A XOR B	0	1	1	0	True iff *A* is not equal to *B*.
A OR B	0	1	1	1	True iff *A* is true, or *B* is true, or both.
A NOR B	1	0	0	0	True iff neither *A* nor *B*.
A XNOR B	1	0	0	1	True iff *A* is equal to *B*.
NOT B	1	0	1	0	True iff *B* is false.
A B	1	0	1	1	*A* is implied by *B*. False if not *A* but *B*, otherwise true.
NOT A	1	1	0	0	True iff *A* is false.
A B	1	1	0	1	*A* implies *B*. False if *A* but not *B*, otherwise true.
A NAND B	1	1	1	0	*A* and *B* are not both true.
TRUE	1	1	1	1	Whatever *A* and *B*, the output is true. Tautology.

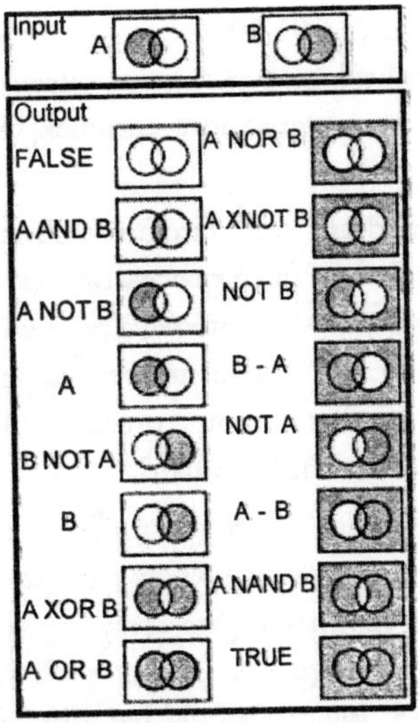

Venn Diagrams for Logic Gates

The four functions denoted by arrows are the logical implication functions. These functions are generally less common, and are usually not implemented directly as logic gates, but rather built out of gates like AND and OR.

Symbols

A synchronous 4-bit up/down decade counter symbol (74LS192) in accordance with ANSI/IEEE Std. 91-1984 and IEC Publication 60617-12.

There are two sets of symbols in common use, both now defined by ANSI/IEEE Std 91-1984 and its supplement ANSI/IEEE Std 91a-1991. The "distinctive shape" set, based on traditional schematics, is used for simple drawings and is quicker to draw by hand. It is sometimes unofficially described as "military", reflecting its origin if not its modern usage.

The "rectangular shape" set, based on IEC 60617-12, has rectangular outlines for all types of gate, and allows representation of a much wider range of devices than is possible with the traditional symbols. The IEC's system has been adopted by other standards, such as EN 60617-12:1999 in Europe and BS EN 60617-12:1999 in the United Kingdom.

The goal of IEEE Std 91-1984 was to provide a uniform method of describing the complex logic functions of digital circuits with schematic symbols. These functions were more complex than simple AND and OR gates.

They could be medium scale circuits such as a 4-bit counter to a large scale circuits such as a microprocessor. The 1984 version did not include the "distinctive shape" symbols. These were added to the 1991 supplement with this note: "The distinctive-shape symbol is, according to IEC Publication 617, Part 12, not preferred, but is not considered to be in contradiction to that standard."

In the 1980s, schematics were the predominant method to design both circuit boards and custom ICs known as gate arrays. Today custom ICs and the field-programmable gate array are typically designed with Hardware Description Languages (HDL) such as Verilog or VHDL. The need for complex logic symbols has diminished and distinctive shape symbols are still the predominate style.

In practice, the cheapest gate to manufacture is usually the NAND gate. Additionally, Charles Sanders Peirce (1880) showed that NAND gates alone (as well as NOR gates alone) can be used to reproduce the functions of all the other logic gates, but his work on it was unpublished until 1935. The first published proof was by Henry M. Sheffer in 1913.

The 7400 chip, containing four NANDs. The two additional pins supply power (+5 V) and connect the ground.

Two more gates are the exclusive-OR or XOR function and its inverse, exclusive-NOR or XNOR. The two input Exclusive-OR is true only when the two input values are *different*, false if they are equal, regardless of the value. If there are more than two inputs, the gate generates a true at its output if the number of trues at its input is *odd* ([2]). In practice, these gates are built from combinations of simpler logic gates.

De Morgan Equivalent Symbols

By use of De Morgan's theorem, an *AND* gate can be turned into an *OR* gate by inverting the sense of the logic at its inputs and outputs. This leads to a separate set of symbols with inverted inputs and the opposite core symbol. These symbols can make circuit diagrams for circuits using active low signals much clearer and help to show accidental connection of an active high output to an active low input or vice-versa.

Symbolically, a NAND gate can also be shown using the OR shape with bubbles on its inputs, and a NOR gate can be shown as an AND gate with bubbles on its inputs.

The bubble signifies a logic inversion. This reflects the equivalency due to De Morgans law, but it also allows a diagram to be read more easily, or a circuit to be mapped onto available physical gates in packages easily, since any circuit node that has bubbles at both ends can be replaced by a simple bubble-less connection and a suitable change of gate.

If the NAND is drawn as OR with input bubbles, and a NOR as AND with input bubbles, this gate substitution occurs automatically in the diagram (effectively, bubbles "cancel"). This is commonly seen in real logic diagrams-thus the reader must not get into the habit of associating the shapes exclusively as OR or AND shapes, but also take into account the bubbles at both inputs and outputs in order to determine the "true" logic function indicated.

All logic relations can be realized by using NAND gates. (This can also be done using NOR gates). De Morgan's theorem is most commonly used to transform all logic gates to NAND gates or NOR gates. This is done mainly since it is easy to buy logic gates in bulk and because many electronics labs stock only NAND and NOR gates.

Storage of Bits

Related to the concept of logic gates (and also built from them) is the idea of storing a bit of information. None of the gates discussed up to here can store a value by itself: when the inputs change, the outputs immediately react.

It is possible to make a storage element either through a capacitor (which stores charge due to its physical properties) or by feedback. Connecting the output of a gate to the input causes it to be put through the logic again, and choosing the feedback correctly allows it to be preserved or modified through the use of other inputs. A set of gates arranged in this fashion is known as a "latch", and more complicated designs that utilize clock signals and change only on the rising edge are called edge-triggered "flip-flops".

The combination of multiple flip-flops in parallel, to store a multiple-bit value, is known as a register. When using any of these gate setups the overall system has memory; it is then called a sequential logic system since its output can be influenced by its previous state(s).

These registers or capacitor-based circuits are known as computer memory. They vary in performance, based on factors of speed, complexity, and reliability of storage, and many different types of designs are used based on the application.

Three-state Logic Gates

A tristate buffer can be thought of as a switch. If *B* is on, the switch is closed. If B is off, the switch is open.

Three-state, or 3-state, logic gates have three states of the output: high (H), low (L) and high-impedance (Z).

The high-impedance state plays no role in the logic, which remains strictly binary. These devices are used on buses to allow multiple chips to send data. A group of three-states driving a line with a suitable control circuit is basically equivalent to a multiplexer, which may be physically distributed over separate devices or plug-in cards.

In electronics, a high output would mean the output is sourcing current from the positive power terminal (positive voltage). A low output would mean the output is sinking current to the negative power terminal (zero voltage).

High impedance would mean that the output is effectively disconnected from the circuit.

'Tri-state', a widely-used synonym of 'three-state', is a trademark of the National Semiconductor Corporation.

Miscellaneous

Logic circuits include such devices as multiplexers, registers, arithmetic logic units (ALUs), and computer memory, all the way up through complete microprocessors, which may contain more than 100 million gates. In practice, the gates are made from field-effect transistors (FETs), particularly MOSFETs.

Compound logic gates AND-OR-Invert (AOI) and OR-AND-Invert (OAI) are often employed in circuit design because their construction using MOSFET's is simpler and more efficient than the sum of the individual gates.

In Reversible logic, Toffoli Gates are Used

History and Development

The earliest logic gates were made mechanically. Charles Babbage, around 1837, devised the Analytical Engine. His logic gates relied on mechanical gearing to perform operations. Electromagnetic relays were later used for logic gates.

In 1891, Almon Strowger patented a device containing a logic gate switch circuit (U.S. Patent 0,447,918). Strowger's patent was not in widespread use until the 1990s. Starting in 1898, Nikola Tesla filed for patents of devices containing logic gate circuits. Eventually, vacuum tubes replaced relays for logic operations.

Lee De Forest's modification, in 1907, of the Fleming valve can be used as AND logic gate. Ludwig Wittgenstein introduced a version of the 16-row truth table, which is shown above, as proposition 5.101 of *Tractatus Logico-Philosophicus* (1921). Claude E. Shannon introduced the use of Boolean algebra in the analysis and design of switching circuits in 1937. Walther Bothe, inventor of the coincidence circuit, got part of the 1954 Nobel Prize in physics, for the first modern electronic AND gate in 1924. Active research is taking place in molecular logic gates.

Implementations

As of 2008, most logic gates are made of CMOS transistors. Often millions of logic gates are packaged in a single integrated circuit.

There are several logic families with different characteristics (power consumption, speed, cost, size) such as: RDL (resistor-diode logic), RTL (resistor-transistor logic), DTL (diode-transistor logic), TTL (transistor-transistor logic) and CMOS (complementary metal oxide semiconductor).

Many early electromechanical digital computers, such as the Harvard Mark I, were built from relay logic gates, using electro-mechanical relays.

It is also possible to make logic gates out of pneumatic devices, such as the Sorteberg relayor mechanical logic gates, including on a molecular scale. Logic gates have been made out of DNA and used to create a computer called MAYA.

Additionally, logic gates can be made from quantum mechanical effects (though quantum computing usually diverges from boolean design). It is also possible to make photonic logic gates using non-linear optical effects.

Combinational Logic With MSI and LSI

The purpose of simplification of Boolean functions is to obtain an algebraic expression with less number of literals and less numbers of logic gates.

This results in low-cost circuit implementation. The design procedure for combinational circuits as described is intended to minimize the number of logic gates to implement a given function. This classical procedure realizes the logic circuit with fewer gates with the assumption that the circuit with fewer gates will cost less. However, in practical design, with the arrival of a variety of integrated circuits (IC), this concept is always true.

Since one single IC package contains several number of logic gates, it is economical to use as many of the gates from an already used package, even if the total number of gates is increased by doing so. Moreover, some of the interconnections among the gates in many ICs are internal to the chip and it is more economical to use such types of ICs to minimize the external interconnections or wirings among the IC pins as much as possible. A typical example of this is if the circuit diagrams are considered. Both circuit diagrams perform the function of Excess-3-to-BCD code conversion and consist of 13 logic gates. However, the circuit needs six ICs (one 3-input OR, one 3-input AND, two 2-input AND, one 2-input OR, and one INVERTER, since one 3-input OR IC package contains three gates,.

Multiplexors

A multiplexor, or MUX, selects one of its data inputs and copies that input to the output, with the selection being made according to its address input.

Multiplexer

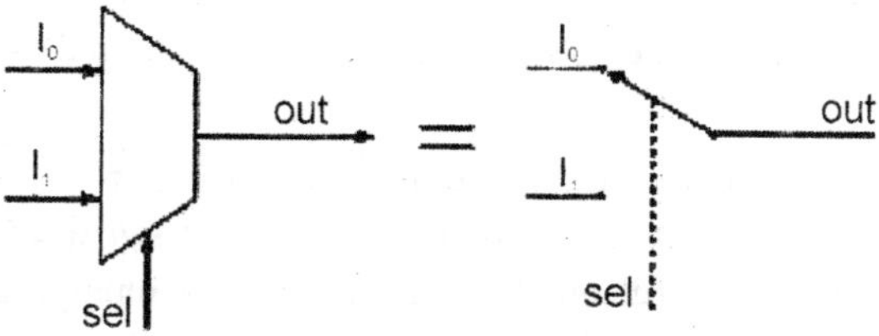

Schematic of a 2-to-1 Multiplexer. It can be equated to a controlled switch.

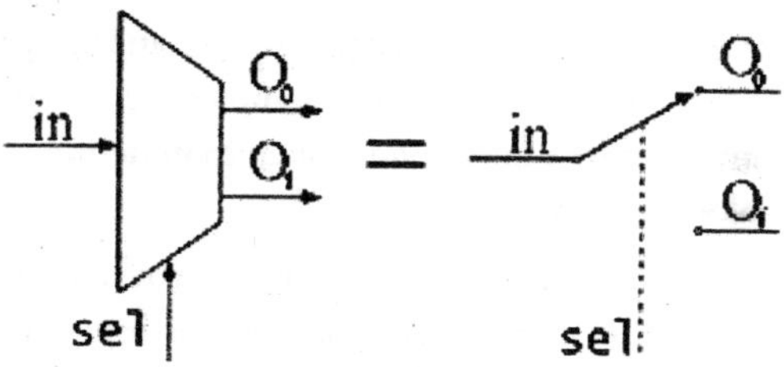

Schematic of a 1-to-2 Demultiplexer. Like a multiplexer, it can be equated to a controlled switch.

In electronics, a multiplexer or mux (occasionally the terms muldex or muldem are also found for a combination multiplexer-demultiplexer) is a device that performs multiplexing; it selects one of many analog or digital input signals and forwards the selected input into a single line. A multiplexer of 2^n inputs has n select lines, which are used to select which input line to send to the output.

An electronic multiplexer makes it possible for several signals to share one device or resource, for example one A/D converter or one communication line, instead of having one device per input signal.

On the other end, a demultiplexer (or demux) is a device taking a single input signal and selecting one of many data-output-lines, which is connected to the single input. A multiplexer is often used with a complementary demultiplexer on the receiving end.

An electronic multiplexer can be considered as a multiple-input, single-output switch, and a demultiplexer as a single-input, multiple-output switch. The schematic symbol for a multiplexer is an isosceles trapezoid with the longer parallel side containing the input pins and the short parallel side containing the output pin. The schematic on the right shows a 2-to-1 multiplexer on the left and an equivalent switch on the right. The *sel* wire connects the desired input to the output.

In telecommunications, a multiplexer is a device that combines several input information signals into one output signal, which carries several communication channels, by means of some multiplex technique. A demultiplexer is in this context a device taking a single input signal that carries many channels and separates those over multiple output signals.

In telecommunications and signal processing, an analog time division multiplexer (TDM) may take several samples of separate analogue signals and combine them into one pulse amplitude modulated (PAM) wide-band analogue signal.

Alternatively, a digital TDM multiplexer may combine a limited number of constant bit rate digital data streams into one data stream of a higher data rate, by forming data frames consisting of one timeslot per channel.

In telecommunications, computer networks and digital video, a statistical multiplexer may combine several variable bit rate data streams into one constant bandwidth signal, for example by means of packet mode communication. An inverse multiplexer may utilize several communication channels for transferring one signal.

Cost Savings

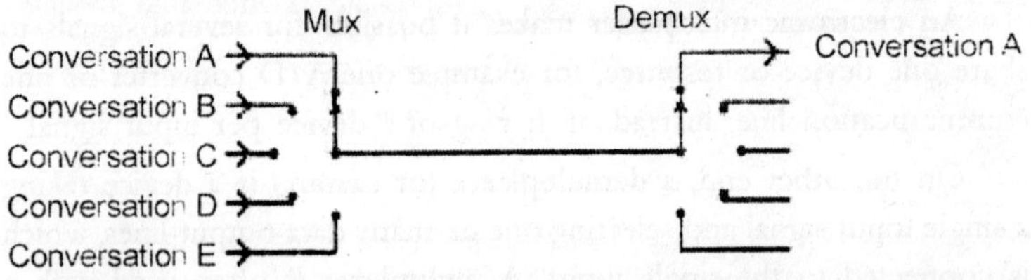

The basic function of a multiplexer: combining multiple inputs into a single data stream. On the receiving side, a demultiplexer splits the single data stream into the original multiple signals. One use for multiplexers is cost savings by connecting a multiplexer and a demultiplexer (or demux) together over a single channel (by connecting the multiplexer's single output to the demultiplexer's single input). The image to the right demonstrates this. In this case, the cost of implementing separate channels for each data source is more expensive than the cost and inconvenience of providing the multiplexing/demultiplexing functions. In a physical analogy, consider the merging behaviour of commuters crossing a narrow bridge; vehicles will take turns using the few available lanes. Upon reaching the end of the bridge they will separate into separate routes to their destinations.

At the receiving end of the data link a complementary *demultiplexer* is normally required to break single data stream back down into the original streams. In some cases, the far end system may have more functionality than a simple demultiplexer and so, whilst the demultiplexing still exists logically, it may never actually happen physically. This would be typical where a multiplexer serves a number of IP network users and then feeds directly into a router which immediately reads the content of the entire link into its routing processor and then does the demultiplexing in memory from where it will be converted directly into IP packets.

Often, a multiplexer and demultiplexer are combined together into a single piece of equipment, which is usually referred to simply as a "multiplexer". Both pieces of equipment are needed at both ends of a transmission link because most communications systems transmit in both directions.

A real world example is the creation of telemetry for transmission from the computer/instrumentation system of a satellite, space craft or other remote vehicle to a ground-based system. In analog circuit design, a multiplexer is a special type of analog switch that connects one signal selected from several inputs to a single output.

Digital Multiplexers

In digital circuit design, the selector wires are of digital value. In the case of a 2-to-1 multiplexer, a logic value of 0 would connect to the output while a logic value of 1 would connect to the output. In larger multiplexers, the number of selector pins is equal to where is the number of inputs.

For example, 9 to 16 inputs would require no fewer than 4 selector pins and 17 to 32 inputs would require no fewer than 5 selector pins.

The binary value expressed on these selector pins determines the selected input pin. A 2-to-1 multiplexer has a boolean equation where and are the two inputs, is the selector input, and is the output:

$$Z = (A \cdot \overline{S}) + (B \cdot S)$$

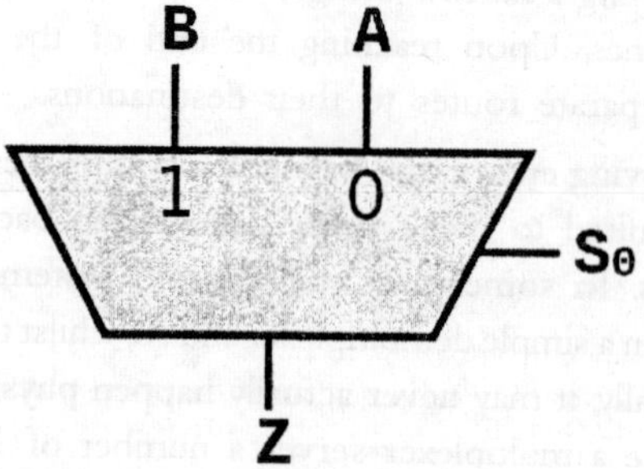

A 2-to-1 mux

Which can be expressed as a truth table:

0	1	1	1
	1	0	1
	0	1	0
	0	0	0
1	1	1	1
	1	0	0
	0	1	1
	0	0	0

This truth table shows that when then but when then. A straightforward realization of this 2-to-1 multiplexer would need 2 AND gates, an OR gate, and a NOT gate. Larger multiplexers are also common and, as stated above, requires selector pins for *n* inputs. Other common sizes are 4-to-1, 8-to-1, and 16-to-1. Since digital logic uses binary values, powers of 2 are used (4, 8, 16) to maximally control a number of inputs for the given number of selector inputs.

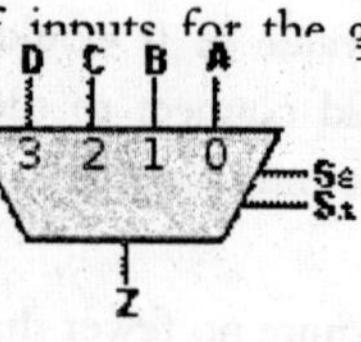

4-to-1 mux

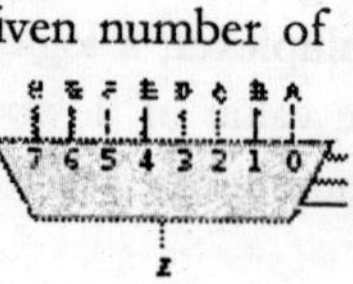

8-to-1 mux

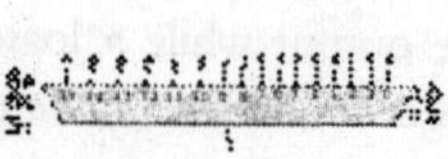

16-to-1 mux

The boolean equation for a 4-to-1 multiplexer is:

$$F = (A \cdot \overline{S_0} \cdot \overline{S_1}) + (B \cdot \overline{S_0} \cdot S_1) + (C \cdot S_0 \cdot \overline{S_1}) + (D \cdot S_0 \cdot S_1)$$

Two realizations for creating a 4-to-1 multiplexer are shown below:

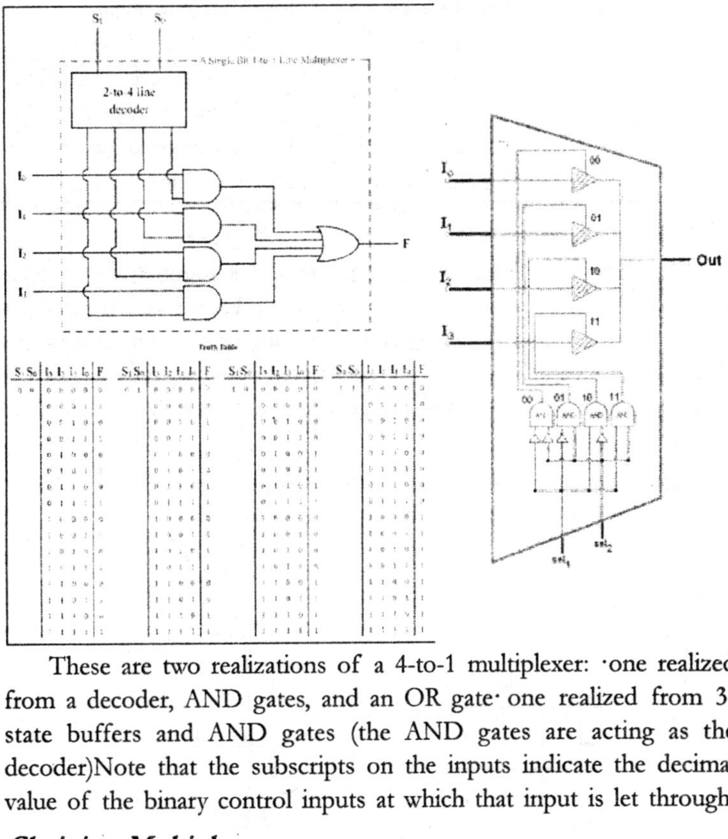

These are two realizations of a 4-to-1 multiplexer: ·one realized from a decoder, AND gates, and an OR gate· one realized from 3-state buffers and AND gates (the AND gates are acting as the decoder)Note that the subscripts on the inputs indicate the decimal value of the binary control inputs at which that input is let through.

Chaining Multiplexers

Larger multiplexers can be constructed by using smaller multiplexers by chaining them together. For example, an 8-to-1 multiplexer can be made with two 4-to-1 and one 2-to-1 multiplexers. The two 4-to-1 multiplexer outputs are fed into the 2-to-1 with the selector pins on the 4-to-1's put in parallel giving a total number of selector inputs to 3, which is equivalent to an 8-to-1.

List of ICs Which Provide Multiplexing

The 7400 series has several ICs that contain multiplexer(s):

S.No.	*IC No.*	*Function*	*Output State*
1	74157	Quad 2:1 mux.	Output same as input given
2	74158	Quad 2:1 mux.	Output is inverted input
3	74153	Dual 4:1 mux.	Output same as input
4	74352	Dual 4:1 mux.	Output is inverted input
5	74151A	8:1 mux.	Both outputs available (i.e., complementary outputs)
6	74151	8:1 mux.	Output is inverted input
7	74150	16:1 mux.	Output is inverted input

Digital Demultiplexers

Demultiplexers take one data input and a number of selection inputs, and they have several outputs. They forward the data input to one of the outputs depending on the values of the selection inputs. Demultiplexers are sometimes convenient for designing general purpose logic, because if the demultiplexer's input is always true, the demultiplexer acts as a decoder.

This means that any function of the selection bits can be constructed by logically OR-ing the correct set of outputs.

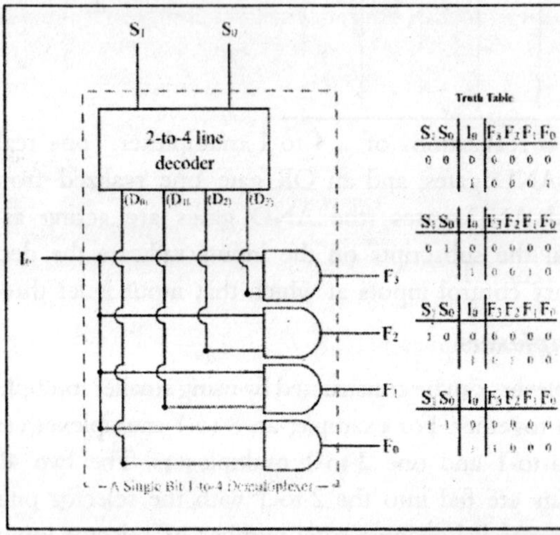

Example: A Single Bit 1-to-4 Line Demultiplexer

List of ICs which provide demultiplexing

The 7400 series has several ICs that contain demultiplexer(s):

S.No.	IC No.	Function	Output State
1	74139	Dual 1:4 demux.	Output is inverted input
3	74156	Dual 1:4 demux.	Output is open collector
4	74138	1:8 demux.	Output is inverted input
5	74154	1:16 demux.	Output is inverted input
6	74159	1:16 demux.	Output is open collector and same as input

In telecommunications and computer networks, multiplexing (also known as muxing) is a process where multiple analog message signals or digital data streams are combined into one signal over a shared medium. The aim is to share an expensive resource. For example, in telecommunications, several phone calls may be transferred using one wire. It originated in telegraphy, and is now widely applied in communications.

The multiplexed signal is transmitted over a communication channel, which may be a physical transmission medium. The multiplexing divides the capacity of the low-level communication channel into several higher-level logical channels, one for each message signal or data stream to be transferred. A reverse process, known as demultiplexing, can extract the original channels on the receiver side. A device that performs the multiplexing is called a multiplexer (MUX), and a device that performs the reverse process is called a demultiplexer (DEMUX). Inverse multiplexing (IMUX) has the opposite aim as multiplexing, namely to break one data stream into several streams, transfer them simultaneously over several Categories communication channels, and recreate the original data stream. The two most basic forms of multiplexing are time-division multiplexing (TDM) and frequency-division multiplexing (FDM), both either in analog or digital form. FDM requires modulation of each signal. In optical communications, FDM is referred to as wavelength-division multiplexing (WDM).

Variable bit rate digital bit streams may be transferred efficiently over a fixed bandwidth channel by means of statistical multiplexing, for example packet mode communication. Packet mode communication is an asynchronous mode time-domain multiplexing, which resembles, but should not be considered as, time-division multiplexing. Digital bit streams can be transferred over an analog channel by means of code-division multiplexing (CDM) techniques such as frequency-hopping spread spectrum (FHSS) and direct-sequence spread spectrum (DSSS).

In wireless communications, multiplexing can also be accomplished through alternating polarization (horizontal/vertical or clockwise/counterclockwise) on each adjacent channel and satellite, or through phased multi-antenna array combined with a Multiple-input multiple-output communications (MIMO) scheme.

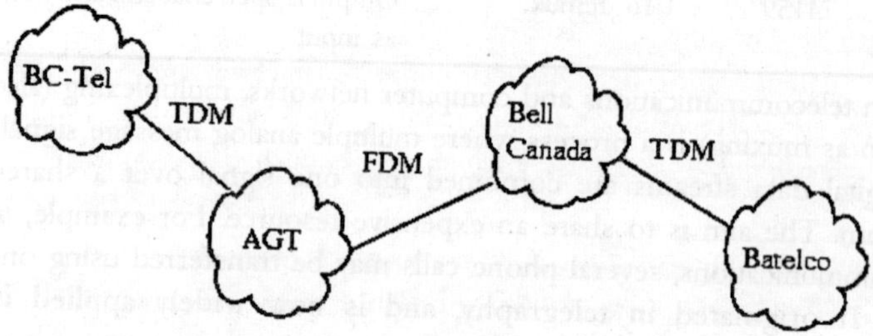

Telecommunication Multiplexing

Relation to Multiple Access

A multiplexing technique may be further extended into a multiple access method or channel access method, for example TDM into Time-division multiple access (TDMA) and statistical multiplexing into carrier sense multiple access (CSMA). A multiple access method makes it possible for several transmitters connected to the same physical medium to share its capacity. Multiplexing is provided by the Physical Layer of the OSI model, while multiple access also involves a media access control protocol, which is part of the Data Link Layer.

Application Areas

Telegraphy

The earliest communication technology using electrical wires, and therefore sharing an interest in the economies afforded by multiplexing, was the electric telegraph. Early experiments allowed two separate messages to travel in opposite directions simultaneously, first using an electric battery at both ends, then at only one end.

- Émile Baudot developed a time-multiplexing system of multiple Hughes machines in the 1990s.
- In 1874, the quadruplex telegraph developed by Thomas Edison transmitted two messages in each direction simultaneously, for a total of four messages transiting the same wire at the same time.

- Several workers were investigating acoustic telegraphy, a frequency-division multiplexing technique, which led to the invention of the telephone.

Telephony

In telephony, a customer's telephone line now typically ends at the remote concentrator box down the street, where it is multiplexed along with other telephone lines for that neighbourhood or other similar area. The multiplexed signal is then carried to the central switching office on significantly fewer wires and for much further distances than a customer's line can practically go. This is likewise also true for digital subscriber lines (DSL).

Fiber in the loop (FITL) is a common method of multiplexing, which uses optical fibre as the backbone. It not only connects POTS phone lines with the rest of the PSTN, but also replaces DSL by connecting directly to Ethernet wired into the home. Asynchronous Transfer Mode is often the communications protocol used.

Because all of the phone (and data) lines have been clumped together, none of them can be accessed except through a demultiplexer. This provides for more-secure communications, though they are not typically encrypted. The concept is also now used in cable TV, which is increasingly offering the same services as telephone companies. IPTV also depends on multiplexing.

Video Processing

In video editing and processing systems, multiplexing refers to the process of interleaving audio and video into one coherent transport stream (time-division multiplexing). In digital video, such a transport stream is normally a feature of a container format which may include metadata and other information, such as subtitles. The audio and video streams may have variable bit rate. Software that produces such a transport stream and/or container is commonly called a statistical multiplexor or muxer. A demuxer is software that extracts or otherwise makes available for separate processing the components of such a stream or container.

Digital Broadcasting

In digital television and digital radio systems, several variable bit-rate data streams are multiplexed together to a fixed bitrate transport stream by means of statistical multiplexing. This makes it possible to transfer several video and audio channels simultaneously over the same frequency channel, together with various services.

In the digital television systems, this may involve several standard definition television (SDTV) programmes (particularly on DVB-T, DVB-S2, ISDB and ATSC-C), or one HDTV, possibly with a single SDTV companion channel over one 6 to 8 MHz-wide TV channel. The device that accomplishes this is called a statistical multiplexer. In several of these systems, the multiplexing results in an MPEG transport stream. The newer DVB standards DVB-S2 and DVB-T2 has the capacity to carry several HDTV channels in one multiplex. Even the original DVB standards can carry more HDTV channels in a multiplex if the most advanced MPEG-4 compressions hardware is used.

On communications satellites which carry broadcast television networks and radio networks, this is known as multiple channel per carrier or MCPC. Where multiplexing is not practical (such as where there are different sources using a single transponder), single channel per carrier mode is used. Signal multiplexing of satellite TV and radio channels is typically carried out in a central signal playout and uplink centre, such as ASTRA Platform Services in Germany, which provides playout, digital archiving, encryption, and satellite uplinks, as well as multiplexing, for hundreds of digital TV and radio channels.

In digital radio, both the Eureka 147 system of digital audio broadcasting and the in-band on-channel HD Radio, FMeXtra, and Digital Radio Mondiale systems can multiplex channels. This is essentially required with DAB-type transmissions (where a multiplex is called an ensemble), but is entirely optional with IBOC systems.

Analog Broadcasting

In FM broadcasting and other analog radio media, multiplexing is a term commonly given to the process of adding subcarriers to the audio signal before it enters the transmitter, where modulation occurs. Multiplexing in this sense is sometimes known as MPX, which in turn is also an old term for stereophonic FM, seen on stereo systems since the 1990s.

Other Meanings

In spectroscopy the term is used in a related sense to indicate that the experiment is performed with a mixture of frequencies at once and their respective response unravelled afterwards using the Fourier transform principle. In computer programming, it may refer to using a single in-memory resource (such as a file handle) to handle multiple external resources (such as on-disk files).

Some electrical multiplexing techniques do not require a physical "multiplexer" device, they refer to a "keyboard matrix" or "Charlieplexing" design style:

- Multiplexing may refer to the design of a multiplexed display (non-multiplexed displays are immune to the Dorito effect).
- Multiplexing may refer to the design of a "switch matrix" (non-multiplexed buttons are immune to "phantom keys" and also immune to "phantom key blocking").

Decoders

This is best explained by example, say for a 3-to-8 decoder. Let's call the 3-bit input lines X2, X1 and X0, and the output lines Z7, Z6,..., Z1 and Z0. The 3-bit input can be considered the binary coding for one of the numbers 0-7. The output lines then tell us which one of the numbers 0-7 is represented by the input. For example, suppose X2 = 0, X1 = 1 and X0 = 1, representing the number 3; then Z3 will be 1, to indicate that fact, and all the other Zi will be 0. Building a decoder from gates is quite straightforward from the equations, which themselves are also straightforward.

Examples

Half Adder

Here we will design logic to add two 1-bit numbers A and B together. Let's call the sum bit Sum. But note also that there may be a carry generated (this will happen if both addends are equal to 1); we will call this Cout, for "carry output."

The logic will look like this: A B Cout Sum (The dark circles represent wire connections. If two lines cross in the picture but there is no dark circle at their intersection, then they do not touch each other.

Full Adder

A full adder has one more input than does a half adder. We will call this input Cin, for "carry in." The reason we need this extra input is that we will be using a full adder as a building block to do multi-bit addition. For example, consider the following addition of two 3-bit numbers, 011 and 001:

Bus-Based Circuits

The input line is visible at the left of the picture. Its quiescent state is 0, but sometimes pulses, i.e. 1s, come in on that line. (The pulses might come at regular intervals, such as from a clock, or at irregular times, depending on what application we needed this circuit for, i.e. depending on what we are counting.) The output pins are M0, M1 and M2, which contain c mod 5, and D0, D1, D2 and D3, which contain c div 5 (though only up to 15 for the latter). There are two boxes labeled CTR; these are 4-bit ripple counters. The pins labeled C in them are for clearing, i.e. resetting; if this pin is pulsed, all bits of the ripple counter will be reset to 0. Similarly, there is an "init" input at the top of the picture, to clear both the mod and div counters.

The box labeled DCD is a 3-to-8 decoder. Its output pins are active low, meaning that 0 means "yes" and 1 means "no." For example, let's label these pins Z7,Z6,...,Z0 from left to right. Then Z7 will be equal to 0 if and only if the three input pins contain 111, the binary representation of 7. Whenever the mod counter reaches 4, Z4 will be 0, which means that the output of the NOT gate we've connected to Z4 will be 1. This 1 is then ANDed with the circuit's input line. So, the next time the input line is pulsed—which will be a count which is a multiple of 5—a pulse will be felt at the c div 5 counter.

That Counter will then Increment, Exactly what we Want.

Note that the gate delay in DCD is helping us here. When the count is 4, the next pulse will change the count momentarily to 5 (and the rest of the circuit will change that to 0). However, even when the count first becomes 5, Z4 will still be equal to 0 (indicating a count of 4, not 5) for a short period of time equal to the gate delay in DCD. This delay is good, because when the pulse comes at count 4, we want Z4 to stay at 0 long enough so that it makes CTR increment. This illustrates the delicate timing issues which can arise in digital circuits.

Bus-Based Circuits

A bus is a set of parallel wires used for transfer of data among various components. You are already familiar with the idea of a system bus for a computer, which connects components such as the CPU, memory and I/O devices. Since several components are attached to the same bus, how do we make sure that only one of them actually is connected to the bus at a time? The answer is that we use tri-state buffers which can connect a component to a bus, or electrically isolate the component away from the bus. To illustrate this, consider the design of a very simple CPU which, for simplicity of exposition, will have only two registers, R0 and R1, each only one bit wide, implemented as a DFF:

Memory Chips and Systems

There are also inputs, again not shown, to the ALU determining which operation we want to perform, e.g. add, subtract, logical-and, logical-or, etc. Thus in the third clock cycle the control logic would also be putting the code for "add" on the control inputs to the ALU.9 During the third cycle we would also enable the connection from the output of the ALU to the bus. Note that this also means that there needs to be circuitry which counts clock pulses. How could we make this faster? Suppose we had two buses, rather than one, with all components (the registers and the ALU) connected to both buses. Then we could load both R2 and R3 at the same time, i.e. during the same clock cycle: R0 would be copied to R2 via the first bus, while at the same time, R1 would be copied to R2 via the second bus. During the second cycle we would enable the output from the ALU to a bus, say the first one, and enable the input to (in this example) R0. The instruction ADD R0,R1 would then take only two clock cycles, rather than three—a 33% speedup!

And by adding a third bus, we could get the time down to only one cycle. Now all of this is somewhat oversimplified (we have not accounted for time needed to fetch the instruction from memory and decode it, etc.), but you can at least begin to see the principle here—a classic computer science time/space tradeoff. If we are willing to use greater amounts of precious space on the CPU chip (more buses take up more room), we can reap a savings in time. With this example, the need for edge-triggering or some other anti-feedback mechanism should be more apparent. It would be worthwhile for you now to go back and review that section earlier in this document.

Example: Memory Chips and Systems

To illustrate the principles developed here, we will consider the design of simple memory chips and memory systems.

An SRAM Memory Chip

First consider the design of a "4x2" memory chip, meaning that it contains four two-bit words. (This is much, much smaller than the sizes of typical commercial memory chips, but the principles are the same.) We will call the four words Word 0, Word 1, Word 2 and Word 3. (Remember, though, that these are word numbers within this chip, not within a system constructed from this chip and others; more on this later.)

The chip will have the following pins: address pins A1 and A0 (two pins encode __ÀÛÜ_____ addresses), which indicate which of the four words is to be accessed; data-in pins DI1 and DI0 (for writing data to the chip); data-out pins DO1 and DO0 (for reading data from the chip); a write-enable pin WE, used to inform the chip that we wish to write to it; an output-enable pin OE, used to inform the chip that we wish to read from it; and a chip-select pin CS, to inform the chip that it, rather than some other memory chip, will be involved in the current memory transaction. Again, the "4x2" designation for this chip means that the chip contains four words, each two bits wide. Note that this might be a quite different viewpoint than that held by the CPU of our system. The CPU might, say, view an "8x4" system would consist of eight four-bit words. The memory for such a system could then be constructed by using in combination four 4x2 chips, as we will do later. (The CPU, though, would be unaware of the chip structure of the system.)

The use of separate pins for data input and output here is not standard, but simplifies the design somewhat.

If we were to have a single set of pins for both functions (as we will assume later), the design below could be modified in a straightforward way. To design this chip, let us first design a one-bit cell which will serve as the basic building block for the chip:

An Introduction to Digital Logic

This section contains a brief overview of digital electronics, it has enough information for you to complete the labs for this course, but is not meant to be all inclusive. Up until now the labs have dealt with electricity in its analog form where a quantity is described by the amount of voltage, or current, or charge... expressed as a real number. However a large proportion of electronic equipment, including computers, uses digital electronics where the quantities (usually voltage) are described by two states; on and off.

These two states can also be represented by true and false, 1 and 0, and in most physical systems are represented by the voltages 5V and 0V, or something close to that. While the restriction to two states seems limiting it makes many things easier because problems due to noise are minimized. It is generally very easy to reliably distinguish between logic 1 or logic 0.

Since many quantities cannot be represented by two states, more than one binary digit can be used to represent a number. For example the number 25_{10} (twenty five base 10) can be represented by the binary number 11001_2. It is easy to convert back and forth from binary to decimal by remembering that each digit in a binary number simply corresponds to a power of 2, as every digit in a decimal number corresponds to a power of 10. Using the previous example:

10^1	10^0		2^4	2^3	2^2	2^1	2^0
(10)	(1)		(16)	(8)	(4)	(2)	(1)
2	5	=	1	1	0	0	1
2*10	+ 5*1	=	1*16	+ 1*8	+ 0*4	+ 0*2	+ 1*1

In general an *n* digit binary number can represent numbers from 0 to 2^n-1. For instance a byte is 8 bits and can represent numbers from 0 to 255 (2^8-1).

Combinatorial Logic

Another advantage of digital electronics is the ability to express signals in terms of logic equations using standard terms from logic: *and*, *or*, and *not*. These functions can be represented by truth tables as shown below with A and B as inputs and C as output.

and			or			not	
A	B	C	A	B	C	A	C
0	0	0	0	0	0	0	1
0	1	0	0	1	1	1	0
1	0	0	1	0	1		
1	1	1	1	1	1		

These logic functions can be represented using a shorthand notation, *and* is represented by. or &, *or* is represented by + or #, and *not* is represented by ~ or ! (there are also other conventions, the most common is to put a bar over the variable). Thus the equation D equals A and B or not C can be represented as:

$$D = A.B + \tilde{}C \text{ or by } D = A \ \& \ B \ \# \ !C$$

Obviously this equation has different meanings depending on whether the *and* or the *or* function is performed first and parentheses can be used in the normal way to get rid of the ambiguity

$$D = (A.B) + \tilde{}C$$

Other functions that are common are *nand* and *nor.* The *nand* function is an *and* function followed by a *not, nor* is an *or* function followed by *not.* The symbols used in schematics for these functions are given below:

Logic equations, like any other, can get complicated quickly. To simplify logic equations a system called Boolean algebra (after the mathematician George Boole) was developed. A short selection of its theorems is listed.

(1) $A \cdot 0 = 0$	(6) $A+1 = 1$	$!A!B$	(11) $(A \cdot B) \cdot C = A \cdot (B \cdot C)$
(2) $A \cdot 1 = A$	(7) $A+\tilde{A} = 1$	1	(12) $A \cdot (B+C) = A \cdot B+B \cdot C$
(3) $A \cdot \tilde{A} = 0$	(8) $A+A = A$	0	(13) $A+(B \cdot C) = (A+B) \cdot (A+C)$
(4) $A+0 = A$	(9) $A+B = B+A$	0	(14) $!(A+B) = !A!B$
(5) $A \cdot A = A$	(10) $(A+B)+C = A+(B+C)$	0	(15) $!(A \cdot B) = !A+!B$

Some of these rules are quite obvious. For example if we make out the truth table for rule (1) we get:

A	A·0
0	0
i	0

Some of the other rules are not so obvious. For example rule 14 yields the truth table shown below

A	B	!A	!B	A+B	!(A+B)	!A·!B
0	0	1	1	0	1	1
0	1	1	0	1	0	0
1	0	0	1	1	0	0
1	1	0	0	1	0	0

The truth table shows that rule 14, $!(A+B) = !A \cdot !B$, is correct.

These theorems can be used to simplify equations. For example if we start off with the expression

$$D = (A \cdot B+(A+C \cdot \tilde{}C)) \cdot A+B,$$

we can apply the rules in turn to simplify it.

D = (A·B+(A+C·~C))·A+B	apply 3
D = (A·B+A)·A+B	apply 2
D = (A·B+A·1)·A+B	apply 12
D = (A.(B+1))·A+B	apply 6
D = A·A+B	apply 5
D = A+B	

As with the algebra you learned in elementary school, this kind of simplification gets tedious, and messy, quickly. Luckily there is a graphical shortcut to doing logic minimizations called a Karnaugh map. This introduction will only cover Karnaugh maps with up to four variables, though the technique can be generalized to larger systems-though these systems are usually simplified using computers. Consider the truth table of the equation given above, which is given in the forma of a truth table and a three variable Karnaugh map:

Truth Table

A	B	C	D
0	0	0	0
0	0	1	0
0	1	0	1
0	1	1	1
1	0	0	1
1	0	1	1
1	1	0	1
1	1	1	1

Karnaugh Map

A \ BC	00	01	11	10
0	0	0	1	1
1	1	1	1	1

One way to get a solution is simply to write an expression for each true result in the table. For example, the lower-leftmost true result from the Karnaugh map represents the case where A=1 and B=0 and C=0 and it can be written as A·~B·~C. The true result next to it can be written as A·~B·C. Now to develop a logic expression, we would just *or* together all of these terms. Thus our result (including an expression for each true term — 6 in all) is:

A·~B·~C + A·~B·C + A·B·C + A·B·~C + ~A·B·C + A·B·~C

This is called the sum-of-products form. Although this expression is correct, it is also unwieldy. We could use the theorems of Boolean algebra to simplify the expression, which is often difficult and does not guarantee a best solution. However we can use a visual technique based on Karnaugh maps to develop a minimal sum-of-products solution. To get the simplified equation one takes the table and encircles as many

1's as possible in rectangular groups that have 1, 2, 4, or 8 elements (i.e., any power of 2). The idea is to make the groupings as large as possible. For the example above this can be accomplished with 2 groupings:

A \ BC	00	01	11	10
0	0	0	1	1
1	1	1	1	1

If you examine these groupings carefully you can see that the red grouping has no dependence on the variables A or C, and is totally described by the statement B=1. The blue group on the other hand has no dependence on B or C and is described by the statement A=1. Therefore to include the elements from both groups we can use the equation A+B.

If you had used smaller groups you would have obtained an equivalent, though more complicated, expression. Try it. This graphical method is clearly easier than the technique used earlier that employed algebraic simplifications. You should examine the map shown above and convince yourself that any grouping of a single element needs all three variables to describe it. For instance the uppermost "1" on the right hand side is described by B·~C· A A grouping of two gets rid of the dependence on one of the variables (the two rightmost ones have no dependence on A and are given by B·~C). A group of four, as you have seen, depends only on one variable. Therefore by choosing the smallest number of groups (i.e., the largest groups), you will come up with the minimal equation describing those groups. The result obtained with the Karnaugh map is called the minimal sum of products form because it generates the smallest number of product (*and*ed) terms.

Also, if you look at the table again you can convince yourself that it is possible to "wrap-around" the ends of the table, as shown

A \ BC	00	01	11	10
0	0	0	0	1
1	1	0	0	1

The two groups are represented by B·C (the red group) and the blue group that wraps around by A·~C.

This technique also works for two variables (trivial), four variables (shown below), and even more (though this gets complicated and will not be described here). A typical four variable map and its groupings are shown here.

AB \ CD	00	01	11	10
00	0	0	1	1
01	1	0	1	1
11	0	1	0	0
10	0	0	1	1

AB \ CD	00	01	11	10
00	0	0	1	1
01	1	0	1	1
11	0	1	0	0
10	0	0	1	1

which simplifies to: $A\cdot B\cdot D\cdot \bar{C} + \tilde{A}\cdot B\cdot \bar{D} + \tilde{A}\cdot C + \bar{B}\cdot C$. Prove it to yourself.

Months in school

Month	**D**	**C**	**B**	**A**	**Output**
January	0	0	0	1	1
February	0.	0	1	0	1
March	0	0	1	1	1
April	0	1	0	0	1
May	0	1	0	1	1
June	0	1	1	0	0
July	0	1	1	1	0
August	1	0	0	0	0
September	1	0	0	1	0
October	1	0	1	0	1
November	1	0	1	1	1
December	1	1	0	0	1

Truth Table and Karnaugh map

DC \ BA	00	01	11	10
00	X	1	1	1
01	1	1	0	0
11	1	X	X	X
10	0	0	1	1

DC \ BA	00	01	11	10
00	X	1	1	1
01	1	1	0	0
11	1	X	X	X
10	0	0	1	1

Alternate solution (others possible)

DC \ BA	00	01	11	10
00	X	1	1	1
01	1	1	0	0
11	1	X	X	X
10	0	0	1	1

Sequential Logic

The digital logic described thus far is called combinatorial logic because the output depends solely upon the presently existing combination of the inputs; *past* values of the inputs are not important. Sequential logic deals with the issue of time dependence and can get much more complicated than combinatorial logic — much in the same way that differential equations are more difficult than algebraic equations. The fundamental building block of sequential circuits is the flip-flop (which flips and flops between different logic states) of which there are several. The simplest flip-flop is the R-S, or Set-Reset flip flop which is made up of two gates:

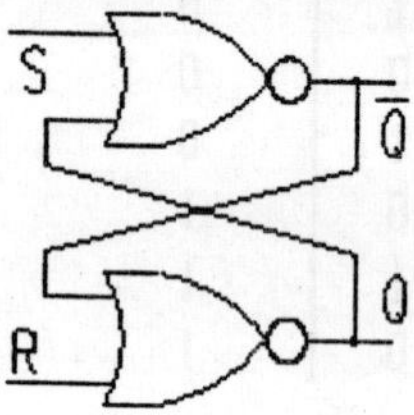

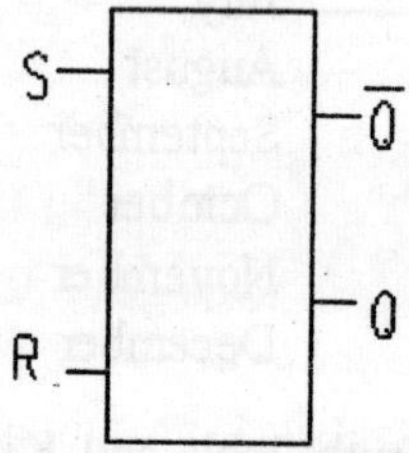

Note that flip flops are often quite complicated at the gate level and are frequently represented by a "black box" with inputs and outputs as shown at right.

Let's see how this device operates by examining the four possible inputs, if S,R=1,0 then Q=1 and ˉQ=0, therefore S=1 *sets* Q.

If S,R=0,1 then Q=1 and ˉQ=0, or R=1 *resets* Q. If S,R=1,1 then Q=0 and ˉQ=0; a result that doesn't seem to make sense, but we will deal with this soon. If S,R=0,0 then you can convince yourself that the outputs are indeterminate — that is you cannot figure out what they are. This is where the time dependence of the circuit is important: if S,R goes from the 1,0 to the 0,0 state then Q=1 and ˜Q=0; if S,R goes from 0,1 to 0,0 then Q=0 and ˜Q=1; but if S,R goes from 1,1 to 0,0 then Q and ˜Q are still indeterminate and so we will call 1,1 the disallowed state and design our circuit so this state is not used. The 0,0 state is called the *hold* state. The truth table for this circuit is given as:

S_n	Rn	Q_n
0	0	Q_{n-1}
0	1	0
1	0	1
1	1	Disallowed

Note that the variables have a subscript associated with them. This subscript denotes time, so that if S,R=0,0 at time n then the output Q retains the value it had at time n-1.

There are several other types of flip-flops, but the most popular are the D and J-K flip-flops which have the following truth tables:

D_{n-1}	Q_n
1	1
0	0

J_{n-1}	K_{n-1}	Q_n
0	0	Q_{n-1}
0	1	0
1	0	1
1	1	$\tilde{Q}_{n-1}$

and the circuit symbols:

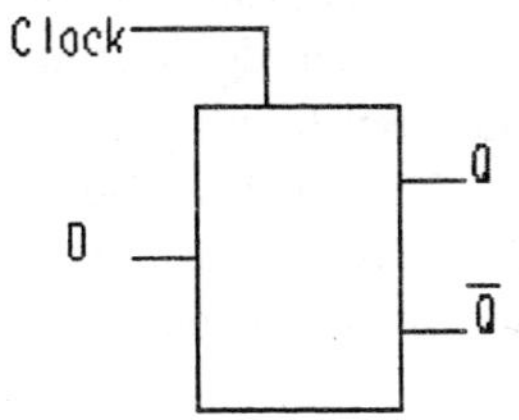

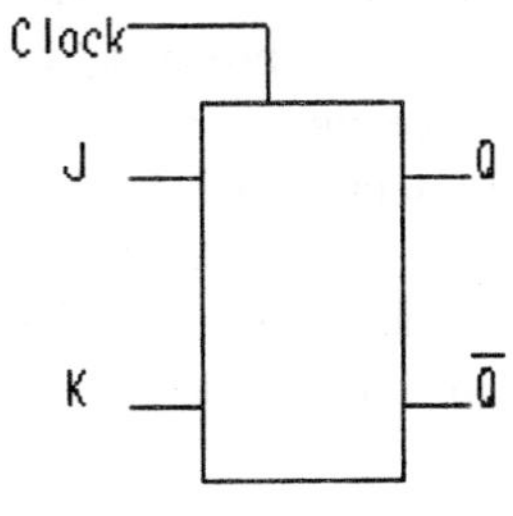

Note that these flip-flops have another input called the "clock". The transition from time *n-1* to time *n* occurs at some transition of the clock; usually when the clock goes from low to high (rising edge) or from high to low (falling edge), but is sometimes level sensitive (for instance the output may do what is required by the input while the clock is high and holds the last value when the clock is low). In addition to the clock there are sometimes *reset* inputs to clear the output to logic 0, and preset inputs to set the outputs to logic 1. To further understand these devices consider the circuit shown below (actually a simplified portion of an integrated circuit, the 7493):

Note: the inverted outputs of the flip-flops aren't shown since we aren't using them.

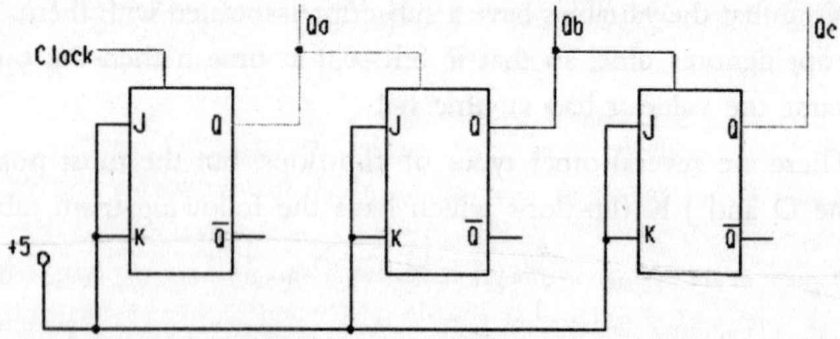

Assume that the flip-flops are falling edge triggered and that the outputs are initially all 0, then if a series of clock pulses is fed into the circuit, Clock, you should be able to convince yourself that the output is given by:

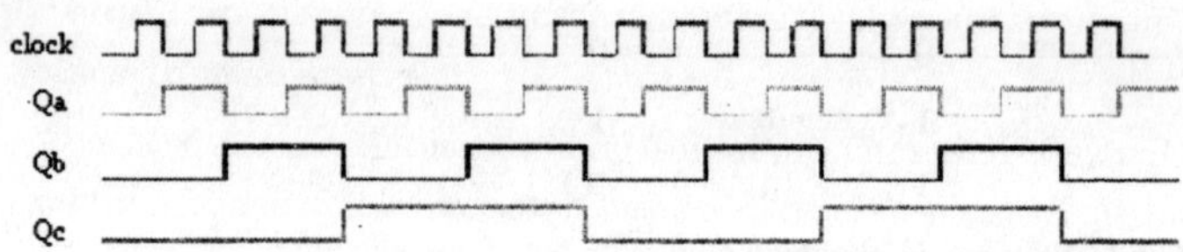

Thus Q_a is half the frequency of the clock, Q_b half that of Q_a, and Q_c half that of Q_b; making Q_c 1/8 the frequency of the clock. Also if you use Q_a through Q_c to represent a number (Q_a=least significant bit), then the output of this circuit cycles repetitively through eight states representing the numbers 0_{10} to 7_{10} (0_2 to 111_2). Therefore this circuit is known as a divide by eight counter. The actual 7493 is a little more complicated and includes a reset signal so that you can reset the counter to 0 at any time.

2

Basic Computer Organization and Design

In computer engineering, microarchitecture (sometimes abbreviated to μarch or uarch) is the way a given instruction set architecture (ISA) is implemented on a processor. A given ISA may be implemented with different microarchitectures Implementations might vary due to different goals of a given design or due to shifts in technology. Computer Architecture is the combination of microarchitecture and instruction set design.

Relation to Instruction Set Architecture

The ISA is roughly the same as the programming model of a processor as seen by an assembly language programmer or compiler writer. The ISA includes the execution model, processor registers, address and data formats among other things. The microarchitecture includes the constituent parts of the processor and how these interconnect and interoperate to implement the ISA.

The microarchitecture of a machine is usually represented as (more or less detailed) diagrams that describe the interconnections of the various microarchitectual elements of the machine, which may be everything from single gates and registers, to complete ALUs and even larger elements. These diagrams generally separate the data path (where data is placed) and the control path (which can be said to steer the data). Machines with different microarchitectures may have the same instruction set architecture, and thus be capable of executing the same programs. New microarchitectures and/or circuitry solutions, along with advances in semiconductor manufacturing, are what allows newer generations of processors to achieve higher performance while using the same ISA.

Aspects of Microarchitecture

The pipelined datapath is the most commonly used datapath design in microarchitecture today. This technique is used in most modern microprocessors, microcontrollers, and DSPs. The pipelined architecture allows multiple instructions to overlap in execution, much like an assembly line. The pipeline includes several different stages which are fundamental in microarchitecture designs. Some of these stages include instruction fetch, instruction decode, execute, and write back. Some architectures include other stages such as memory access. The design of pipelines is one of the central microarchitectural tasks.

Execution units are also essential to microarchitecture. Execution units include arithmetic logic units (ALU), floating point units (FPU), load/store units, branch prediction, and SIMD. These units perform the operations or calculations of the processor. The choice of the number of execution units, their latency and throughput is a central microarchitectural design task. The size, latency, throughput and connectivity of memories within the system are also microarchitectural decisions.

System-level design decisions such as whether or not to include peripherals, such as memory controllers, can be considered part of the microarchitectural design process. This includes decisions on the performance-level and connectivity of these peripherals. Unlike architectural design, where achieving a specific performance level is the main goal, microarchitectural design pays closer attention to other constraints. Since microarchitecture design decisions directly affect what goes into a system, attention must be paid to such issues as:

- chip area/cost
- power consumption
- logic complexity
- ease of connectivity
- manufacturability
- ease of debugging
- testability.

Microarchitectural Concepts

In general, all CPUs, single-chip microprocessors or multi-chip implementations run programs by performing the following steps:

1. read an instruction and decode it
2. find any associated data that is needed to process the instruction
3. process the instruction
4. write the results out.

Complicating this simple-looking series of steps is the fact that the memory hierarchy, which includes caching, main memory and non-volatile storage like hard disks, (where the program instructions and data reside) has always been slower than the processor itself. Step (2) often introduces a lengthy (in CPU terms) delay while the data arrives over the computer bus. A considerable amount of research has been put into designs that avoid these delays as much as possible. Over the years, a central goal was to execute more instructions in parallel, thus increasing the effective execution speed of a program. These efforts introduced complicated logic and circuit structures. Initially these techniques could only be implemented on expensive mainframes or supercomputers due to the amount of circuitry needed for these techniques. As semiconductor manufacturing progressed, more and more of these techniques could be implemented on a single semiconductor chip.

What follows is a survey of micro-architectural techniques that are common in modern CPUs.

Instruction Set Choice

Instruction sets have shifted over the years, from originally very simple to sometimes very complex (in various respects). In recent years, load-store architectures, VLIW and EPIC types have been in fashion. Architectures that are dealing with data parallelism include SIMD and Vectors. Some labels used to denote classes of CPU architectures are not particularity descriptive, especially so the CISC label; many early designs, retroactively denoted "CISC" are in fact significantly simpler than modern RISC processors (in several respects).

However, the choice of instruction set architecture may greatly affect the complexity of implementing high performance devices. The prominent strategy, used to develop the first RISC processors, was to simplify instructions to a minimum of individual semantic complexity combined with high encoding regularity and simplicity. Such uniform instructions were easily fetched, decoded and executed in a pipelined fashion and a simple strategy to reduce the number of logic levels in order to reach high operating frequencies; instruction cache-memories compensated for the higher operating frequency and inherently low code density while large register sets were used to factor out as much of the (slow) memory accesses as possible.

Instruction Pipelining

One of the first, and most powerful, techniques to improve performance is the use of the instruction pipeline. Early processor designs would carry out all of the steps above for one instruction before moving onto the next. Large portions of the circuitry were left idle at any one step; for instance, the instruction decoding circuitry would be idle during execution and so on.

Pipelines improve performance by allowing a number of instructions to work their way through the processor at the same time. In the same basic example, the processor would start to decode (step 1) a new instruction while the last one was waiting for results. This would allow up to four instructions to be "in flight" at one time, making the processor look four times as fast. Although any one instruction takes just as long to complete (there are still four steps) the CPU as a whole "retires" instructions much faster and can be run at a much higher clock speed.

RISC make pipelines smaller and much easier to construct by cleanly separating each stage of the instruction process and making them take the same amount of time — one cycle. The processor as a whole operates in an assembly line fashion, with instructions coming in one side and results out the other. Due to the reduced complexity of the Classic RISC pipeline, the pipelined core and an instruction cache could be placed on the same size die that would otherwise fit the core alone on a CISC design. This was the real reason that RISC was faster. Early designs like the SPARC and MIPS often ran over 10 times as fast as Intel and Motorola CISC solutions at the same clock speed and price.

Pipelines are by no means limited to RISC designs. By 1986 the top-of-the-line VAX implementation (VAX 8800) was a heavily pipelined design, slightly predating the first commercial MIPS and SPARC designs. Most modern CPUs (even embedded CPUs) are now pipelined, and microcoded CPUs with no pipelining are seen only in the most area-constrained embedded processors. Large CISC machines, from the VAX 8800 to the modern Pentium 4 and Athlon, are implemented with both microcode and pipelines. Improvements in pipelining and caching are the two major microarchitectural advances that have enabled processor performance to keep pace with the circuit technology on which they are based.

Cache

It was not long before improvements in chip manufacturing allowed for even more circuitry to be placed on the die, and designers started looking for ways to use it. One of the most common was to add an ever-increasing amount of cache memory on-die. Cache is simply very fast memory, memory that can be accessed in a few cycles as opposed to "many" needed to talk to main memory. The CPU includes a cache controller which automates reading and writing from the cache, if the data is already in the cache it simply "appears," whereas if it is not the processor is "stalled" while the cache controller reads it in.

RISC designs started adding cache in the mid-to-late 1980s, often only 4 KB in total. This number grew over time, and typical CPUs now have at least 512 KB, while more powerful CPUs come with 1 or 2 or even 4, 6, 8 or 12 MB, organized in multiple levels of a memory hierarchy. Generally speaking, more cache means more performance, thanks to reduced stalling.

Caches and pipelines were a perfect match for each other. Previously, it didn't make much sense to build a pipeline that could run faster than the access latency of off-chip memory. Using on-chip cache memory instead, meant that a pipeline could run at the speed of the cache access latency, a much smaller length of time. This allowed the operating frequencies of processors to increase at a much faster rate than that of off-chip memory.

Branch Prediction

One barrier to achieving higher performance through instruction-level parallelism stems from pipeline stalls and flushes due to branches. Normally, whether a conditional branch will be taken isn't known until late in the pipeline as conditional branches depend on results coming from a register. From the time that the processor's instruction decoder has figured out that it has encountered a conditional branch instruction to the time that the deciding register value can be read out, the pipeline needs to be stalled for several cycles, or if it's not and the branch is taken, the pipeline needs to be flushed. As clock speeds increase the depth of the pipeline increases with it, and some modern processors may have 20 stages or more. On average, every fifth instruction executed is a branch, so without any intervention, that's a high amount of stalling.

Techniques such as branch prediction and speculative execution are used to lessen these branch penalties. Branch prediction is where the hardware makes educated guesses on whether a particular branch will be taken. In reality one side or the other of the branch will be called much more often than the other. Modern designs have rather complex statistical prediction systems, which watch the results of past branches to predict the future with greater accuracy. The guess allows the hardware to prefect instructions without waiting for the register read. Speculative execution is a further enhancement in which the code along the predicted path is not just perfected but also executed before it is known whether the branch should be taken or not. This can yield better performance when the guess is good, with the risk of a huge penalty when the guess is bad because instructions need to be undone.

Superscalar

Even with all of the added complexity and gates needed to support the concepts outlined above, improvements in semiconductor manufacturing soon allowed even more logic gates to be used.

In the outline above the processor processes parts of a single instruction at a time. Computer programs could be executed faster if multiple instructions were processed simultaneously. This is what superscalar processors achieve, by replicating functional units such as ALUs. The replication of functional units was only made possible when the die area of a single-issue processor no longer stretched the limits of what could be reliably manufactured. By the late 1980s, superscalar designs started to enter the market place.

In modern designs it is common to find two load units, one store (many instructions have no results to store), two or more integer math units, two or more floating point units, and often a SIMD unit of some sort. The instruction issue logic grows in complexity by reading in a huge list of instructions from memory and handing them off to the different execution units that are idle at that point. The results are then collected and re-ordered at the end.

Out-of-Order Execution

The addition of caches reduces the frequency or duration of stalls due to waiting for data to be fetched from the memory hierarchy, but does not get rid of these stalls entirely. In early designs a *cache miss* would force the cache controller to stall the processor and wait. Of course there may be some other instruction in the program whose data *is* available in the cache at that point. Out-of-order execution allows that ready instruction to be processed while an older instruction waits on the cache, then re-orders the results to make it appear that everything happened in the programmed order. This technique is also used to avoid other operand dependency stalls, such as an instruction awaiting a result from a long latency floating-point operation or other multi-cycle operations.

Register Renaming

Register renaming refers to a technique used to avoid unnecessary serialized execution of program instructions because of the reuse of the same registers by those instructions. Suppose we have two groups of instruction that will use the same register, one set of instruction is executed first to leave the register to the other set, but if the other set is assigned to a different similar register both sets of instructions can be executed in parallel.

Multiprocessing and Multithreading

Computer architects have become stymied by the growing mismatch in CPU operating frequencies and DRAM access times. None of the techniques that exploited instruction-level parallelism within one program could make up for the long stalls that occurred when data had to be fetched from main memory. Additionally, the large transistor counts and high operating frequencies needed for the more advanced ILP techniques required power dissipation levels that could no longer be cheaply cooled. For these reasons, newer generations of computers have started to exploit higher levels of parallelism that exist outside of a single program or program thread.

This trend is sometimes known as *throughput computing*. This idea originated in the mainframe market where online transaction processing emphasized not just the execution speed of one transaction, but the capacity to deal with massive numbers of transactions. With transaction-based applications such as network routing and website serving greatly increasing in the last decade, the computer industry has re-emphasized capacity and throughput issues.

One technique of how this parallelism is achieved is through multiprocessing systems, computer systems with multiple CPUs. Once reserved for high-end mainframes and supercomputers, small scale (2-8) multiprocessors servers have become commonplace for the small business market. For large corporations, large scale (16-256) multiprocessors are common. Even personal computers with multiple CPUs have appeared since the 1990s.

With further transistor size reductions made available with semiconductor technology advances, multicore CPUs have appeared where multiple CPUs are implemented on the same silicon chip. Initially used in chips targeting embedded markets, where simpler and smaller CPUs would allow multiple instantiations to fit on one piece of silicon. By 2005, semiconductor technology allowed dual high-end desktop CPUs *CMP* chips to be manufactured in volume. Some designs, such as Sun Microsystems' UltraSPARC T1 have reverted back to simpler (scalar, in-order) designs in order to fit more processors on one piece of silicon.

Another technique that has become more popular recently is multithreading. In multithreading, when the processor has to fetch data from slow system memory, instead of stalling for the data to arrive, the processor switches to another program or program thread which is ready to execute. Though this does not speed up a particular program/ thread, it increases the overall system throughput by reducing the time the CPU is idle.

Conceptually, multithreading is equivalent to a context switch at the operating system level. The difference is that a multithreaded CPU can do a thread switch in one CPU cycle instead of the hundreds or thousands of CPU cycles a context switch normally requires. This is achieved by replicating the state hardware (such as the register file and program counter) for each active thread.

A further enhancement is simultaneous multithreading. This technique allows superscalar CPUs to execute instructions from different programs/threads simultaneously in the same cycle.

Microprocessor

A microprocessor incorporates most or all of the functions of a central processing unit (CPU) on a single integrated circuit (IC). The first microprocessors emerged in the early 1970s and were used for electronic calculators, using binary-coded decimal (BCD) arithmetic on 4-bit words. Other embedded uses of 4-and 8-bit microprocessors, such as terminals, printers, various kinds of automation etc, followed rather quickly. Affordable 8-bit microprocessors with 16-bit addressing also led to the first general purpose microcomputers in the mid-1970s.

Computer processors were for a long period constructed out of small and medium-scale ICs containing the equivalent of a few to a few hundred transistors. The integration of the whole CPU onto a single chip therefore greatly reduced the cost of processing capacity. From their humble beginnings, continued increases in microprocessor capacity have rendered other forms of computers almost completely obsolete (see history of computing hardware), with one or more microprocessor as processing element in everything from the smallest embedded systems and handheld devices to the largest mainframes and supercomputers.

Since the early 1970s, the increase in capacity of microprocessors has been known to generally follow Moore's Law, which suggests that the complexity of an integrated circuit, with respect to minimum component cost, doubles every two years. In the late 1990s, and in the high-performance microprocessor segment, heat generation (TDP), due to switching losses, static current leakage, and other factors, emerged as a leading developmental constraint.

History

First Types

Three projects arguably delivered a complete microprocessor at about the same time, namely Intel's 4004, the Texas Instruments (TI) *TMS* 1000, and Garrett AiResearch's Central Air Data Computer (CADC). Intel's 4004 is considered the first microprocesor, and cost in the thousands of dollars. The first known advertisement for the 4004 is dated to November 1971; it appeared in Electronic News. The project that produced the 4004 originated in 1969, when Busicom, a Japanese calculator manufacturer, asked Intel to build a chipset for high-performance desktop calculators. Busicom's original design called for a dozen different logic and memory chips. Ted Hoff, the Intel engineer assigned to the project, believed the design was not cost effective. His solution was to simplify the design and produce a programmable processor capable of creating a set of complex special-purpose calculator chips. Together with Masatoshi Shima and Federico Faggin, later the founder of Zilog, Hoff came up with a four-chip design; a ROM for custom application programs, a RAM for processing data, an I/O device, and an unnamed 4-bit central processing unit which would become known as a "microprocessor."

The Smithsonian Institution says TI engineers Gary Boone and Michael Cochran succeeded in creating the first microcontroller (also called a microcomputer) in 1971. The result of their work was the TMS 1000 which went commercial in 1974.

In early 1971 Pico Electronics. and General Instrument introduced their first collaboration in ICs, a complete single chip calculator IC for the Monroe Royal Digital III calculator. This IC could also arguably lay claim to be one of the first microprocessors or microcontrollers having ROM, RAM and a RISC instruction set on-chip. Pico was a spinout by five GI design engineers whose vision was to create single chip calculator ICs. They had significant previous design experience on multiple calculator chipsets with both GI and Marconi-Elliott. Pico and GI went on to have significant success in the burgeoning handheld calculator market.

The design engineer Ray Holt, a graduate of California Polytechnical University in 1968, began his computer design career with the F14 CADC. The central air data computer was shrouded in secrecy for over 30 years from its creation (the year being 1968), it was not publicly known until 1998 at which time, at the request of Mr. Ray Holt, the US Navy allowed the documents into the public domain. Since then many debates have argued that this was, in fact, the first microprocessor. The scientific papers and literature published around 1971 reveal that the MP944 digital processor used for the F-14 Tomcat aircraft of the US Navy qualifies as the "first microprocessor". Although interesting, it was not a single-chip processor, and was not general purpose – it was more like a set of parallel building blocks you could use to make a special-purpose DSP form. It indicates that today's industry theme of converging DSP-microcontroller architectures was started in 1971. This convergence of DSP and microcontroller architectures is known as a Digital Signal Controller.

In 1968, Garrett AiResearch, with designer Ray Holt and Steve Geller, were invited to produce a digital computer to compete with electromechanical systems then under development for the main flight control computer in the US Navy's new F-14 Tomcat fighter. The design was complete by 1970, and used a MOS-based chipset as the core CPU. The design was significantly (approximately 20 times) smaller and much more reliable than the mechanical systems it competed against, and was used in all of the early Tomcat models. This system contained a "a 20-bit, pipelined, parallel multi-microprocessor". However, the system was considered so advanced that the Navy refused to allow publication of the design until 1997. For this reason the CADC, and the MP944 chipset it used, are fairly unknown even today. TI developed the 4-bit TMS 1000, and stressed pre-programmed embedded applications, introducing a version called the TMS1802NC on September 17, 1971, which implemented a calculator on a chip. The Intel chip was the 4-bit 4004, released on November 15, 1971, developed by Federico Faggin and Ted Hoff. The manager of the design team was Leslie L. Vadász.

TI filed for the patent on the microprocessor. Gary Boone was awarded U.S. Patent 3,757,306 for the single-chip microprocessor architecture on September 4, 1973. It may never be known which company actually had the first working microprocessor running on the lab bench. In both 1971 and 1976, Intel and TI entered into broad patent cross-licensing agreements, with Intel paying royalties to TI for the microprocessor patent. A nice history of these events is contained in court documentation from a legal dispute between Cyrix and Intel, with TI as intervenor and owner of the microprocessor patent.

Interestingly, a third party (Gilbert Hyatt) was awarded a patent which might cover the "microprocessor". See a webpage claiming an invention pre-dating both TI and Intel, describing a "microcontroller". According to a rebuttal and a commentary, the patent was later invalidated, but not before substantial royalties were paid out.

A computer-on-a-chip is a variation of a microprocessor which combines the microprocessor core (CPU), some memory, and I/O (input/output) lines, all on one chip.It is also called as micro-controller. The computer-on-a-chip patent, called the "microcomputer patent" at the time, U.S. Patent 4,074,351, was awarded to Gary Boone and Michael J. Cochran of TI. Aside from this patent, the standard meaning of microcomputer is a computer using one or more microprocessors as its CPU(s), while the concept defined in the patent is perhaps more akin to a microcontroller. According to *A History of Modern Computing*, (MIT Press), pp. 220–21, Intel entered into a contract with Computer

Terminals Corporation, later called Datapoint, of San Antonio TX, for a chip for a terminal they were designing. Datapoint later decided not to use the chip, and Intel marketed it as the 8008 in April, 1972. This was the world's first 8-bit microprocessor. It was the basis for the famous "Mark-8" computer kit advertised in the magazine Radio-Electronics in 1974. The 8008 and its successor, the world-famous 8080, opened up the microprocessor component marketplace.

Notable 8-bit Designs

The 4004 was later followed in 1972 by the 8008, the world's first 8-bit microprocessor. These processors are the precursors to the very successful Intel 8080 (1974), Zilog Z80 (1976), and derivative Intel 8-bit processors. The competing Motorola 6800 was released August 1974 and the similar MOS Technology 6502 in 1975 (designed largely by the same people). The 6502 rivaled the Z80 in popularity during the 1980s.

A low overall cost, small packaging, simple computer bus requirements, and sometimes circuitry otherwise provided by external hardware (the Z80 had a built in memory refresh) allowed the home computer "revolution" to accelerate sharply in the early 1980s, eventually delivering such inexpensive machines as the Sinclair ZX-81, which sold for US$99.

The Western Design Centre, Inc. (WDC) introduced the CMOS 65C02 in 1982 and licensed the design to several firms. It was used as the CPU in the Apple IIc and IIe personal computers as well as in medical implantable grade pacemakers and defibrilators, automotive, industrial and consumer devices. WDC pioneered the licensing of microprocessor designs, later followed by ARM and other microprocessor Intellectual Property (IP) providers in the 1990's.

Motorola introduced the MC6809 in 1978, an ambitious and thought through 8-bit design source compatible with the 6800 and implemented using purely hard-wired logic. (Subsequent 16-bit microprocessors typically used microcode to some extent, as design requirements were getting too complex for purely hard-wired logic only.)

Another early 8-bit microprocessor was the Signetics 2650, which enjoyed a brief surge of interest due to its innovative and powerful instruction set architecture.

A seminal microprocessor in the world of spaceflight was RCA's RCA 1802 (aka CDP1802, RCA COSMAC) (introduced in 1976) which was used in NASA's Voyager and Viking spaceprobes of the 1970s, and onboard the Galileo probe to Jupiter (launched 1989, arrived 1995). RCA COSMAC was the first to implement C-MOS technology. The CDP1802 was used because it could be run at very low power, and because its production process (Silicon on Sapphire) ensured much better protection against cosmic radiation and electrostatic discharges than that of any other processor of the era. Thus, the 1802 is said to be the first radiation-hardened microprocessor.

The RCA 1802 had what is called a *static design*, meaning that the clock frequency could be made arbitrarily low, even to 0 Hz, a total stop condition. This let the Voyager/Viking/Galileo spacecraft use minimum electric power for long uneventful stretches of a voyage. Timers and/or sensors would awaken/improve the performance of the processor in time for important tasks, such as navigation updates, attitude control, data acquisition, and radio communication.

16-bit Designs

The first multi-chip 16-bit microprocessor was the National Semiconductor IMP-16, introduced in early 1973. An 8-bit version of the chipset was introduced in 1974 as the IMP-8. During the same year, National introduced the first 16-bit single-chip microprocessor, the National Semiconductor PACE, which was later followed by an NMOS version, the INS8900.

Other early multi-chip 16-bit microprocessors include one used by Digital Equipment Corporation (DEC) in the LSI-11 OEM board set and the packaged PDP 11/03 minicomputer, and the Fairchild Semiconductor MicroFlame 9440, both of which were introduced in the 1975 to 1976 timeframe.

The first single-chip 16-bit microprocessor was TI's TMS 9900, which was also compatible with their TI-990 line of minicomputers. The 9900 was used in the TI 990/4 minicomputer, the TI-99/4A home computer, and the TM990 line of OEM microcomputer boards. The chip was packaged in a large ceramic 64-pin DIP package, while most 8-bit microprocessors such as the Intel 8080 used the more common, smaller, and less expensive plastic 40-pin DIP. A follow-on chip, the TMS 9980, was designed to compete with the Intel 8080, had the full TI 990 16-bit instruction set, used a plastic 40-pin package, moved data 8 bits at a time, but could only address 16 KB. A third chip, the TMS

9995, was a new design. The family later expanded to include the 99105 and 99110.

The Western Design Centre, Inc. (WDC) introduced the CMOS 65816 16-bit upgrade of the WDC CMOS 65C02 in 1984. The 65816 16-bit microprocessor was the core of the Apple IIgs and later the Super Nintendo Entertainment System, making it one of the most popular 16-bit designs of all time.

Intel followed a different path, having no minicomputers to emulate, and instead "upsized" their 8080 design into the 16-bit Intel 8086, the first member of the x86 family which powers most modern PC type computers. Intel introduced the 8086 as a cost effective way of porting software from the 8080 lines, and succeeded in winning much business on that premise. The 8088, a version of the 8086 that used an external 8-bit data bus, was the microprocessor in the first IBM PC, the model 5150. Following up their 8086 and 8088, Intel released the 80186, 80286 and, in 1985, the 32-bit 80386, cementing their PC market dominance with the processor family's backwards compatibility.

The integrated microprocessor memory management unit (MMU) was developed by Childs et al. of Intel, and awarded US patent number 4,442,484.

32-bit Designs

The most significant of the 32-bit designs is the MC68000, introduced in 1979. The 68K, as it was widely known, had 32-bit registers but used 16-bit internal data paths and a 16-bit external data bus to reduce pin count, and supported only 24-bit addresses. Motorola generally described it as a 16-bit processor, though it clearly has 32-bit architecture. The combination of high performance, large (16 megabytes or 2^{24} bytes) memory space and fairly low cost made it the most popular CPU design of its class. The Apple Lisa and Macintosh designs made use of the 68000, as did a host of other designs in the mid-1980s, including the Atari ST and Commodore Amiga.

The world's first single-chip fully-32-bit microprocessor, with 32-bit data paths, 32-bit buses, and 32-bit addresses, was the AT&T Bell Labs BELLMAC-32A, with first samples in 1980, and general production in 1982. After the divestiture of AT&T in 1984, it was renamed the WE 32000 (WE for Western Electric), and had two follow-on generations, the WE 32100 and WE 32200. These microprocessors were used in the AT&T 3B5 and 3B15 minicomputers; in the 3B2, the world's first desktop supermicrocomputer; in the "Companion", the world's first 32-bit laptop computer; and in "Alexander", the world's first book-sized supermicrocomputer, featuring ROM-pack memory cartridges similar to today's gaming consoles. All these systems ran the UNIX System V operating system.

Intel's first 32-bit microprocessor was the iAPX 432, which was introduced in 1981 but was not a commercial success. It had an advanced capability-based object-oriented architecture, but poor performance compared to contemporary architectures such as Intel's own 80286 (introduced 1982), which was almost four times as fast on typical benchmark tests. However, the results for the iAPX432 was partly due to a rushed and therefore suboptimal Ada compiler.

Motorola's success with the 68000 led to the MC68010, which added virtual memory support. The MC68020, introduced in 1985 added full 32-bit data and address busses. The 68020 became hugely popular in the Unix supermicrocomputer market, and many small companies (e.g., Altos, Charles River Data Systems) produced desktop-size systems. The MC68030 was introduced next, improving upon the previous design by integrating the MMU into the chip. The continued success led to the MC68040, which included an FPU for better math performance. A 68050 failed to achieve its performance goals and was not released, and the follow-up MC68060 was released into a market saturated by much faster RISC designs. The 68K family faded from the desktop in the early 1990s.

Other large companies designed the 68020 and follow-ons into embedded equipment. At one point, there were more 68020s in embedded equipment than there were Intel Pentiums in PCs. The ColdFire processor cores are derivatives of the venerable 68020.

During this time (early to mid 1980s), National Semiconductor introduced a very similar 16-bit pinout, 32-bit internal microprocessor called the NS 16032 (later renamed 32016), the full 32-bit version named the NS 32032, and a line of 32-bit industrial OEM microcomputers. By the mid-1980s, Sequent introduced the first symmetric multiprocessor (SMP) server-class computer using the NS 32032. This was one of the design's few wins, and it disappeared in the late 1980s.

The MIPS R2000 (1984) and R3000 (1989) were highly successful 32-bit RISC microprocessors. They were used in high-end workstations and servers by SGI, among others.

Other designs included the interesting Zilog Z8000, which arrived too late to market to stand a chance and disappeared quickly.

In the late 1980s, "microprocessor wars" started killing off some of the microprocessors. Apparently, with only one major design win, Sequent, the NS 32032 just faded out of existence, and Sequent switched to Intel microprocessors.

From 1985 to 2003, the 32-bit x86 architectures became increasingly dominant in desktop, laptop, and server markets, and these microprocessors became faster and more capable. Intel had licensed early versions of the architecture to other companies, but declined to license the Pentium, so AMD and Cyrix built later versions of the architecture based on their own designs. During this span, these processors increased in complexity (transistor count) and capability (instructions/second) by at least three orders of magnitude. Intel's Pentium line is probably the most famous and recognizable 32-bit processor model, at least with the public at large.

64-bit Designs in Personal Computers

While 64-bit microprocessor designs have been in use in several markets since the early 1990s, the early 1990s. saw the introduction of 64-bit microprocessors targeted at the PC market.

With AMD's introduction of a 64-bit architecture backwards-compatible with x86, x86-64 (now called AMD64), in September 2003, followed by Intel's near fully compatible 64-bit extensions (first called IA-32e or EM64T, later renamed Intel 64), the 64-bit desktop era began. Both versions can run 32-bit legacy applications without any performance penalty as well as new 64-bit software. With operating systems Windows XP x64, Windows Vista x64, Linux, BSD and Mac OS X that run 64-bit native, the software is also geared to fully utilize the capabilities of such processors. The move to 64 bits is more than just an increase in register size from the IA-32 as it also doubles the number of general-purpose registers.

The move to 64 bits by PowerPC processors had been intended since the processors' design in the early 90s and was not a major cause of incompatibility. Existing integer registers are extended as are all related data pathways, but, as was the case with IA-32, both floating point and vector units had been operating at or above 64 bits for several years. Unlike what happened when IA-32 was extended to x86-64, no new general purpose registers were added in 64-bit PowerPC, so any performance gained when using the 64-bit mode for applications making no use of the larger address space is minimal.

Multicore Designs

A different approach to improving a computer's performance is to add extra processors, as in symmetric multiprocessing designs which have been popular in servers and workstations since the early 1990s. Keeping up with Moore's Law is becoming increasingly challenging as chip-making technologies approach the physical limits of the technology.

In response, the microprocessor manufacturers look for other ways to improve performance, in order to hold on to the momentum of constant upgrades in the market.

A multi-core processor is simply a single chip containing more than one microprocessor core, effectively multiplying the potential performance with the number of cores (as long as the operating system and software is designed to take advantage of more than one processor). Some components, such as bus interface and second level cache, may be shared between cores. Because the cores are physically very close they interface at much faster clock rates compared to discrete multiprocessor systems, improving overall system performance.

In 2005, the first personal computer dual-core processors were announced and as of 2009 dual-core and quad-core processors are widely used in servers, workstations and PCs while six and eight-core processors will be available for high-end applications in both the home and professional environments.

Sun Microsystems has released the Niagara and Niagara 2 chips, both of which feature an eight-core design. The Niagara 2 supports more threads and operates at 1.6 GHz.

High-end Intel Xeon processors that are on the LGA771 socket are DP (dual processor) capable, as well as the Intel Core 2 Extreme QX9775 also used in the Mac Pro by Apple and the Intel Skulltrail motherboard. With the transition to the LGA1366 socket and the Intel i7 chip quad core is now considered mainstream and the upcoming i9 chip will introduce six and possibly dual-die hex-core (12-cores), processors.

Risc

In the mid-1980s to early-1990s, a crop of new high-performance Reduced Instruction Set Computer (RISC) microprocessors appeared, influenced by discrete RISC-like CPU designs such as the IBM 801 and others. RISC microprocessors were initially used in special-purpose machines and Unix workstations, but then gained wide acceptance in other roles.

In 1986, HP released its first system with a PA-RISC CPU. The first commercial microprocessor design was released either by MIPS Computer Systems, the 32-bit R2000 (the R1000 was not released) or by Acorn computers, the 32-bit ARM2 in 1987. The R3000 made the design truly practical, and the R4000 introduced the world's first commercially available 64-bit RISC microprocessor. Competing projects would result in the IBM POWER and Sun SPARC architectures. Soon every major vendor was releasing a RISC design, including the AT&T CRISP, AMD 29000, Intel i860 and Intel i960, Motorola 88000, DEC Alpha.

As of 2007, two 64-bit RISC architectures are still produced in volume for non-embedded applications: SPARC and Power ISA. The Itanium is produced in smaller quantities. The vast majority of 64-bit microprocessors are now x86-64 CISC designs from AMD and Intel.

Special-Purpose Designs

Though the term "microprocessor" has traditionally referred to a single-or multi-chip CPU or system-on-a-chip (SoC), several types of specialized processing devices have followed from the technology. The most common examples are microcontrollers, digital signal processors (DSP) and graphics processing units (GPU).

Many examples of these are either not programmable, or have limited programming facilities. For example, in general GPUs through the 1990s were mostly non-programmable and have only recently gained limited facilities like programmable vertex shaders. There is no universal consensus on what defines a "microprocessor", but it is usually safe to assume that the term refers to a general-purpose CPU of some sort and not a special-purpose processor unless specifically noted.

Market Statistics

In 2003, about $44 billion (USD) worth of microprocessors were manufactured and sold. Although about half of that money was spent on CPUs used in desktop or laptop personal computers, those count for only about 0.2% of all CPUs sold.

About 55% of all CPUs sold in the world are 8-bit microcontrollers, over two billion of which were sold in 1997. As of 2002, less than 10% of all the CPUs sold in the world are 32-bit or more. Of all the 32-bit CPUs sold, about 2% are used in desktop or laptop personal computers. Most microprocessors are used in embedded control applications such as household appliances, automobiles, and computer peripherals. Taken as a whole, the average price for a microprocessor, microcontroller, or DSP is just over $6.

About ten billion CPUs were manufactured in 2008. About 98% of new CPUs produced each year are embedded.

Microcontroller

A microcontroller (also microcontroller unit, MCU or μC) is a small computer on a single integrated circuit consisting of a relatively simple CPU combined with support functions such as a crystal oscillator, timers, watchdog timer, serial and analog I/O etc. Program memory in the form of NOR flash or OTP ROM is also often included on chip, as well as a typically small amount of RAM. Microcontrollers are designed for small or dedicated applications. Thus, in contrast to the microprocessors used in personal computers and other high-performance or general purpose applications, simplicity is emphasized. Some microcontrollers may operate at clock rate frequencies as low as 4 kHz, as this is adequate for many typical applications, enabling low power consumption (milliwatts or microwatts). They will generally have the ability to retain functionality while waiting for an event such as a button press or other interrupt; power consumption while sleeping (CPU clock and most peripherals off) may be just nanowatts, making many of them well suited for long lasting battery applications. Other microcontrollers may serve performance-critical roles, where they may need to act more like a digital signal processor (DSP), with higher clock speeds and power consumption.

Microcontrollers are used in automatically controlled products and devices, such as automobile engine control systems, remote controls, office machines, appliances, power tools, and toys. By reducing the size and cost compared to a design that uses a separate microprocessor, memory, and input/output devices, microcontrollers make it economical to digitally control even more devices and processes. Mixed signal microcontrollers are common, integrating analog components needed to control non-digital electronic systems.

Embedded Design

A microcontroller can be considered a self-contained system with a processor, memory and peripherals and can be used with an embedded system. (Only the software needs be added.) The majority of computer systems in use today are embedded in other machinery, such as automobiles, telephones, appliances, and peripherals for computer systems. These are called embedded systems. While some embedded systems are very sophisticated, many have minimal requirements for memory and program length, with no operating system, and low software complexity. Typical input and output devices include switches, relays, solenoids, LEDs, small or custom LCD displays, radio frequency devices, and sensors for data such as temperature, humidity, light level etc. Embedded systems usually have no keyboard, screen, disks, printers, or other recognizable I/O devices of a personal computer, and may lack human interaction devices of any kind.

Interrupts

Microcontrollers must provide real time (predictable, though not necessarily fast) response to events in the embedded system they are controlling. When certain events occur, an interrupt system can signal the processor to suspend processing the current instruction sequence and to begin an interrupt service routine (ISR, or "interrupt handler"). The ISR will perform any processing required based on the source of the interrupt before returning to the original instruction sequence. Possible interrupt sources are device dependent, and often include events such as an internal timer overflow, completing an analog to digital conversion, a logic level change on an input such as from a button being pressed, and data received on a communication link. Where power consumption is important as in battery operated devices, interrupts may also wake a microcontroller from a low power sleep state where the processor is halted until required to do something by a peripheral event.

Programs

Microcontroller programs must fit in the available on-chip program memory, since it would be costly to provide a system with external, expandable, memory. Compilers and assembler are used to turn high-level language and assembler language codes into a compact machine code for storage in the microcontroller's memory. Depending on the device, the program memory may be permanent, read-only memory that can only be programmed at the factory, or program memory may be field-alterable flash or erasable read-only memory.

Other Microcontroller Features

Since embedded processors are usually used to control devices, they sometimes need to accept input from the device they are controlling. This is the purpose of the analog to digital converter. Since processors are built to interpret and process digital data, i.e. 1s and 0s, they won't be able to do anything with the analog signals that may be being sent to it by a device. So the analog to digital converter is used to convert the incoming data into a form that the processor can recognize. There is also a digital to analog converter that allows the processor to send data to the device it is controlling.

In addition to the converters, many embedded microprocessors include a variety of timers as well. One of the most common types of timers is the Programmable Interval Timer (PIT). A PIT just counts down from some value to zero. Once it reaches zero, it sends an interrupt to the processor indicating that it has finished counting. This is useful for devices such as thermostats, which periodically test the temperature around them to see if they need to turn the air conditioner on, the heater on, etc.

Time Processing Unit (TPU) is a sophisticated timer. In addition to counting down, the TPU can detect input events, generate output events, and perform other useful operations. A dedicated Pulse Width Modulation (PWM) block makes it possible for the CPU to control power converters, resistive loads, motors, etc., without using lots of CPU resources in tight timer loops.

Universal Asynchronous Receiver/Transmitter (UART) block makes it possible to receive and transmit data over a serial line with very little load on the CPU. For those wanting Ethernet one can use an external chip like Crystal Semiconductor CS8900A, Realtek RTL8019, or

Microchip ENC 28J60. All of them allow easy interfacing with low pin count.

Higher Integration

In contrast to general-purpose CPUs, microcontrollers may not implement an external address or data bus as they integrate RAM and non-volatile memory on the same chip as the CPU. Using fewer pins, the chip can be placed in a much smaller, cheaper package.

Integrating the memory and other peripherals on a single chip and testing them as a unit increases the cost of that chip, but often results in decreased net cost of the embedded system as a whole. Even if the cost of a CPU that has integrated peripherals is slightly more than the cost of a CPU and external peripherals, having fewer chips typically allows a smaller and cheaper circuit board, and reduces the labour required to assemble and test the circuit board.

A Microcontroller is a Single Integrated Circuit, Commonly with the Following Features

- Central processing unit-ranging from small and simple 4-bit processors to complex 32-or 64-bit processors
- Discrete input and output bits, allowing control or detection of the logic state of an individual package pin
- Serial input/output such as serial ports (UARTs)
- Other serial communications interfaces like I²C, Serial Peripheral Interface and Controller Area Network for system interconnect
- Peripherals such as timers, event counters, PWM generators, and watchdog
- Volatile memory (RAM) for data storage
- ROM, EPROM, EEPROM or Flash memory for program and operating parameter storage
- Clock generator-often an oscillator for a quartz timing crystal, resonator or RC circuit
- Many include analog-to-digital converters
- In-circuit programming and debugging support.

This integration drastically reduces the number of chips and the amount of wiring and circuit board space that would be needed to produce equivalent systems using separate chips. Furthermore, and on low pin count devices in particular, each pin may interface to several internal peripherals, with the pin function selected by software. This allows a part to be used in a wider variety of applications than if pins had dedicated functions. Microcontrollers have proved to be highly popular in embedded systems since their introduction in the 1970s.

Some microcontrollers use a Harvard architecture: separate memory buses for instructions and data, allowing accesses to take place concurrently. Where a Harvard architecture is used, instruction words for the processor may be a different bit size than the length of internal memory and registers; for example: 12-bit instructions used with 8-bit data registers.

The decision of which peripheral to integrate is often difficult. The microcontroller vendors often trade operating frequencies and system design flexibility against time-to-market requirements from their customers and overall lower system cost. Manufacturers have to balance the need to minimize the chip size against additional functionality.

Microcontroller architectures vary widely. Some designs include general-purpose microprocessor cores, with one or more ROM, RAM, or I/O functions integrated onto the package. Other designs are purpose built for control applications. A microcontroller instruction set usually has many instructions intended for bit-wise operations to make control programs more compact. For example, a general purpose processor might require several instructions to test a bit in a register and branch if the bit is set, where a microcontroller could have a single instruction to provide that commonly-required function. Microcontrollers typically do not have a math coprocessor, so floating point arithmetic is performed by software.

Volumes

About 55% of all CPUs sold in the world are 8-bit microcontrollers and microprocessors. According to Semico, Over four billion 8-bit microcontrollers were sold in 2006.

A typical home in a developed country is likely to have only four general-purpose microprocessors but around three dozen microcontrollers. A typical mid-range automobile has as many as 30 or more microcontrollers. They can also be found in many electrical device such as washing machines, microwave ovens, and telephones.

Manufacturers have often produced special versions of their

microcontrollers in order to help the hardware and software development of the target system. Originally these included EPROM versions that have a "window" on the top of the device through which program memory can be erased by ultraviolet light, ready for reprogramming after a programming ("burn") and test cycle. Since 1998, EPROM versions are rare and have been replaced by EEPROM and flash, which are easier to use (can be erased electronically) and cheaper to manufacture.

Other versions may be available where the ROM is accessed as an external device rather than as internal memory, however these are becoming increasingly rare due to the widespread availability of cheap microcontroller programmers.

The use of field-programmable devices on a microcontroller may allow field update of the firmware or permit late factory revisions to products that have been assembled but not yet shipped. Programmable memory also reduces the lead time required for deployment of a new product.

Where hundreds of thousands of identical devices are required, using parts programmed at the time of manufacture can be an economical option. These 'mask programmed' parts have the program laid down in the same way as the logic of the chip, at the same time.

Programming Environments

Microcontrollers were originally programmed only in assembly language, but various high-level programming languages are now also in common use to target microcontrollers. These languages are either designed specially for the purpose, or versions of general purpose languages such as the C programming language. Compilers for general purpose languages will typically have some restrictions as well as enhancements to better support the unique characteristics of microcontrollers. Some microcontrollers have environments to aid developing certain types of applications. Microcontroller vendors often make tools freely available to make it easier to adopt their hardware.

Many microcontrollers are so quirky that they effectively require their own non-standard dialects of C, such as SDCC for the 8051, which prevent using standard tools (such as code libraries or static analysis tools) even for code unrelated to hardware features. Interpreters are often used to hide such low level quirks.

Interpreter firmware is also available for some microcontrollers.

For example, BASIC on the early microcontrollers Intel 8052; BASIC and FORTH on the Zilog Z8 as well as some modern devices. Typically these interpreters support interactive programming.

Simulators are available for some microcontrollers, such as in Microchip's MPLAB environment. These allow a developer to analyze what the behaviour of the microcontroller and their program should be if they were using the actual part. A simulator will show the internal processor state and also that of the outputs, as well as allowing input signals to be generated. While on the one hand most simulators will be limited from being unable to simulate much other hardware in a system, they can exercise conditions that may otherwise be hard to reproduce at will in the physical implementation, and can be the quickest way to debug and analyze problems.

Recent microcontrollers are often integrated with on-chip debug circuitry that when accessed by an in-circuit emulator via JTAG, allow debugging of the firmware with a debugger.

Types of Microcontrollers

As of 2008 there are several dozen microcontroller architectures and vendors including:

- 68HC11
- 8051
- ARM processors (from many vendors) using ARM7 or Cortex-M3 cores are generally microcontrollers
- STMicroelectronics STM8S (8-bit), and STM32 (32-bit)
- Atmel AVR (8-bit), AVR32 (32-bit), and AT91SAM
- Freescale ColdFire (32-bit) and S08 (8-bit)
- Hitachi H8, Hitachi SuperH
- Hyperstone E1/E2 (32-bit, First full integration of RISC and DSP on one processor core [1996] [1])
- MIPS (32-bit PIC32)
- NEC V850
- PIC (8-bit PIC16, PIC18, 16-bit dsPIC33/PIC24)
- PowerPC ISE
- PSoC (Programmable System-on-Chip)
- Rabbit 2000

- Texas Instruments MSP430 (16-bit), C2000 (32-bit), and Stellaris (32-bit)
- Toshiba TLCS-870
- Zilog eZ8, eZ80.

and many others, some of which are used in very narrow range of applications or are more like applications processors than microcontrollers. The microcontroller market is extremely fragmented, with numerous vendors, technologies, and markets. Note that many vendors sell (or have sold) multiple architectures. In mid-2009, some consolidation is evident, with vendors pruning product lines.

Interrupt Latency

In contrast to general-purpose computers, microcontrollers used in embedded systems often seek to optimize interrupt latency over instruction throughput. Issues include both reducing the latency, and making it be more predictable (to support real-time control).

When an electronic device causes an interrupt, the intermediate results (registers) have to be saved before the software responsible for handling the interrupt can run. They must also be restored after that software is finished. If there are more registers, this saving and restoring process takes more time, increasing the latency. Ways to reduce such context/restore latency include having relatively few registers in their central processing units (undesirable because it slows down most non-interrupt processing substantially), or at least not having hardware save them all (hoping that the software doesn't then need to compensate by saving the rest "manually"). Another technique involves spending silicon gates on "shadow registers": one or more duplicate registers used only by the interrupt software, perhaps supporting a dedicated stack.

Other Factors Affecting Interrupt Latency Include

- Cycles needed to complete current CPU activities. To minimize those costs, microcontrollers tend to have short pipelines (often three instructions or less), small write buffers, and ensure that longer instructions are continuable or restartable. RISC design principles ensure that most instructions take the same number of cycles, helping avoid the need for most such continuation/restart logic.
- The length of any critical section that needs to be interrupted.

Entry to a critical section restricts concurrent data structure access. When a data structure must be accessed by an interrupt handler, the critical section must block that interrupt. Accordingly, interrupt latency is increased by however long that interrupt is blocked. When there are hard external constraints on system latency, developers often need tools to measure interrupt latencies and track down which critical sections cause slowdowns.

- One common technique just blocks all interrupts for the duration of the critical section. This is easy to implement, but sometimes critical sections get uncomfortably long.
- A more complex technique just blocks the interrupts that may trigger access to that data structure. This often based on interrupt priorities, which tend to not correspond well to the relevant system data structures. Accordingly, this technique is used mostly in very constrained environments.
- Processors may have hardware support for some critical sections. Examples include supporting atomic access to bits or bytes within a word, or other atomic access primitives like the LDREX/STREX exclusive access primitives introduced in the ARMv6 architecture.
- Interrupt nesting. Some microcontrollers allow higher priority interrupts to interrupt lower priority ones. This allows software to manage latency by giving time-critical interrupts higher priority (and thus lower and more predictable latency) than less-critical ones.
- Trigger rate. When interrupts occur back-to-back, microcontrollers may avoid an extra context save/restore cycle by a form of tail call optimization.

Lower end microcontrollers tend to support fewer interrupt latency controls than higher end ones.

History

The first single-chip microprocessor was the 4-bit Intel 4004 released in 1971, with the Intel 8008 and more capable microprocessors available over the next several years.

These however all required external chip(s) to implement a working system, raising total system cost, and making it impossible to economically computerise appliances.

The first computer system on a chip optimised for control applications-microcontroller was the Intel 8048 released in 1975, with both RAM and ROM on the same chip. This chip would find its way into over one billion PC keyboards, and other numerous applications.

Most microcontrollers at this time had two variants. One had an erasable EEPROM program memory, which was significantly more expensive than the PROM variant which was only programmable once.

In 1993, the introduction of EEPROM memory allowed microcontrollers (beginning with the Microchip PIC16x84)) to be electrically erased quickly without an expensive package as required for EPROM, allowing both rapid prototyping, and In System Programming.

The same year, Atmel introduced the first microcontroller using Flash memory..

Other companies rapidly followed suit, with both memory types.

Cost has plummeted over time, with the cheapest 8-bit microcontrollers being available for under $0.25 in quantity (thousands) in 2009, and some 32-bit microcontrollers around $1 for similar quantities.

Nowadays microcontrollers are low cost and readily available for hobbyists, with large online communities around certain processors.

In the future, MRAM could potentially be used in microcontrollers as it has infinite endurance and its incremental semiconductor wafer process cost is relatively low.

Microcontroller Embedded Memory Technology

Since the emergence of microcontrollers, many different memory technologies have been used. Almost all microcontrollers have at least two different kinds of memory, a non-volatile memory for storing firmware and a read-write memory for temporary data.

Data

From the earliest microcontrollers to today, six-transistor SRAM almost always used as the read/write working memory, with a few more transistors per bit used in the register file. MRAM could potentially replace it as it is 4-10 times denser which would make it more cost effective.

In addition to the SRAM, some microcontrollers also have internal EEPROM for data storage; and even ones that don't have any (or don't have enough) are often connected to external serial EEPROM chip (such as the BASIC Stamp) or external serial flash memory chip.

A few recent microcontrollers beginning in 2003 have "self-programmable" flash memory.

Firmware

The earliest microcontrollers used hard-wired or mask ROM to store firmware. Later microcontrollers (such as the early versions of the Freescale 68HC11 and early PIC microcontrollers) had quartz windows that allowed ultraviolet light in to erase the EPROM.

The Microchip PIC16C84, introduced in 1993, was the first microcontroller to use EEPROM to store firmware.

Also in 1993, Atmel introduced the first microcontroller using NOR Flash memory to store firmware. PSoC microcontrollers, introduced in 2002, store firmware in SONOS flash memory. MRAM could potentially be used to store firmware.

Digital Signal Processor

A digital signal processor (DSP) is a specialized microprocessor with an optimized architecture for the fast operational needs of digital signal processing.

Typical Characteristics

Digital signal processing algorithms typically require a large number of mathematical operations to be performed quickly on a set of data. Signals are converted from analog to digital, manipulated digitally, and then converted again to analog form, as diagrammed below. Many DSP applications have constraints on latency; that is, for the system to work, the DSP operation must be completed within some time constraint.

A Simple Digital Processing System

Most general-purpose microprocessors and operating systems can execute DSP algorithms successfully. But these microprocessors are not suitable for application of mobile telephone and pocket PDA systems etc. because of power supply and space limit. A specialized digital signal processor, however, will tend to provide a lower-cost solution, with better performance and lower latency.

The architecture of a digital signal processor is optimized specifically for digital signal processing work. Some useful features for optimizing DSP algorithms are outlined below.

Architecture

By the standards of general purpose processors, DSP instruction sets are often highly irregular. One implication for software architecture is that hand optimized assembly is commonly packaged into libraries for re-use, instead of relying on unusually advanced compiler technologies to handle essential algorithms.

Hardware Features Visible Through DSP Instruction sets Commonly Include

- Hardware modulo addressing, allowing circular buffers to be implemented without having to constantly test for wrapping.
- A memory architecture designed for streaming data, using DMA extensively and expecting code to be written to know about cache hierarchies and the associated delays.
- Driving multiple arithmetic units may require memory architectures to support several accesses per instruction cycle
- Separate program and data memories (Harvard architecture)
- Special SIMD (single instruction, multiple data) operations
- Some processors use VLIW techniques so each instruction drives multiple arithmetic units in parallel
- Special arithmetic operations, such as fast multiply-accumulates (MACs). Many fundamental DSP algorithms, such as FIR filters or the Fast Fourier transform (FFT) depend heavily on multiply-accumulate performance.
- Bit-reversed addressing, a special addressing mode useful for calculating FFTs
- Special loop controls, such as architectural support for executing a few instruction words in a very tight loop without overhead for instruction fetches or exit testing

- Deliberate exclusion of a memory management unit. DSPs frequently use multi-tasking operating systems, but have no support for virtual memory or memory protection. Operating systems that use virtual memory require more time for context switching among processes, which increases latency.

Program Flow

- Floating-point unit integrated directly into the datapath
- Pipelined architecture
- Highly parallel multiplier–accumulators (MAC units)
- Hardware-controlled looping, to reduce or eliminate the overhead required for looping operations.

Memory Architecture

- DSPs often use special memory architectures that are able to fetch multiple data and/or instructions at the same time:
  - Harvard architecture
  - Modified von Neumann architecture
- Use of direct memory access
- Memory-address calculation unit.

Data Operations

- Saturation arithmetic, in which operations that produce overflows will accumulate at the maximum (or minimum) values that the register can hold rather than wrapping around (maximum+1 doesn't overflow to minimum as in many general-purpose CPUs, instead it stays at maximum). Sometimes various sticky bits operation modes are available.
- Fixed-point arithmetic is often used to speed up arithmetic processing
- Single-cycle operations to increase the benefits of pipelining.

Instruction Sets

- Multiply-accumulate (MAC, aka fused multiply-add, FMA) operations, which are used extensively in all kinds of matrix operations, such as convolution for filtering, dot product, or even polynomial evaluation
- ***Instructions to Increase Parallelism:*** SIMD, VLIW, superscalar architecture

- Specialized instructions for modulo addressing in ring buffers and bit-reversed addressing mode for FFT cross-referencing
- Digital signal processors sometimes use time-stationary encoding to simplify hardware and increase coding efficiency.

History

Prior to the advent of stand-alone DSP chips discussed below, most DSP applications were implemented using bit slice processors. The AMD2901 bit slice chip with its family of components was a very popular choice. There were reference designs from AMD, but very often the specifics of a particular design were application specific. These bit slice architecture would sometimes include a peripheral multiplier chip. Examples of these multipliers were a series from TRW including the TRW1008 and TRW1010, some of which included an accumulator, providing the requisite multiply-accumulate (MAC) function.

In 1978, Intel released the 2920 as an "analog signal processor". It had an on-chip ADC/DAC with an internal signal processor, but it didn't have a hardware multiplier and was not successful in the market. In 1979, AMI released the S2811. It was designed as a microprocessor peripheral, and it had to be initialized by the host. The S2811 was likewise not successful in the market.

In 1980 the first stand-alone, complete DSPs – the NEC µPD7720 and AT&T DSP1 – were presented at the International Solid-State Circuits Conference '80. Both processors were inspired by the research in PSTN telecommunications.

The Altamira DX-1 was another early DSP, utilizing quad integer pipelines with delayed branches and branch prediction.

The first DSP produced by Texas Instruments (TI), the TMS32010 presented in 1983, proved to be an even bigger success. It was based on the Harvard architecture, and so had separate instruction and data memory. It already had a special instruction set, with instructions like load-and-accumulate or multiply-and-accumulate. It could work on 16-bit numbers and needed 390ns for a multiply-add operation. TI is now the market leader in general-purpose DSPs. Another successful design was the Motorola 56000.

About five years later, the second generation of DSPs began to spread. They had 3 memories for storing two operands simultaneously and included hardware to accelerate tight loops, they also had an addressing unit capable of loop-addressing. Some of them operated on 24-bit variables and a typical model only required about 21ns for a MAC (multiply-accumulate). Members of this generation were for example the AT&T DSP16A or the Motorola DSP56001.

The main improvement in the third generation was the appearance of application-specific units and instructions in the data path, or sometimes as coprocessors. These units allowed direct hardware acceleration of very specific but complex mathematical problems, like the Fourier-transform or matrix operations. Some chips, like the Motorola MC68356, even included more than one processor core to work in parallel. Other DSPs from 1995 are the TI TMS320C541 or the TMS 320C80.

The fourth generation is best characterized by the changes in the instruction set and the instruction encoding/decoding. SIMD and MMX extensions were added, VLIW and the superscalar architecture appeared. As always, the clock-speeds have increased, a 3ns MAC now became possible.

Modern DSPs

Modern signal processors yield greater performance. This is due in part to both technological and architectural advancements like lower design rules, fast-access two-level cache, (E)DMA circuit and a wider bus system. Of course, not all DSPs provide the same speed and many kinds of signal processors exist, each one of them being better suited for a specific task, ranging in price from about US$1.50 to US$300.

A Texas Instruments C6000 series DSP clocks at 1.2 GHz and implements separate instruction and data caches as well as an 8 MiB 2nd level cache, and its I/O speed is rapid thanks to its 64 EDMA channels. The top models are capable of as many as 8000 MIPS (million instructions per second), use VLIW (very long instruction word) encoding, perform eight operations per clock-cycle and are compatible with a broad range of external peripherals and various buses (PCI/serial/etc). TMS320C6474 chips each have three such DSPs, and the newest generation C6000 chips support floating point as well as fixed point processing.

Another player at the high-end signal processor manufacturer today is Freescale. The company provides a multi-core DSPs family MSC81xx. The MSC81xx is based on StarCore Architecture processors. The latest

MSC8144 DSP combines four programmable SC3400 StarCore DSP cores. Each SC3400 StarCore DSP core runs at 1 GHz. The SC3400 performed higher than any other programmable DSP at 1 GHz on BDTIsimMark2000 results published by Berkeley Design Technology, Inc. (BDTI).

Another major signal processor manufacturer today is Analog Devices. The company provides a broad range of DSPs, but its main portfolio is multimedia processors, such as codecs, filters and digital-analog converters. Its SHARC-based processors range in performance from 66 MHz/198 MFLOPS (million floating-point operations per second) to 400 MHz/2400MFLOPS. Some models even support multiple multipliers and ALUs, SIMD instructions and audio processing-specific components and peripherals. Another product of the company is the Blackfin family of embedded digital signal processors, with models like the ADSP-BF531 to ADSP-BF536. These processors combine the features of a DSP with those of a general use processor. As a result, these processors can run simple operating systems like ìCLinux, velocity and Nucleus RTOS while operating relatively efficiently on real-time data.

Another player is NXP Semiconductors based on TriMedia VLIW technology, optimized for audio and video processing. In some products the DSP core is hidden as a fixed-function block into an SoC, but NXP also provides a range of flexible single core media processors, such as the with a complete software development kit and a library of codecs and filters. The TriMedia media processors support both fixed-point arithmetic as well as floating-point arithmetic, and have specific instructions to deal with complex filters and entropy coding.

Most DSPs use fixed-point arithmetic, because in real world signal processing the additional range provided by floating point is not needed, and there is a large speed benefit and cost benefit due to reduced hardware complexity. Floating point DSPs may be invaluable in applications where a wide dynamic range is required. Product developers might also use floating point DSPs to reduce the cost and complexity of software development in exchange for more expensive hardware, since it is generally easier to implement algorithms in floating point.

Generally, DSPs are dedicated integrated circuits, however DSP functionality can also be realized using Field Programmable Gate Array chips.

Embedded general-purpose RISC processors are becoming increasingly DSP like in functionality. For example, ARM Cortex-A8 has a 128-bit wide SIMD unit that can have impressive 16-and 8-bit performance for industry standard benchmarks. OMAP3 processors include a Cortex-A8, and optionally incorporate a C6000 DSP, so designs can choose the best approach: higher end DSP, or ARM-based "DSP lite". Machine code or machine language is a system of instructions and data executed directly by a computer's central processing unit. Machine code may be regarded as a primitive (and cumbersome) programming language or as the lowest-level representation of a compiled and/or assembled computer program. Programs in interpreted languages are not represented by machine code however, although their *interpreter* (which may be seen as a processor executing the higher level program) often is. Machine code is sometimes called native code when referring to platform-dependent parts of language features or libraries. Machine code should not be confused with so called "bytecode", which is executed by an interpreter.

Machine Code Instructions

Every processor or processor family has its own machine code instruction set. Instructions are patterns of bits that by physical design correspond to different commands to the machine. The instruction set is thus specific to a class of processors using (much) the same architecture. Successor or derivative processor designs often include all the instructions of a predecessor and may add additional instructions. Occasionally a successor design will discontinue or alter the meaning of some instruction code (typically because it is needed for new purposes), affecting code compatibility to some extent; even nearly completely compatible processors may show slightly different behaviour for some instructions but this is seldom a problem. Systems may also differ in other details, such as memory arrangement, operating systems, or peripheral devices; because a program normally relies on such factors, different systems will typically not run the same machine code, even when the same type of processor is used.

A machine code instruction set may have all instructions of the same length, or it may have variable-length instructions. How the patterns are organized varies strongly with the particular architecture and often also with the type of instruction. Most instructions have one or more opcode fields which specifies the basic instruction type (such as arithmetic, logical, jump, etc) and the actual operation (such as add or compare) and other fields that may give the type of the operand(s), the addressing mode(s), the addressing offset(s) or index, or the actual value itself (such constant operands contained in an instruction are called *immediates*).

Programs

A computer program is a sequence of instructions that are executed by a CPU. While simple processors execute instructions one after the other, superscalar processors are capable of executing several instructions at once. Program flow may be influenced by special 'jump' instructions that transfer execution to an instruction other than the following one. Conditional jumps are taken (execution continues at another address) or not (execution continues at the next instruction) depending on some condition.

Assembly Languages

A much more readable rendition of machine language, called assembly language, uses mnemonic codes to refer to machine code instructions, rather than simply using the instructions' numeric values. For example, on the Zilog Z80 processor, the machine code 00000101, which causes the CPU to decrement the B processor register, would be represented in assembly language as DEC B.

Relationship to Microcode

In some computer architectures, the machine code is implemented by a more fundamental underlying layer of programs called microprograms, providing a common machine language interface across a line or family of different models of computer with widely different underlying dataflows. This is done to facilitate porting of machine language programs between different models. An example of this use is the IBM System/360 family of computers and their successors. With dataflow path widths of 8 bits to 64 bits and beyond, they nevertheless present a common architecture at the machine language level across the entire line. Using a microcode layer to implement an emulator enables the computer to present the architecture of an entirely different computer. The System/360 line used this to allow porting programs from earlier IBM machines to the new family of computers, e.g. an IBM 1401/1440/1460 emulator on the IBM S/360 model 40.

3

Programming the Basic Computer

In computer programming, BASIC (an acronym for Beginner's All-purpose Symbolic Instruction Code) is a family of high-level programming languages. The original BASIC was designed in 1964 by John George Kemeny and Thomas Eugene Kurtz at Dartmouth in New Hampshire, USA to provide computer access to non-science students. At the time, nearly all use of computers required writing custom software, which was something only scientists and mathematicians tended to be able to do. The language and its variants became widespread on microcomputers in the late 1970s and 1980s. BASIC remains popular to this day in a handful of highly modified dialects and new languages influenced by BASIC such as Microsoft Visual Basic. As of 2006, 59% of developers for the.NET platform used Visual Basic.NET as their only language

History

Before the mid-1960s, computers were extremely expensive and used only for special-purpose tasks. A simple batch processing arrangement ran only a single "job" at a time, one after another. But during the 1990s. faster and more affordable computers became available. With this extra processing power, computers would sometimes sit idle, without jobs to run.

Programming languages in the batch programming era tended to be designed, like the machines on which they ran, for specific purposes (such as scientific formula calculations or business data processing or eventually for text editing). Since even the newer, less expensive machines were still major investments, there was a strong tendency to consider efficiency to be the most important feature of a language. In general, these specialized languages were difficult to use and had widely disparate syntax.

As prices decreased, the possibility of sharing computer access began to move from research labs to commercial use. Newer computer systems supported time-sharing, a system which allows multiple users or processes to use the RAM and memory. In such a system the operating system alternates between running processes, giving each one running time on the RAM before switching to another. The machines had become fast enough that most users could feel they had the machine all to themselves. In theory, timesharing reduced the cost of computing tremendously, as a single machine could be shared among hundreds of users.

Early Years: the Mainframe and Mini-Computer Era

The original BASIC language was designed in 1963 by John Kemeny and Thomas Kurtz and implemented by a team of Dartmouth students under their direction. BASIC was designed to allow students to write programs for the Dartmouth Time-Sharing System. It was intended to address the complexity issues of older languages with a new language design specifically for the new class of users that time-sharing systems allowed—that is, a less technical user who did not have the mathematical background of the more traditional users and was not interested in acquiring it. Being able to use a computer to support teaching and research was quite novel at the time. In the following years, as other dialects of BASIC appeared, Kemeny and Kurtz's original BASIC dialect became known as *Dartmouth BASIC*. The eight design principles of BASIC were:

1. Be easy for beginners to use.
2. Be a general-purpose programming language.
3. Allow advanced features to be added for experts (while keeping the language simple for beginners).
4. Be interactive.
5. Provide clear and friendly error messages.
6. Respond quickly for small programs.
7. Not to require an understanding of computer hardware.
8. Shield the user from the operating system.

The language was based partly on the FORTRAN II and partly

on the ALGOL 60, with additions to make it suitable for timesharing. (The features of other time-sharing systems such as JOSS and CORC, and to a lesser extent LISP, were also considered.) It had been preceded by other teaching-language experiments at Dartmouth such as the DARSIMCO (1956) and DOPE (1962 implementations of SAP and DART (1963) which was a simplified FORTRAN II). Initially, BASIC concentrated on supporting straightforward mathematical work, with matrix arithmetic support from its initial implementation as a batch language and full string functionality being added by 1965. BASIC was first implemented on the GE-265 mainframe which supported multiple terminals. At the time of its introduction, it was a compiled language. It was also quite efficient, beating FORTRAN II and ALGOL 60 implementations on the 265 at several fairly computationally intensive (at the time) programming problems such as numerical integration by Simpson's Rule.

The designers of the language decided to make the compiler available free of charge so that the language would become widespread. They also made it available to high schools in the Dartmouth area and put a considerable amount of effort into promoting the language. As a result, knowledge of BASIC became relatively widespread (for a computer language) and BASIC was implemented by a number of manufacturers, becoming fairly popular on newer minicomputers like the DEC PDP series and the Data General Nova. The BASIC language was also central to the HP Time-Shared BASIC system in the late 1990s. and early 1970s, and the Pick operating system. In these instances the language tended to be implemented as an interpreter, instead of (or in addition to) a compiler.

Several years after its release, highly respected computer professionals, notably Edsger W. Dijkstra, expressed their opinions that the use of GOTO statements, which existed in many languages including BASIC, promoted poor programming practices. Some have also derided BASIC as too slow (most interpreted versions are slower than equivalent compiled versions) or too simple (many versions, especially for small computers, left out important features and capabilities).

Explosive Growth: the home Computer Era

Notwithstanding the language's use on several minicomputers, it was the introduction of the MITS Altair 8800 "kit" microcomputer in

1975 that provided BASIC a path to universality. Most programming languages required suitable text editors, large amounts of memory and available disk space, whereas the early microcomputers had no resident editors, limited memory and often substituted recordable audio tapes for disk space. All these issues allowed a language like BASIC, in its interpreted form with a built-in code editor, to operate within those constraints.

BASIC also had the advantage that it was fairly well-known to the young designers and computer hobbyists who took an interest in microcomputers, and generally worked in the electronics industries of the day. Kemeny and Kurtz's earlier proselytizing paid off in this respect and the few hobbyists' journals of the era were filled with columns that made mentions of the language or focused entirely on one version compared to others.

One of the first to appear for the 8080 machines like the Altair was Tiny BASIC, a simple BASIC implementation originally written by Dr. Li-Chen Wang, and then ported onto the Altair by Dennis Allison at the request of Bob Albrecht (who later founded Dr. Dobb's Journal). The Tiny BASIC design and the full source code were published in 1976 in DDJ.

In 1975, MITS released Altair BASIC, developed by college drop-outs Bill Gates and Paul Allen as the company Micro-Soft, which grew into today's corporate giant, Microsoft. The first Altair version was co-written by Gates, Allen, and Monte Davidoff in a burst of enthusiasm and neglect of studies. Versions of Microsoft BASIC (also known then, and most widely as M BASIC or MBASIC) was soon bundled with the original floppy disk-based CP/M computers, which became widespread in small business environments. As the popularity of BASIC on CP/M spread, newer computer designs also introduced their own version of the language, or had Micro-Soft port its version to their platform.

When three major new computers were introduced in what Byte Magazine would later call the "1977 Trinity", all three had BASIC as their primary programming language and operating environment. The Commodore PET licensed a version of Micro-Soft BASIC that was ported to the MOS 6502, while Apple II and TRS-80 both introduced new, largely similar versions of the language. As new companies entered the field, additional versions were added that subtly changed the BASIC family. The Atari 8-bit family had their own Atari BASIC that was modified in order to fit on an 8 kB ROM cartridge. The BBC published BBC BASIC, developed for them by Acorn Computers Ltd, incorporating many extra structuring keywords. Most of the home computers of the 1980s had a ROM-resident BASIC interpreter, allowing the machines to boot directly into BASIC. Because of this legacy, there are more dialects of BASIC than there are of any other programming language.

As BASIC grew in this period, many magazines such as *Creative Computing Magazine* published complete source code in BASIC for games, utilities, and other programs. Given BASIC's straightforward nature, it was simple matter to type in the code from the magazine and execute the program. Different magazines were published featuring programs for specific computers, though some BASIC programs were universal and could be used in machines running any variant of BASIC. A logical extension of the magazine idea was the publishing of BASIC source code in full-fledged books: probably the classic example was David Ahl's series of Basic Computer Games.

Maturity: the Personal Computer Era

As early as 1979 Microsoft was in negotiations with IBM to supply their IBM PCs with an IBM Cassette BASIC (BASIC C) inside BIOS. Microsoft sold several versions of BASIC for MS-DOS/PC-DOS including IBM Disk BASIC (BASIC D), IBM BASICA (BASIC A), GW-BASIC (a BASICA-compatible version that did not need IBM's ROM) and QuickBASIC. Turbo Pascal-publisher Borland published Turbo BASIC 1.0 in 1985 (successor versions are still being marketed by the original author under the name PowerBASIC). Microsoft wrote the windowing based AmigaBASIC that was supplied with version 1.1 of the pre-emptive multitasking GUI Amiga computers (late 1985/early 1986), although the product unusually did not bear any Microsoft marks.

These languages introduced many extensions to the original home computer BASIC, such as improved string manipulation and graphics support, access to the file system and additional data types. More important were the facilities for structured programming, including additional control structures and proper subroutines supporting local variables.

However, by the latter half of the 1980s newer computers were far more capable with more resources. At the same time, computers had progressed from a hobbyist interest to tools used primarily for applications written by others, and programming became less important for most users. BASIC started to recede in importance, though numerous versions remained available. Compiled BASIC or CBASIC is still used in many IBM 4690 OS point of sale systems.

BASIC's fortunes reversed once again with the introduction of Visual Basic by Microsoft. It is somewhat difficult to consider this language to be BASIC, because of the major shift in its orientation towards an object-oriented and event-driven perspective. The only significant similarity to older BASIC dialects was familiar syntax. Syntax itself no longer "fully defined" the language, since much development was done using "drag and drop" methods without exposing all code for commonly used objects such as buttons and scrollbars to the developer. While this could be considered an evolution of the language, few of the distinctive features of early Dartmouth BASIC, such as line numbers and the INPUT keyword, remain (although Visual Basic still uses INPUT to read data from files, and INPUTBOX is available for direct user input; line numbers can also optionally be used in all VB versions, even VB.NET, albeit they cannot be used in certain places, for instance before SUB).

Ironically given the origin of BASIC as a "beginner's" language, and apparently even to the surprise of many at Microsoft who still initially marketed Visual Basic or "VB" as a language for hobbyists, the language had come into widespread use for small custom business applications shortly after the release of VB version 3.0, which is widely considered the first relatively stable version. While many advanced programmers still scoffed at its use, VB met the needs of small businesses efficiently wherever processing speed was less of a concern than easy development. By that time, computers running Windows 3.1 had become fast enough that many business-related processes could be completed "in the blink of an eye" even using a "slow" language, as long as massive amounts of data were not involved. Many small business owners found they could create their own small yet useful applications in a few evenings to meet their own specialized needs. Eventually, during the lengthy lifetime of VB3, knowledge of Visual Basic had become a marketable job skill.

Many BASIC dialects have also sprung up in the last few years, including Bywater BASIC and True BASIC (the direct successor to

Dartmouth BASIC from a company controlled by Kurtz). One notable variant is RealBasic which although first released in 1998 for Macintosh computers, has since 2005 fully compiled programs for Microsoft Windows, Mac OS X and 32-bit x86 Linux, from the same object-oriented source code. RealBasic compiled programs may execute natively on these platforms as services, consoles or windowed applications. However in keeping with BASIC tradition, single-platform hobbyist versions are also still maintained. Many other BASIC variants and adaptations have been written by hobbyists, equipment developers, and others, as it is a relatively simple language to develop translators for. An example of an open source interpreter, written in C, is MiniBasic. More complex examples of free software BASIC implementations (development tools and compilers) includes Gambas and FreeBASIC.

The ubiquity of BASIC interpreters on personal computers was such that textbooks once included simple "Try It In BASIC" exercises that encouraged students to experiment with mathematical and computational concepts on classroom or home computers. Futurist and sci-fi writer David Brin mourns the loss of ubiquitous BASIC in a recent *Salon* article.

Types of Input Statement

a. Ordinary Input

b. Prompted Input-(String Variable Name is used)

3. If... Then Statement-is used in comparison or decision making.

4. Tab Function-allows the computer user to have complete control on the position where the next character will be shown on the screen or printed on paper.

Argument-represents the position where printing will be made.

5. GOSUB Command-is used to avoid repetitive typing of the same set of instructions in the program.

6. REM (Remarks)-is used to assign/give title to the program and to help identify the purpose of a given section of code.

7. ON... GOTO Command-allows the program to choose from a list of line numbers where to go depending on certain conditions. It is the variation of If... Then Statement and GOTO Command.

It is very important to have an appreciation for how the computer is going to look at your program. The fact of the matter is that, when your program is executed, the computer will do nothing unless your program tells it to do so. This includes reading input from the user or a file, doing something with that input, and giving the results in a predictable manner (usually either to screen or to print). None of this happens unless you, the programmer, tell the computer to do it. You do not need to tell it the fine details of *how* to do it, but you must tell it to *do* it.

At their core, computers are machines. Machines operate on the basis of command: you tell them to do something and they do it. This is an essential aspect of computers to be recognised by anyone who wants to program: the computer does what you tell it to do and does it faster than you could. But if it receives bad input, it will give bad output. In the early days of computing, programmers used an acronym for this: GIGO (*Garbage In, Garbage Out*). Like speaking Swahili to a Parisian, if you do not give the computer the right commands in the expected way, you will not get the right results in the way you expect.

There are two parts to every executing program: data and code. The first is fairly obvious; it is the information to be processed. The second is comprised of three kinds of statements: assignment, iteration, and operation. The kind of statement determines what the computer will do with it. Unlike in human speech, computers do not understand polite tones. There is no such thing as "I would like you to print now" in computer programming. Instead, one simply tells the computer "print", and it does it.

Programming happens when one tells the computer to do something in a way that the computer understands. So, the secret of programming is how to tell a computer to do something. This differs by programming language. No one programs in the language that the computer itself uses (binary). Instead every language is translated for the computer. Exactly which words are translated and how depends on the vocabulary of the programming language. This vocabulary is a set of terms called "reserved words".

Reserved words are trigger words. When the Python interpreter or computer reads them, it triggers a response, an action. Depending on what the term is, the computer will do something immediately (e.g., 'break') or will look for more information. If two reserved words begin with some of the same letters, the computer reads the program until it is clear which word is meant; only then does the computer do something.

Picking an Argument-Part 1

The concept of looking for more information, however, needs further unpacking. Programming languages have a lot of the same characteristics as human languages. If we want to tell someone to do something, we need to communicate a couple of things:

- Who is going to do it (a subject like "Jack")
- What is going to be done (a verb like "threw")

In addition, sometimes we need to communicate two more pieces of information:

- to what they are going to do something (a direct object like "ball")
- who will receive the effect of that action (an indirect object like "Jane")

When we put these items together, we get a sentence. Consider the following:

Jack threw the Ball to Jane

We know that the person doing the task is the subject, Jack. What is being done is 'threw'. What is being thrown (or acted upon) is 'ball'. And the one receiving the effect, or output, of the action is 'Jane'. Computer languages are no different.

In programming, the computer is always the one that does things. What is to be done is, obviously, what you tell Jack, or the computer, to do. In most instances, however, if you do not tell the computer *what* you want it to act upon, it will not know what you mean. However, the computer, being a bit clueless without your help, will still not know what to do. 'Throwing' carries a sense of direction with it, and the computer will want to know where you want the ball thrown. If the command was 'hold', Jack (and the computer) would know to simply sit still and hold the ball. But throwing requires direction and so one must give Jack (and the computer) an endpoint: Jane. Just like in human language, if we leave out any part of the sentence, confusion fills the gap. These pieces of more information are what computer programmers call "arguments". Commands can require no arguments or several. Sometimes a command knows to assume information, a default setting, if other information is not given. Other times, however, the Python interpreter will look for more information, not find any, and quit without finishing the program (aka, "throw an error").

In Python, the command to print is simply "print". Like the example of "throw" above, "print" needs an argument, something to print (e.g., "ball"). In Python, this is offset by quotations.

print "ball"

The output from this statement would be simply (note: no print command and no quotation marks): ball

By default, the output from print goes to the screen. There are ways to redirect the output, but we shall save that for a later tutorial.

There are three kinds of statements in programming: assignment, control, and operation. I shall discuss each of them in greater depth in the respective tutorials on Python. In the next couple of pages, however, I will discuss their basic characteristics.

Assignment statements are perhaps the simplest of the three. In assignment, the value on the right side of the equal sign ('=') is assigned to a variable name on the left. The more common way of describing the statement "x = 25" is to say that 'x equals 25'. As long as x is equivalent to '25', one may refer to the variable 'x' instead of '25' wherever needed. However, one must be careful. If a program is dependent upon x being '25' and x is later assigned a new value, perhaps '26', then every calculation that relies upon x being equivalent to '25' will change, sometimes with unpredictable results.

Control statements have the sole purpose of regulating the flow of the program. Like a traffic signal, a control statement, or loop, tells the computer whether to go or stop. It does this by expressing the conditions under which an action should occur. If the conditions are not met, the entire loop is ignored by the computer.

Operation statements are the lifeblood of a program. These statements tell the computer what to do. Like the example about Jack and Jane above, operation statements are commands to do an action on a certain input and to produce a certain output. Some commands expect to be told explicitly upon which input to act or where it should to direct the output. If this information is expected and not given, the command will be unclear to the computer, and the program will quit unexpectedly.

Logical Instructions

1. In order to program a computer, you must think and write clearly and logically. A computer can only do exactly what you tell it and cannot make assumptions. It is often difficult to think in very clear and detailed ways to ensure the computer knows what you want, which is what makes computer programmers valuable. The computer will only do exactly what you ask it to do, and will never do any more.

Machine Language

2. Machine language is the basic language that the computer understands. Machine language consists of nothing but a long combination of zeros and ones. All other programming languages and computer instructions have to be converted into machine language in order for the computer to process the instructions. Few people ever actually write program in machine language because it is so difficult for people to understand. Instead, there are usually programs that convert other programming languages into machine language.

Assembly Language

3. The next level "up" from machine language is assembly language. This computer programming language is still considered a low level language because the computer can understand the language rather easily. Assembly language is a series of short 3-letter commands. Assembly language is still very difficult to use to program a computer, because it takes a large number of 3-letter commands to do even a simple task for the computer.

High Level Languages

4. Most people who program computers use high level languages. Many people who start out in computer programming use a program called Visual Basic, which is a high level language. High level programming languages are easier for humans to understand, but impossible for computers to understand. Instead, an interpreter or compiler is used to convert the high level programming language into machine language so the computer can understand it. High level languages can still be very complex.

Fourth Generation Languages

Fourth Generation Languages (4GLs) are an attempt to make computer programming even easier. While high level languages are easy for experienced computer programmers to understand, fourth generation languages are designed to be used by people without computer programming experience. These programming languages are designed to respond to natural English speaking instructions which are converted to machine language so the computer can understand them. Because of the complexity of the English language, few fourth generation programming languages are effective.

Microprogrammed Control

A control unit with its binary control values stored as words in memory is called a *microprogrammed control.* Each word in the control memory contains a *microinstruction* that specifies one or more microoperations for the system. A sequence of microinstructions constitutes a *microprogram.* The latter is often fixed at the time of the system design and so is usually stored in ROM. Microprogramming involves placing some representation for combinations of values of control variables in words of ROM for use by the rest of the control logic via successive read operations.

The contents of a word in ROM at a given address specify the microoperations to be performed for both the datapath and the control unit. A microprogram can also be stored in RAM. In this case, it is loaded initially at system startup from the computer console or from some form of nonvolatile storage, such as a magnetic disk. With either ROM or RAM, the memory in the control unit is called *control memory;* if RAM is used, the memory is referred to as *writable control memory.*

The general configuration of a microprogrammed control. The control memory is assumed to be a ROM within which all control information is permanently stored. The *control address register* (*CAR*) specifies the address of the microinstruction. The *control data register (CDR),* which is optional, may hold the microinstruction currently being executed by the datapath and the control unit.

One of the functions of the control word is to determine the address of the next microinstruction to be executed. This microinstruction may be the next one in sequence, or it may be located somewhere else in the control memory. Therefore, one or more bits that specify how to determine the address of the next microinstruction must be present in the current microinstruction. The next address may also be a function of status and external control inputs. While a microinstruction is being executed, the *next-address generator* produces the next address. This address is transferred to the *CAR* on the next clock pulse and is used to read the next microinstruction to be executed from ROM. Thus, the microinstructions contain bits for activating microoperations in the datapath and bits that specify the sequence of microinstructions executed.

The next-address generator, in combination with the *CAR*, is sometimes called a microprogram *sequencer*, as it determines the sequence of instructions that is read from control memory. The address of the next microinstruction can be specified in several ways, depending on the sequencer inputs. Typical functions of a microprogram sequencer are incrementing the *CAR* by one and loading the *CAR*. Possible sources for the load operation include an address from control memory, an externally provided address, and an initial address to start control unit operation.

The *CDR* holds the present microinstruction while the next address is being computed and the next microinstruction is being read from memory. The *CDR* breaks up a long combinational delay path through the control memory and the datapath. Insertion of this register is just like inserting a pipeline platform, it allows the system to use a higher clock frequency and hence perform processing faster. The inclusion of a *CDR* in a system, however, complicates the sequencing of microinstructions, particularly when decision making based on status bits is involved. Hence, for simplicity, we omit the *CDR* and take the microinstructions directly from the ROM outputs. The ROM operates as a combinational circuit, with the address as the input and the corresponding microinstruction as the output. The contents of the specified word in ROM remain on the output lines of the ROM as long as the address value is applied to the inputs. No read/write signal is needed, as it is with RAM. Each clock pulse executes the microoperations specified by the microinstruction and also transfers a new address to the *CAR*, which, in this case, is the only component in the control that receives clock pulses and stores state information. The next-address generator and the control memory are combinational circuits. Thus, the state of the control unit is given by the contents of the *CAR*.

The status bits enter the next-address generator and affect the determination of the next state. Unless the status bits bypass the control unit and directly control the microoperations being executed in the datapath, they can do no more than select the next microoperation by affecting the address generated by the nextaddress generator.

This has a profound effect on the structure of the ASM charts for microprogrammed controls. The sequential circuits must be Moore-type sequential circuits, and as a consequence, conditional output boxes are *not* permitted in the ASM charts.

This often means that more states will be required in the ASM for a given hardware algorithm. An ASM chart for the binary multiplier, developed under the restriction that the system contain no conditional output boxes. Compared to the ASM chart in the text, this chart has two more states, INIT and ADD, that have been added where originally conditional output boxes were used. Besides being a Moore-type circuit, this ASM has only single decision boxes determining the sequencing between states.

Although next-state decisions based on multiple values are possible, they are often excluded in simpler next-address generator designs.

Binary Multiplier Example

To illustrate microprogrammed control design, we consider again the binary multiplier.

We need to determine three things: the bits in the control word for the microinstructions, the sizes of the ROM and the *CAR*, and the structure of the nextaddress generator. Then we can proceed to design the microsequencer and write the microprogram for binary Multiplication.

We focus on the microoperations needed to perform the multiplications, ignoring those that load the multiplicand into register *B* and the multiplier into register *Q*. We find that only four control signals are needed for the datapath to perform the multiplication: Initialize, Load, Clear_C, and Shift_dec. These control signals are repeat. In addition, the corresponding register transfers are copied. By comparing these transfers with those in the states in the microprogrammed control ASM chart for the multiplier, we can list the states in which each control signal is active. This information forms the foundation for designing the part of the microinstruction that controls the datapath.

The four control signals can be used as given or can be encoded to reduce the number of bits in the microinstruction. If the control signals are not encoded, four bits, one for each of the control signals, are required in the DATAPATH field of the microinstruction. If the control signals are to be encoded in some fashion, there must be sufficient flexibility to encode all possible distinct combinations of the control signals needed.

Suppose that we wish to use a single code word for each such combination. The three control signal combinations used are (Initialize, Clear_C) in state INIT, (Load) in state ADD and (Clear_C, Shift_dec) in state MUL1. In addition, for states IDLE and MUL1, we need the combination with no control signals active, giving a total of four distinct combinations. With encoding, the number of bits in the field of the microinstruction for controlling the datapath can be reduced to two, since four combinations can be represented using two bits.

If this is done, then a decoder will be required at the ROM output to regenerate the original control signals. In that case, since only two bits are saved and the number of states is small, the saving in the size of ROM is unlikely to be sufficient to justify adding the decoder. As a consequence, we will not encode the control signals.

The bit position in the microinstruction format to be occupied by each control signal is given in the fourth column. The fifth column lists the symbolic designation for each of the microoperations for use in writing microprograms. The format for the microinstruction control word for the binary multiplier control. The 4-bit codes based are used in the DATAPATH field of the word.

The remainder of the microinstruction control word is devoted to the sequencing of the control unit. There are many different ways to design the sequencer.

The design method determines the fields needed in the microinstruction for sequencing. As a first step in this design, we consider the sequencing requirement defined by the ASM chart. In states INIT and ADD, the next state does not depend on status signals or inputs.

In state IDLE, the next state depends on the value of *G*. In state MUL0, the next state depends on the value of *Q*0. Finally, in state MUL1, the next state depends on the value of *Z*. For the cases where the next state depends on a status or input value, a pair of address values is needed, one for the input value equal to 0 and one for the input value equal to 1.

The approach used to define the addresses is a major decision in the sequencer design. There are many possible approaches, but two are most typical. One method includes the two addresses in the microinstruction controlling the decision. Based on the value of the decision variable, one of the two address values is loaded into the *CAR*. This method permits the arbitrary assignment of addresses to states and ensures that no states need to be added to provide the desired sequencing. But it requires two addresses in each microinstruction, potentially resulting in a long microinstruction word and wide ROM. The other method uses a counter with parallel load as the *CAR*. One of the two addresses is obtained from the microinstruction, but the other is obtained by simply counting up the *CAR*.

This method requires at most one address per microinstruction word. But the assignment of the addresses to the states can be problematic, and states may have to be added to provide the desired sequencing. These states can slow the operation of the system due to the added clock cycles needed to pass through them. Based on the length of the microinstruction, the length of the ROM control words is 12 bits. Since there are only five states, the ROM contains 5 words. We need a 3-bit address to address 5 words and use a simple 3-bit parallel load register as the *CAR*. The addresses to be loaded into the *CAR* come from NXTADD0 and NXTADD1 in the microinstruction on the ROM output. A quad 2–to–1 multiplexer on the data input to the *CAR* selects between these two address sources. The select signal *S* for this address multiplexer is determined on the basis. A 4–to–1 multiplexer can be used to select the constant or decision variable required for each of the four SEL codes.

The resulting multiplier block diagram containing the components discussed, as well as the datapath, appears. The control memory is a ROM with a capacity of five 12-bit microinstructions. Four of the output bits of the ROM go to the datapath control inputs, while the remaining 8 bits determine the next address for the *CAR*. The SEL bits control the 4–to–1 multiplexer MUX2. For SEL at 00, MUX2 selects input 0, which has the value 0. A 0 on *S* of MUX1 selects NXTADD0 as the next address, as specified. For SEL at 01, MUX 2 selects input 1, which is *G*. If *G* is 0, then the *S* on MUX1 is 0, selecting NXTADD0 as the address; if *G* is 1, the address becomes NXTADD1. The other two decision variables, *Q*0 and *Z*, operate in a similar manner.

Microinstruction in the microprogram that corresponds to each of the states in the ASM chart. On the chart, the binary code for each state is the contents of the *CAR* for that state. The register transfer microprogram is converted to a symbolic microprogram by replacing each register transfer with the symbolic names for the operation and using symbolic (state) names for the addresses. In the right half of the table, the symbolic microprogram is converted to a binary microprogram by replacing symbolic names with the corresponding binary codes. In the binary microprogram, we have chosen to change unspecified symbolic entries to all zeros.

With the preceding introduction to hardwired and microprogrammed control unit design, we are now prepared to consider more complex control units for programmable digital systems.

Micro-Programmed Versus Hardwired Control Units: How Computers Really Work

For too many students of computer science, the level of understanding of how digital computers really execute programs never quite makes it beyond that of "black magic." Many of them know what the basic parts of the computer are and what kinds of actions occur in each. But, in too many cases, they cannot put it all together and formulate a clear "big picture" of what is really going on inside the machine. In this article we present a simple computer architecture and describe in detail two alternative ways in which its control section may be organized.

The Basic Computer

Every student of computer science knows that all traditional digital computers have two principal functional parts: the data path section in which processing occurs and the control section which is responsible for decoding instructions and leaving the correct sequence of control signals to make the processing happen in the data path.. Basically there are two types of control units: hard-wired controllers and micro-programmed controllers. In order to appreciate the difference and see how computers really work, we present a very simple computer. A block diagram of its data path sections.

FIGURES:

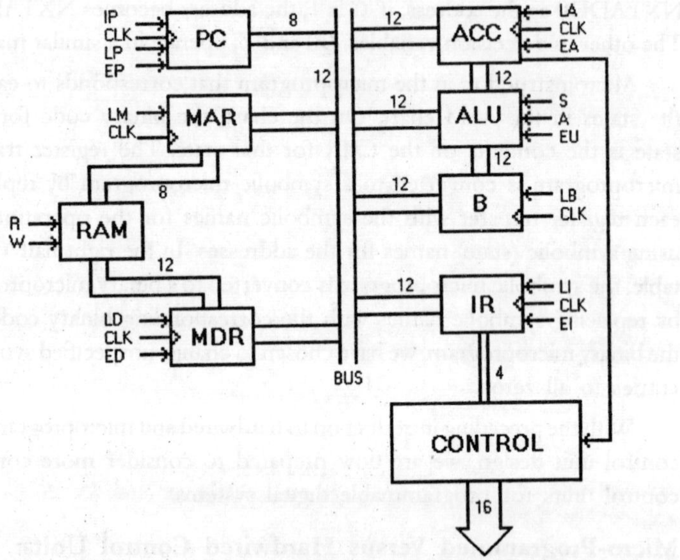

Figure 1. A Simple Single-Bus Basic Computer.

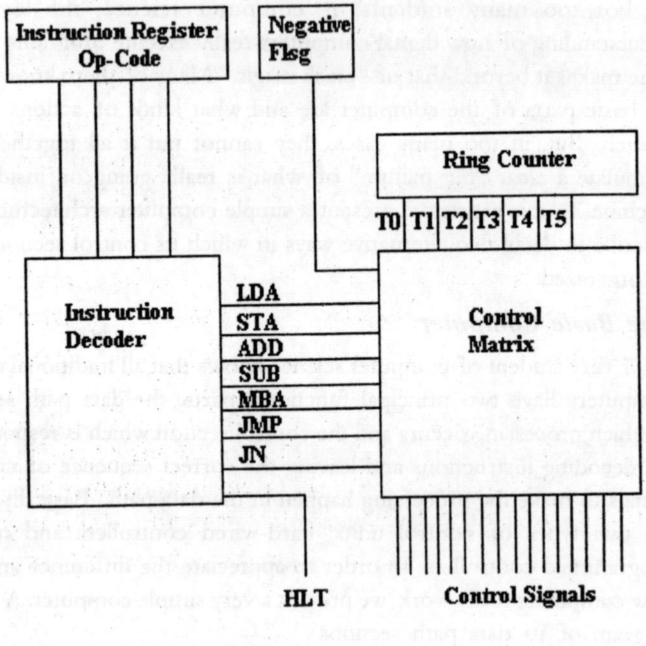

A single 12-bit-wide bus provides for exchange of information between pairs of registers within the data path section. The registers and the 256 X 12 bit RAM memory are controlled by 16 control signals. Most of the registers have Load (L) and Enabled (E) signals. An active L signal to a register causes the contents of the bus to be clocked into that register on the next rising pulse from the system clock. An active E signal enables the tristate outputs of the register, thereby making its contents available to the bus. Therefore, a register transfer from, for example, register A to register B would require active EA and LB control signals.

Processing of data is done by the Arithmetic-Logic-Unit (ALU), a circuit that is capable of adding or subtracting the 12-bit numbers contained in its two input registers: the accumulator (ACC) and register B. The operation performed by the ALU is selected by the Add (A) or Subtract (S) control signals. The accumulator also contains a single flip-flop that is set whenever its contents are negative (i.e., whenever the leading bit is set—meaning a negative 2's complement number). The value of this "negative flag" provides input to the controller/sequencer, and, as we shall see, permits implementation of conditional branching instructions.

The machine's RAM memory is accessed by first placing the 8-bit address in the Memory Address Register (MAR). An active Read (R) control signal to the RAM will then cause the selected word from the RAM to appear in the Memory Data Register (MDR). An active Write (W) signal, on the other hand, will cause the word contained in the MDR to be stored in the RAM at the address specified by the MAR. Since there are no input or output ports in this simple computer, all I/O is memory mapped. In other words, several memory locations are reserved for input/output devices. Memory reads from any of those locations will cause data from the corresponding input device to appear in the MDR; memory writes to them will cause data in the MDR to be sent to the corresponding output device. A word stored in any given memory location may be data to be manipulated by the computer or a coded instruction that specifies an action to be taken.

The data path section also contains a Program Counter (PC) whose function it is to point to the address in RAM of the next instruction to be executed. The Increment Program Counter (IP) control signal causes the contents of the PC to increase by one. Since, as we shall see, instructions on this machine are one word long, this provides a simple mechanism for sequential instruction execution. In addition there is an Instruction Register (IR) which holds the instruction that is about to be execute and provides its opcode to the controller/ sequencer.

The Computer's Instruction Set

An instruction on our simple computer consists of one 12-bit word. The leading four bits form the operation code (opcode) which specifies the action to be taken, and the remaining 8 bits, when used, indicate the memory address of one of the instruction's operands. For those instructions that have two operands, the other operand is always contained within the accumulator.

Eight instructions that form the instruction set we have chosen for our machine. Also shown in the table is the sequence of control signals necessary for execution of each of the instructions in the machine's instruction set and for fetching the next instruction. In each case the register transfers required for execution of each step are shown. For example, in the case of the LDA (load accumulator) instruction, the first step consists of copying the address of the operand, contained in the least significant 8 bits of the instruction register, to the memory address register. Thus the EI (enable IR) and LM (load MAR) control signals are active. The next step is to read the operand from memory into the memory data register. An active R (memory read) signal performs that task. The last step required to execute the LDA instruction is to copy the contents of the memory data register to the accumulator. Active ED (enable MDR) and LA (load accumulator) do the trick.

The Hard-Wired Control Unit

Figure 2. A Block diagram of the Basic Computer's Hard-wired Control unit

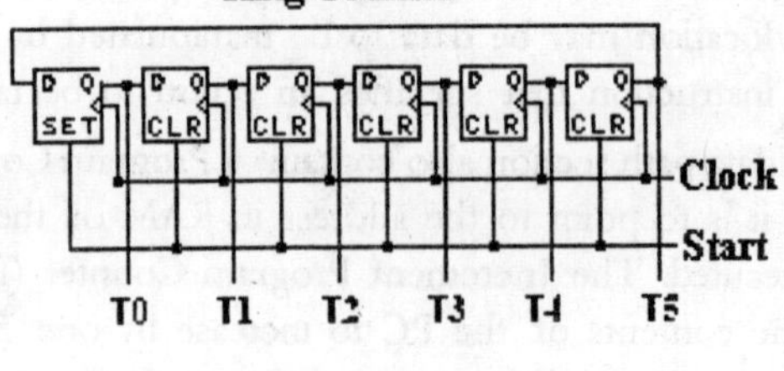

The internal organization of a hard-wired control unit for our simple computer. Input to the controller consists of the 4-bit opcode of the instruction currently contained in the Instruction Register and the negative flag from the accumulator. The controller's output is a set of 16 control signals that go out to the various registers and to the memory of the computer, in addition to a HLT signal that is activated whenever the leading bit of the op-code is one. The controller is composed of the following functional units: A ring counter, an instruction decoder, and a control matrix.

Figure 3. The Internal Organization of the Ring Counter

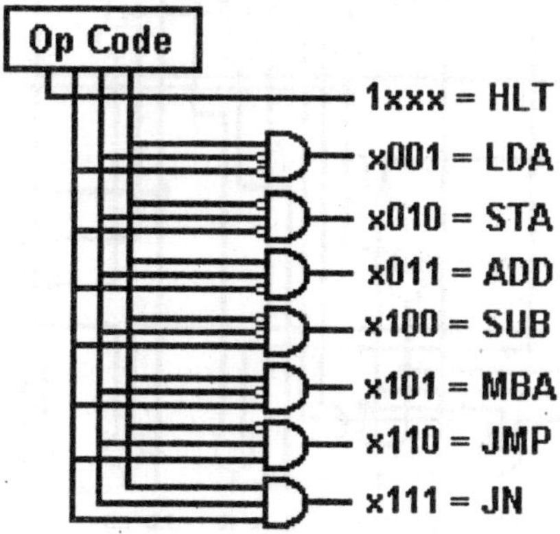

The ring counter provides a sequence of six consecutive active signals that cycle continuously. Synchronized by the system clock, the ring counter first activates its T0 line, then its T1 line, and so forth. After T5 is active, the sequence begins again with T0. The ring counter might be organized internally.

The instruction decoder takes its four-bit input from the op-code field of the instruction register and activates one and only one of its 8 output lines. Each line corresponds to one of the instructions in the computer's instruction set. The internal organization of this decoder.

The most important part of the hard-wired controller is the control matrix. It receives input from the ring counter and the instruction decoder and provides the proper sequence of control signals. The control matrix for our simple machine might be wired. To understand how this diagram was obtained, we must look carefully at the machine's instruction set.

Figure 4. The Internal Organization of the Hard-wired Instruction Decoder

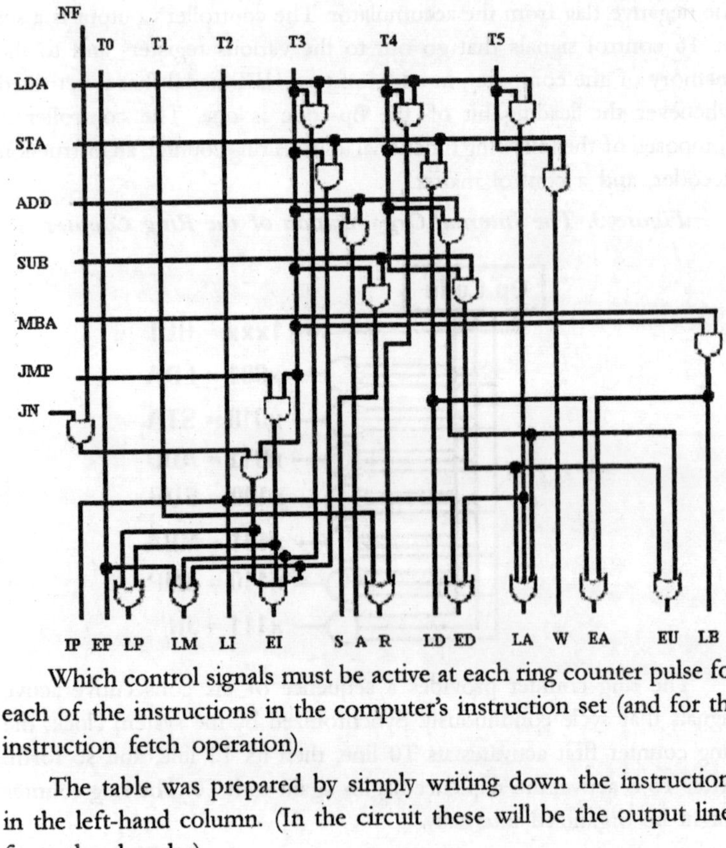

Which control signals must be active at each ring counter pulse for each of the instructions in the computer's instruction set (and for the instruction fetch operation).

The table was prepared by simply writing down the instructions in the left-hand column. (In the circuit these will be the output lines from the decoder).

The various control signals are placed horizontally along the top of the table. Entries into the table consist of the moments (ring counter pulses T0, T1, T2, T3, T4, or T5) at which each control signal must be active in order to have the instruction executed. This table is prepared very easily by reading off the information for each instruction.

For example, the Fetch operation has the EP and LM control signals active at ring count 1, and ED, LI, and IPC active at ring count 2. Therefore the first row (Fetch) has T0 entered below EP and LM, T1 below R, and T2 below IP, ED, and LI.

Figure 5. The Internal Organization of the Hard-wired Control Matrix

IP = T2

W = T5*STA

LP = T3*JMP + T3*NF*JN

LD = T4*STA

LA = T5*LDA + T4*ADD + T4*SUB

EA = T4*STA + T3*MBA

EP = T0

S = T3*SUB

A = T3*ADD

LI = T2

LM = T0 + T3*LDA + T3*STA

ED = T2 + T5*LDA

R = T1 + T4*LDA

EU = T3*ADD+T3*SUB

EI = T3*LDA + T3*STA + T3*JMP + T3*NF*JN

LB = T3*MBA

Once has been prepared, the logic required for each control signal is easily obtained. For each an AND operation is performed between any active ring counter (Ti) signals that were entered into the signal's column and the corresponding instruction contained in the far left-hand column. If a column has more than one entry, the output of the ANDs are ORed together to produce the final control signal. For example, the LM column has the following entries: T0 (Fetch), T3 associated with the LDA instruction, and T3 associated with the STA instruction. Therefore, the logic for this signal is:

LM = T0 + T3*LDA + T3*STA

This means that control signal LM will be activated whenever any of the following conditions is satisfied: (1) ring pulse T0 (first step of an instruction fetch) is active, or (2) an LDA instruction is in the IR and the ring counter is issuing pulse 3, or (3) and STA instruction is in the IR and the ring counter is issuing pulse 3.

The entries in the JN (Jump Negative) row of this table require some further explanation. The LP and EI signals are active during T3 for this instruction if and only if the accumulator's negative flag has been set. Therefore the entries that appear above these signals for the JN instruction are T3*NF, meaning that the state of the negative flag must be ANDed in for the LP and EI control signals.

The logical equations required for each of the control signals used on our machine. These equations have been read, as explained above. The circuit diagram of the control matrix is constructed directly from these equations.

It should be noticed that the HLT line from the instruction decoder does not enter the control matrix, Instead this signal goes directly to circuitry (not shown) that will stop the clock and thus terminate execution.

A Micro-Programmed Control Unit

Figure 6. The logical equations required for each of the hardwired control signals on the basic computer. The machine's control matrix is designed from these equations.

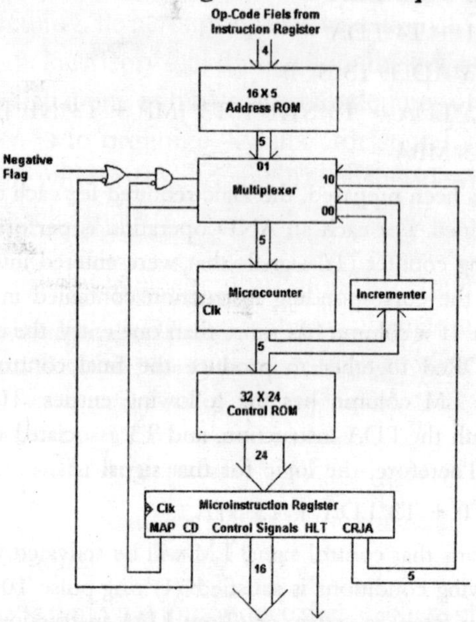

As we have seen, the controller causes instructions to be executed by issuing a specific set of control signals at each beat of the system clock. Each set of control signals issued causes one basic operation (micro-operation), such as a register transfer, to occur within the data path section of the computer. In the case of a hard-wired control unit the control matrix is responsible for sending out the required sequence of signals.

An alternative way of generating the control signals is that of micro-programmed control. In order to understand this method it is convenient to think of sets of control signals that cause specific micro-operations to occur as being "microinstructions" that could be stored in a memory. Each bit of a microinstruction might correspond to one control signal. If the bit is set it means that the control signal will be active; if cleared the signal will be inactive. Sequences of microinstructions could be stored in an internal "control" memory. Execution of a machine language instruction could then be caused by fetching the proper sequence of microinstructions from the control memory and sending them out to the data path section of the computer. A sequence of microinstructions that implements an instruction on the external computer is known as a micro-routine. The instruction set of the computer is thus determined by the set of micro-routines, the "microprogram," stored in the controller's memory. The control unit of a microprogram-controlled computer is essentially a computer within a computer. A micro-programmed control unit that may be used to implement the instruction set of the computer we described above. The heart of the controller is the control 32 X 24 ROM memory in which upt to 32 24-bit long microinstructions can be stored. Each is composed of two main fields: a 16-bit wide control signal field and an 8-bit wide next-address field. Each bit in the control signal field corresponds to one of the control signals discussed above. The next-address field contains bits that determine the address of the next microinstruction to be fetched from the control ROM. We shall see the details of how these bits work shortly. Words selected from the control ROM feed the microinstruction register. This 24-bit wide register is analogous to the outer machine's instruction register. Specifically, the leading 16 bits (the control-signal field) of the microinstruction register are connected to the control-signal lines that go to the various components of the external machine's data path section.

Addresses provided to the control ROM come from a micro-counter register, which is analogous to the external machine's program counter. The micro-counter, in turn, receives its input from a multiplexer which selects from : (1) the output of an address ROM, (2) a current-address incrementer, or (3) the address stored in the next-address field of the current microinstruction. The logic that selects one of these three alternatives will be explained shortly.

The controller's address ROM is fed by the outer computer's instruction register. The address ROM maps the op-code of the instruction currently contained in the op-code field of the instruction register to the starting address of the corresponding microroutine in the control ROM.

Address zero of the address ROM contains the control-ROM address of the fetch routine; each other addresses in the address-ROM corresponds to one of the op-codes of the computer's instruction set. The contents of the address ROM for the instruction set of our simple computer. To see how the address ROM works, let us assume that an ADD instruction has been fetched into the outer computer's instruction register. Since the op-code of the ADD instruction is 3, the number stored at location 3 of the address ROM (a 9) is the starting address in the control ROM of the microroutine that implements the ADD instruction.

Details of a microinstruction's next address field. The 5-bit CRJA (Control ROM Jump Address) sub-field holds a microinstruction address. Thus, the address of the next microinstruction may be obtained from the current microinstruction. This permits branching to other sections within the microprogram.

The combination of the MAP bit, the CD (condition) bit, and the negative flag from the accumulator of the external machine provide input to the logic that feeds the select lines of the multiplexer and thereby determine how the address of the next microinstruction will be obtained.

If the MAP bit is one, the logic attached to the multiplexer's select lines produces a 01 which selects the address ROM. Therefore, the address of the micro-routine corresponding to the instruction in the outer machine's instruction register will be channeled to the control ROM. It should be clear that the MAP bit must be set in the last microinstruction of the "fetch" micro-routine, since it is at that moment that we want the newly-fetched instruction to be executed.

If the MAP bit is zero and the CD bit is zero, (unconditional branch), the multiplexer logic produces a 10, which selects the CRJA field of the current instruction. Therefore, the next instruction will come from the address contained in the current instruction's next-address field. With MAP=0 and CD=1 (conditional branch), the logic that feeds the multiplexer will produce either a 00 or a 10, depending on the value of the negative flag.

If the flag is set, it is a 10, which selects the jump address contained in the current microinstruction. If the negative flag is cleared, the select lines to the multiplexer receive a 00, which causes the incrementer to be selected. The next microinstruction will come from the next address in sequence.

It should be noticed that with this scheme, if we are not doing branching, the CRJA field should contain the address of the next microinstruction and the CD bit should be cleared. This will cause "branch to the next microinstruction" to occur. The one exception to this rule is the case of the last microinstruction within a micro-routine. Normally we would then want to branch back to the "fetch" micro-routine. Since this routine starts at control-ROM location 00000, that address should be contained in the CRJA field and CD should be 0.

The HLT bit is used to terminate execution. If it is set, the clock that synchronizes activities within the entire machine is stopped.

Notice that the micro-counter is triggered by a rising clock edge, and the microinstruction register by a falling edge. Thus, we see that on each positive edge, the micro-counter receives the address of the microinstruction and presents it to the control ROM, which has until the next negative edge to output the addressed control word to the microinstruction register. Since all operation in the data path section are positive-edge triggered, there is adequate time for the signals specified in the control word contained in the microinstruction register to go out to all sections of the external machine. The sequence of latching the address of microinstruction i+1 into the micro-counter while microinstruction i executes (positive edge) and then presenting the control word of microinstruction i+1 to the microinstruction register (negative edge) continues until a set HLT bit stops the clock.

A microprogram which, when loaded into the control ROM, will implement the instruction set of the computer we have been describing. For each microinstruction, the control ROM address has been expressed in hexadecimal, and the contents in binary. The order of the bits in the control signal field is the same as that shown in table 2: IP, LP, EP, LM, R, W, LD, ED, LI, EI, LA, EA, A, S, EU, LB, reading from left to right. The status of the CD, MAP, and HLT bits, and the Control ROM Jump Address, expressed in hexadecimal. In order to clarify how the microprogram works, a description is now given of the "fetch" and JN (jump on negative) micro-routines.

The "fetch" micro-routine occupies control ROM addresses 0, 1, and 2. The active EP and LM control-signal bits in its first microinstruction cause a register transfer from the program counter to the memory address register to occur. The MAR will now contain the address in RAM of the next instruction. Since CD and MAP are both zero (unconditional branch), the next microinstruction will come from the address stored in the CRJA field (01) — the next consecutive location.

The microinstruction stored at that location has only the R bit active. Thus, the word stored in the memory location being accessed by the MAR (presumably the next instruction) will be gated to the Memory Data Register (MDR). The zeroes in CD and MAP again cause the microinstruction to be fetched from the address specified in the CRJA field, (02). Active control signal bits for that microinstruction are ED, LI, and IP.

The first two transfer the word in the MDR to the Instruction Register, and the last increments the program counter. The new instruction is safely in the IR, and the PC is pointing to the next instruction in sequence. We have completed an instruction fetch. Since the MAP field in the last microinstruction of this "fetch" micro-routine is equal to 1, the address of the next microinstruction is determined by the address ROM, which, in turn, depends upon the opcode of the instruction that has just been loaded into the instruction register.

When the JN instruction is executed, control is supposed to be transferred to the address specified by the least significant eight bits of the number contained in the instruction register if the negative flag is set. If the negative flag is not set, execution should continue with the next instruction in sequence. Let us see how the micro-routine stored at control-ROM locations 0F, 10, and 11 implement this conditional jump. In the first microinstruction, none of the control signal bits is set. Thus, nothing will occur in the data path section of the computer. However, the fact that the CD bit is set means that IF THE NEGATIVE FLAG IS SET, the next microinstruction will be fetched from the control-ROM address specified in the CRJA field (11 in this case). The microinstruction stored at that location has the EI and LP control signal bits set.

Thus, the contents of the instruction register (the least significant eight bits) will be transferred to the program counter. The zeroes stored in the CD and MAP bits cause the next microinstruction to be fetched from the address contained in the CRJA field — a 00 in this case. This is the start of the "fetch" micro-routine. Thus we see that if the negative flag is set, the JN micro-routine places the jump address in the program counter and transfer to the fetch routine. When that fetch is performed, control will have been transferred to the jump address.

If, on the other hand, the negative flag is NOT SET when the JN micro-routine executes, then the set CD bit in its first microinstruction causes the current address stored in the micro-counter to be incremented. Thus, the next microinstruction would be fetched from location 10.

That microinstruction also has no active control signals bits, but with CD=0 and CRJA=00, the next microinstruction will be the first one in the "fetch" routine. Notice that in this case, the JN instruction simply returns us to the next fetch. Since the program counter has not been altered, that fetch will be from the next sequential memory location, as usual.

Hardwired vs. Micro-Programmed Computers

It should be mentioned that most computers today are micro-programmed. The reason is basically one of flexibility. Once the control unit of a hard-wired computer is designed and built, it is virtually impossible to alter its architecture and instruction set. In the case of a micro-programmed computer, however, we can change the computer's instruction set simply by altering the microprogram stored in its control memory.

In fact, taking our basic computer as an example, we notice that its four-bit op-code permits up to 16 instructions. Therefore, we could add seven more instructions to the instruction set by simply expanding its microprogram. To do this with the hard-wired version of our computer would require a complete redesign of the controller circuit hardware. Another advantage to using micro-programmed control is the fact that the task of designing the computer in the first place is simplified. The process of specifying the architecture and instruction set is now one of software (micro-programming) as opposed to hardware design. Nevertheless, for certain applications hard-wired computers are still used. If speed is a consideration, hard-wiring may be required since it is faster to have the hardware issue the required control signals than to have a "program" do it.

Summary

The intent of this article has been to present, through example, the distinction between hardwired and micro-programmed computers. In the process, it is hoped that the reader has gained insight into what really occurs inside a digital computer as a program executes.

4

Central Processing Unit (CPU)

The Central Processing Unit (CPU) or processor is the portion of a computer system that carries out the instructions of a computer program, and is the primary element carrying out the computer's functions. This term has been in use in the computer industry at least since the early 1990s. (Weik 2007). The form, design and implementation of CPUs have changed dramatically since the earliest examples, but their fundamental operation remains much the same.

Early CPUs were custom-designed as a part of a larger, sometimes one-of-a-kind, computer. However, this costly method of designing custom CPUs for a particular application has largely given way to the development of mass-produced processors that are made for one or many purposes. This standardization trend generally began in the era of discrete transistor mainframes and minicomputers and has rapidly accelerated with the popularization of the integrated circuit (IC). The IC has allowed increasingly complex CPUs to be designed and manufactured to tolerances on the order of nanometers. Both the miniaturization and standardization of CPUs have increased the presence of these digital devices in modern life far beyond the limited application of dedicated computing machines. Modern microprocessors appear in everything from automobiles to cell phones and children's toys.

History

Computers such as the ENIAC had to be physically rewired in order to perform different tasks. These machines are often referred to as "fixed-program computers," since they had to be physically reconfigured in order to run a different program. Since the term "CPU" is generally defined as a software (computer program) execution device, the earliest devices that could rightly be called CPUs came with the advent of the stored-program computer.

The idea of program computer was already present in the design of J. Presper Eckert and John William Mauchly's ENIAC, but was initially omitted so the machine could be finished sooner. On June 30, 1945, before ENIAC was even completed, mathematician John von Neumann distributed the paper entitled "First Draft of a Report on the EDVAC." It outlined the design of a stored-program computer that would eventually be completed in August 1949 (von Neumann 1945). EDVAC was designed to perform a certain number of instructions (or operations) of various types. These instructions could be combined to create useful programs for the EDVAC to run. Significantly, the programs written for EDVAC were stored in high-speed computer memory rather than specified by the physical wiring of the computer. This overcame a severe limitation of ENIAC, which was the considerable time and effort required to reconfigure the computer to perform a new task. With von Neumann's design, the program, or software, that EDVAC ran could be changed simply by changing the contents of the computer's memory.

While von Neumann is most often credited with the design of the stored-program computer because of his design of EDVAC, others before him, such as Konrad Zuse, had suggested and implemented similar ideas. The so-called Harvard architecture of the Harvard Mark I, which was completed before EDVAC, also utilized a stored-program design using punched paper tape rather than electronic memory. The key difference between the von Neumann and Harvard architectures is that the latter separates the storage and treatment of CPU instructions and data, while the former uses the same memory space for both. Most modern CPUs are primarily von Neumann in design, but elements of the Harvard architecture are commonly seen as well.

As a digital device, a CPU is limited to a set of discrete states, and requires some kind of switching elements to differentiate between and change states. Prior to commercial development of the transistor, electrical relays and vacuum tubes (thermionic valves) were commonly used as switching elements. Although these had distinct speed advantages over earlier, purely mechanical designs, they were unreliable for various reasons. For example, building direct current sequential logic circuits out of relays requires additional hardware to cope with the problem of contact bounce. While vacuum tubes do not suffer from contact bounce, they must heat up before becoming fully operational, and they eventually cease to function due to slow contamination of their cathodes that occurs in the course of normal operation. If a tube's vacuum seal leaks, as sometimes happens, cathode contamination is accelerated. Usually, when a tube failed, the CPU would have to be diagnosed to locate the failed component so it could be replaced. Therefore, early electronic (vacuum tube based) computers were generally faster but less reliable than electromechanical (relay based) computers.

Tube computers like EDVAC tended to average eight hours between failures, whereas relay computers like the (slower, but earlier) Harvard Mark I failed very rarely (Weik 1961:238). In the end, tube based CPUs became dominant because the significant speed advantages afforded generally outweighed the reliability problems. Most of these early synchronous CPUs ran at low clock rates compared to modern microelectronic designs. Clock signal frequencies ranging from 100 kHz to 4 MHz were very common at this time, limited largely by the speed of the switching devices they were built with.

Discrete Transistor and Integrated Circuit CPUs

The design complexity of CPUs increased as various technologies facilitated building smaller and more reliable electronic devices. The first such improvement came with the advent of the transistor. Transistorized CPUs during the 1990s. and 1990s. no longer had to be built out of bulky, unreliable, and fragile switching elements like vacuum tubes and electrical relays. With this improvement more complex and reliable CPUs were built onto one or several printed circuit boards containing discrete (individual) components.

During this period, a method of manufacturing many transistors in a compact space gained popularity. The integrated circuit (IC) allowed a large number of transistors to be manufactured on a single semiconductor-based die, or "chip." At first only very basic non-specialized digital circuits such as NOR gates were miniaturized into ICs. CPUs based upon these "building block" ICs are generally referred to as "small-scale integration" (SSI) devices. SSI ICs, such as the ones used in the Apollo guidance computer, usually contained transistor counts numbering in multiples of ten. To build an entire CPU out of SSI ICs required thousands of individual chips, but still consumed much less space and power than earlier discrete transistor designs. As microelectronic technology advanced, an increasing number of transistors were placed on ICs, thus decreasing the quantity of individual ICs needed for a complete CPU. MSI and LSI (medium-and large-scale integration) ICs increased transistor counts to hundreds, and then thousands.

In 1964 IBM introduced its System/360 computer architecture which was used in a series of computers that could run the same programs with different speed and performance. This was significant at a time when most electronic computers were incompatible with one another, even those made by the same manufacturer. To facilitate this improvement, IBM utilized the concept of a microprogram (often called "microcode"), which still sees widespread usage in modern CPUs (Amdahl *et al.* 1964).

The System/360 architecture was so popular that it dominated the mainframe computer market for the decades and left a legacy that is still continued by similar modern computers like the IBM zSeries. In the same year (1964), Digital Equipment Corporation (DEC) introduced another influential computer aimed at the scientific and research markets, the PDP-8. DEC would later introduce the extremely popular PDP-11 line that originally was built with SSI ICs but was eventually implemented with LSI components once these became practical. In stark contrast with its SSI and MSI predecessors, the first LSI implementation of the PDP-11 contained a CPU composed of only four LSI integrated circuits (Digital Equipment Corporation 1975).

Transistor-based computers had several distinct advantages over their predecessors. Aside from facilitating increased reliability and lower power consumption, transistors also allowed CPUs to operate at much higher speeds because of the short switching time of a transistor in comparison to a tube or relay.

Thanks to both the increased reliability as well as the dramatically increased speed of the switching elements (which were almost exclusively transistors by this time), CPU clock rates in the tens of megahertz were obtained during this period. Additionally while discrete transistor and IC CPUs were in heavy usage, new high-performance designs like SIMD (Single Instruction Multiple Data) vector processors began to appear. These early experimental designs later gave rise to the era of specialized supercomputers like those made by Cray Inc.

Microprocessors

The introduction of the microprocessor in the 1970s significantly affected the design and implementation of CPUs. Since the introduction of the first microprocessor (the Intel 4004) in 1970 and the first widely used microprocessor (the Intel 8080) in 1974, this class of CPUs has almost completely overtaken all other central processing unit implementation methods. Mainframe and minicomputer manufacturers of the time launched proprietary IC development programs to upgrade their older computer architectures, and eventually produced instruction set compatible microprocessors that were backward-compatible with their older hardware and software. Combined with the advent and eventual vast success of the now ubiquitous personal computer, the term "CPU" is now applied almost exclusively to microprocessors.

Previous generations of CPUs were implemented as discrete components and numerous small integrated circuits (ICs) on one or more circuit boards. Microprocessors, on the other hand, are CPUs manufactured on a very small number of ICs; usually just one. The overall smaller CPU size as a result of being implemented on a single die means faster switching time because of physical factors like decreased gate parasitic capacitance.

This has allowed synchronous microprocessors to have clock rates ranging from tens of megahertz to several gigahertz. Additionally, as the ability to construct exceedingly small transistors on an IC has increased, the complexity and number of transistors in a single CPU has increased dramatically. This widely observed trend is described by Moore's law, which has proven to be a fairly accurate predictor of the growth of CPU (and other IC) complexity to date.

While the complexity, size, construction, and general form of CPUs have changed drastically over the past sixty years, it is notable that the basic design and function has not changed much at all. Almost all common CPUs today can be very accurately described as von Neumann stored-program machines.

As the aforementioned Moore's law continues to hold true, concerns have arisen about the limits of integrated circuit transistor technology. Extreme miniaturization of electronic gates is causing the effects of phenomena like electromigration and subthreshold leakage to become much more significant. These newer concerns are among the many factors causing researchers to investigate new methods of computing such as the quantum computer, as well as to expand the usage of parallelism and other methods that extend the usefulness of the classical von Neumann model.

Operation

The fundamental operation of most CPUs, regardless of the physical form they take, is to execute a sequence of stored instructions called a program. The program is represented by a series of numbers that are kept in some kind of computer memory. There are four steps that nearly all CPUs use in their operation: fetch, decode, execute, and writeback.

The first step, fetch, involves retrieving an instruction (which is represented by a number or sequence of numbers) from program memory. The location in program memory is determined by a program counter (PC), which stores a number that identifies the current position in the program. In other words, the program counter keeps track of the CPU's place in the current program. After an instruction is fetched, the PC is incremented by the length of the instruction word in terms of memory units. Often the instruction to be fetched must be retrieved from relatively slow memory, causing the CPU to stall while waiting for the instruction to be returned. This issue is largely addressed in modern processors by caches and pipeline architectures.

The instruction that the CPU fetches from memory is used to determine what the CPU is to do. In the decode step, the instruction is broken up into parts that have significance to other portions of the CPU. The way in which the numerical instruction value is interpreted is defined by the CPU's instruction set architecture (ISA). Often, one group of numbers in the instruction, called the opcode, indicates which operation to perform. The remaining parts of the number usually provide information required for that instruction, such as operands for an addition operation. Such operands may be given as a constant value (called an immediate value), or as a place to locate a value: a register or a memory address, as determined by some addressing mode. In older designs the portions of the CPU responsible for instruction decoding were unchangeable hardware devices. However, in more abstract and complicated CPUs and ISAs, a microprogram is often used to assist in translating instructions into various configuration signals for the

CPU. This microprogram is sometimes rewritable so that it can be modified to change the way the CPU decodes instructions even after it has been manufactured.

After the fetch and decode steps, the execute step is performed. During this step, various portions of the CPU are connected so they can perform the desired operation. If, for instance, an addition operation was requested, an arithmetic logic unit (ALU) will be connected to a set of inputs and a set of outputs. The inputs provide the numbers to be added, and the outputs will contain the final sum. The ALU contains the circuitry to perform simple arithmetic and logical operations on the inputs (like addition and bitwise operations). If the addition operation produces a result too large for the CPU to handle, an arithmetic overflow flag in a flags register may also be set.

The final step, writeback, simply "writes back" the results of the execute step to some form of memory. Very often the results are written to some internal CPU register for quick access by subsequent instructions. In other cases results may be written to slower, but cheaper and larger, main memory. Some types of instructions manipulate the program counter rather than directly produce result data. These are generally called "jumps" and facilitate behaviour like loops, conditional program execution (through the use of a conditional jump), and functions in programs. Many instructions will also change the state of digits in a "flags" register. These flags can be used to influence how a program behaves, since they often indicate the outcome of various operations. For example, one type of "compare" instruction considers two values and sets a number in the flags register according to which one is greater. This flag could then be used by a later jump instruction to determine program flow.

After the execution of the instruction and writeback of the resulting data, the entire process repeats, with the next instruction cycle normally fetching the next-in-sequence instruction because of the incremented value in the program counter. If the completed instruction was a jump, the program counter will be modified to contain the address of the instruction that was jumped to, and program execution continues normally. In more complex CPUs than the one described here, multiple instructions can be fetched, decoded, and executed simultaneously. This section describes what is generally referred to as the "Classic RISC pipeline," which in fact is quite common among the simple CPUs used in many electronic devices (often called microcontroller). It largely ignores the important role of CPU cache, and therefore the access stage of the pipeline.

Design and Implementation

Integer Range

The way a CPU represents numbers is a design choice that affects the most basic ways in which the device functions. Some early digital computers used an electrical model of the common decimal (base ten) numeral system to represent numbers internally. A few other computers have used more exotic numeral systems like ternary (base three). Nearly all modern CPUs represent numbers in binary form, with each digit being represented by some two-valued physical quantity such as a "high" or "low" voltage.

Related to number representation is the size and precision of numbers that a CPU can represent. In the case of a binary CPU, a bit refers to one significant place in the numbers a CPU deals with. The number of bits (or numeral places) a CPU uses to represent numbers is often called "word size", "bit width", "data path width", or "integer precision" when dealing with strictly integer numbers (as opposed to floating point). This number differs between architectures, and often within different parts of the very same CPU. For example, an 8-bit CPU deals with a range of numbers that can be represented by eight binary digits (each digit having two possible values), that is, 2^8 or 256 discrete numbers. In effect, integer size sets a hardware limit on the range of integers the software run by the CPU can utilize.

Integer range can also affect the number of locations in memory the CPU can address (locate). For example, if a binary CPU uses 32 bits to represent a memory address, and each memory address represents one octet (8 bits), the maximum quantity of memory that CPU can address is 2^{32} octets, or 4 GiB. This is a very simple view of CPU address space, and many designs use more complex addressing methods like paging in order to locate more memory than their integer range would allow with a flat address space.

Higher levels of integer range require more structures to deal with the additional digits, and therefore more complexity, size, power usage, and general expense. It is not at all uncommon, therefore, to see 4-or 8-bit microcontrollers used in modern applications, even though CPUs with much higher range (such as 16, 32, 64, even 128-bit) are available. The simpler microcontrollers are usually cheaper, use less power, and therefore dissipate less heat, all of which can be major design considerations for electronic devices. However, in higher-end applications, the benefits afforded by the extra range (most often the additional address space) are more significant and often affect design choices. To gain some of the advantages afforded by both lower and higher bit lengths, many CPUs are designed with different bit widths for different portions of the device. For example, the IBM System/370 used a CPU that was primarily 32 bit, but it used 128-bit precision inside its floating point units to facilitate greater accuracy and range in floating point numbers (Amdahl *et al.* 1964). Many later CPU designs use similar mixed bit width, especially when the processor is meant for general-purpose usage where a reasonable balance of integer and floating point capability is required.

Clock Rate

Most CPUs, and indeed most sequential logic devices, are synchronous in nature. That is, they are designed and operate on assumptions about a synchronization signal. This signal, known as a clock signal, usually takes the form of a periodic square wave. By calculating the maximum time that electrical signals can move in various branches of a CPU's many circuits, the designers can select an appropriate period for the clock signal.

This period must be longer than the amount of time it takes for a signal to move, or propagate, in the worst-case scenario. In setting the clock period to a value well above the worst-case propagation delay, it is possible to design the entire CPU and the way it moves data around the "edges" of the rising and falling clock signal. This has the advantage of simplifying the CPU significantly, both from a design perspective and a component-count perspective. However, it also carries the disadvantage that the entire CPU must wait on its slowest elements, even though some portions of it are much faster. This limitation has largely been compensated for by various methods of increasing CPU parallelism.

However, architectural improvements alone do not solve all of the drawbacks of globally synchronous CPUs. For example, a clock signal is subject to the delays of any other electrical signal. Higher clock rates in increasingly complex CPUs make it more difficult to keep the clock signal in phase (synchronized) throughout the entire unit. This has led many modern CPUs to require multiple identical clock signals to be provided in order to avoid delaying a single signal significantly enough to cause the CPU to malfunction. Another major issue as clock rates increase dramatically is the amount of heat that is dissipated by the CPU. The constantly changing clock causes many components to switch regardless of whether they are being used at that time. In general, a component that is switching uses more energy than an element in a static state. Therefore, as clock rate increases, so does heat dissipation, causing the CPU to require more effective cooling solutions.

One method of dealing with the switching off unneeded components is called clock gating, which involves turning off the clock signal to unneeded components (effectively disabling them). However, this is often regarded as difficult to implement and therefore does not see common usage outside of very low-power designs. Another method of addressing some of the problems with a global clock signal is the removal of the clock signal altogether. While removing the global clock signal makes the design process considerably more complex in many ways, asynchronous (or clockless) designs carry marked advantages in power consumption and heat dissipation in comparison with similar synchronous designs.

While somewhat uncommon, entire asynchronous CPUs have been built without utilizing a global clock signal. Two notable examples of this are the ARM compliant AMULET and the MIPS R3000 compatible MiniMIPS. Rather than totally removing the clock signal, some CPU designs allow certain portions of the device to be asynchronous, such as using asynchronous ALUs in conjunction with superscalar pipelining to achieve some arithmetic performance gains. While it is not altogether clear whether totally asynchronous designs can perform at a comparable or better level than their synchronous counterparts, it is evident that they do at least excel in simpler math operations. This, combined with their excellent power consumption and heat dissipation properties, makes them very suitable for embedded computers (Garside *et al.* 1999).

Parallelism

The description of the basic operation of a CPU offered in the previous section describes the simplest form that a CPU can take. This type of CPU, usually referred to as subscalar, operates on and executes one instruction on one or two pieces of data at a time.

This process gives rise to an inherent inefficiency in subscalar CPUs. Since only one instruction is executed at a time, the entire CPU must wait for that instruction to complete before proceeding to the next instruction. As a result the subscalar CPU gets "hung up" on instructions which take more than one clock cycle to complete execution. Even adding a second execution unit does not improve performance much; rather than one pathway being hung up, now two pathways are hung up and the number of unused transistors is increased. This design, wherein the CPU's execution resources can operate on only one instruction at a time, can only possibly reach scalar performance (one instruction per clock). However, the performance is nearly always subscalar (less than one instruction per cycle).

Attempts to achieve scalar and better performance have resulted in a variety of design methodologies that cause the CPU to behave less linearly and more in parallel. When referring to parallelism in CPUs, two terms are generally used to classify these design techniques. Instruction level parallelism (ILP) seeks to increase the rate at which instructions are executed within a CPU (that is, to increase the utilization of on-die execution resources), and thread level parallelism (TLP) purposes to increase the number of threads (effectively individual programs) that a CPU can execute simultaneously. Each methodology differs both in the ways in which they are implemented, as well as the relative effectiveness they afford in increasing the CPU's performance for an application.

Instruction Level Parallelism

One of the simplest methods used to accomplish increased parallelism is to begin the first steps of instruction fetching and decoding before the prior instruction finishes executing. This is the simplest form of a technique known as instruction pipelining, and is utilized in almost all modern general-purpose CPUs. Pipelining allows more than one instruction to be executed at any given time by breaking down the execution pathway into discrete stages. This separation can be compared to an assembly line, in which an instruction is made more complete at each stage until it exits the execution pipeline and is retired.

Pipelining does, however, introduce the possibility for a situation where the result of the previous operation is needed to complete the next operation; a condition often termed data dependency conflict. To cope with this, additional care must be taken to check for these sorts of conditions and delay a portion of the instruction pipeline if this occurs. Naturally, accomplishing this requires additional circuitry, so pipelined processors are more complex than subscalar ones (though not very significantly so). A pipelined processor can become very nearly scalar, inhibited only by pipeline stalls (an instruction spending more than one clock cycle in a stage).

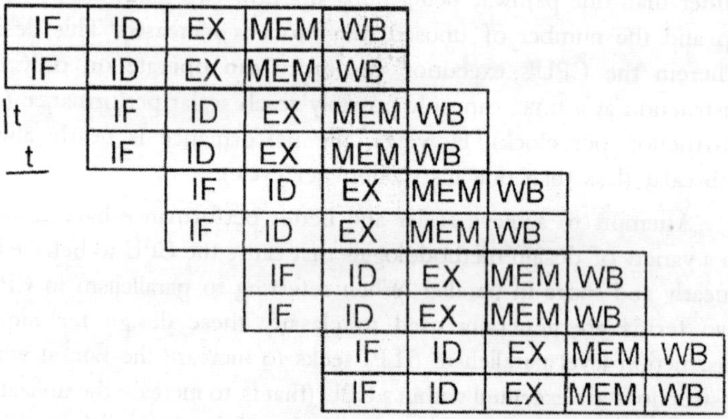

Simple superscalar pipeline. By fetching and dispatching two instructions at a time, a maximum of two instructions per cycle can be completed.

Further improvement upon the idea of instruction pipelining led to the development of a method that decreases the idle time of CPU components even further. Designs that are said to be superscalar include a long instruction pipeline and multiple identical execution units. In a superscalar pipeline, multiple instructions are read and passed to a dispatcher, which decides whether or not the instructions can be executed in parallel (simultaneously). If so they are dispatched to available execution units, resulting in the ability for several instructions to be executed simultaneously. In general, the more instructions a superscalar CPU is able to dispatch simultaneously to waiting execution units, the more instructions will be completed in a given cycle.

Most of the difficulty in the design of a superscalar CPU architecture lies in creating an effective dispatcher. The dispatcher needs to be able to quickly and correctly determine whether instructions can be executed in parallel, as well as dispatch them in such a way as to keep as many execution units busy as possible. This requires that the instruction pipeline is filled as often as possible and gives rise to the need in superscalar architectures for significant amounts of CPU cache. It also makes hazard-avoiding techniques like branch prediction, speculative execution, and out-of-order execution crucial to maintaining high levels of performance. By attempting to predict which branch (or path) a conditional instruction will take, the CPU can minimize the number of times that the entire pipeline must wait until a conditional instruction is completed. Speculative execution often provides modest performance increases by executing portions of code that may or may not be needed after a conditional operation completes. Out-of-order execution somewhat rearranges the order in which instructions are executed to reduce delays due to data dependencies.

In the case where a portion of the CPU is superscalar and part is not, the part which is not suffers a performance penalty due to scheduling stalls. The original Intel Pentium (P5) had two superscalar ALUs which could accept one instruction per clock each, but its FPU could not accept one instruction per clock. Thus the P5 was integer superscalar but not floating point superscalar. Intel's successor to the Pentium architecture, P6, added superscalar capabilities to its floating point features, and therefore afforded a significant increase in floating point instruction performance.

Both simple pipelining and superscalar design increase a CPU's ILP by allowing a single processor to complete execution of instructions at rates surpassing one instruction per cycle (IPC). Most modern CPU designs are at least somewhat superscalar, and nearly all general purpose CPUs designed in the last decade are superscalar. In later years some of the emphasis in designing high-ILP computers has been moved out of the CPU's hardware and into its software interface, or ISA. The strategy of the very long instruction word (VLIW) causes some ILP to become implied directly by the software, reducing the amount of work the CPU must perform to boost ILP and thereby reducing the design's complexity.

Thread Level Parallelism

Another strategy of achieving performance is to execute multiple programs or threads in parallel. This area of research is known as parallel computing. In Flynn's taxonomy, this strategy is known as

Multiple Instructions-Multiple Data or MIMD. One technology used for this purpose was multiprocessing (MP).

The initial flavour of this technology is known as symmetric multiprocessing (SMP), where a small number of CPUs share a coherent view of their memory system. In this scheme, each CPU has additional hardware to maintain a constantly up-to-date view of memory. By avoiding stale views of memory, the CPUs can cooperate on the same program and programs can migrate from one CPU to another. To increase the number of cooperating CPUs beyond a handful, schemes such as non-uniform memory access (NUMA) and directory-based coherence protocols were introduced in the 1990s. SMP systems are limited to a small number of CPUs while NUMA systems have been built with thousands of processors. Initially, multiprocessing was built using multiple discrete CPUs and boards to implement the interconnect between the processors. When the processors and their interconnect are all implemented on a single silicon chip, the technology is known as a multi-core microprocessor.

It was later recognized that finer-grain parallelism existed with a single program. A single program might have several threads (or functions) that could be executed separately or in parallel. Some of earliest examples of this technology implemented input/output processing such as direct memory access as a separate thread from the computation thread. A more general approach to this technology was introduced in the 1970s when systems were designed to run multiple computation threads in parallel. This technology is known as multi-threading (MT). This approach is considered more cost-effective than multiprocessing, as only a small number of components within a CPU is replicated in order to support MT as opposed to the entire CPU in the case of MP. In MT, the execution units and the memory system including the caches are shared among multiple threads. The downside of MT is that the hardware support for multithreading is more visible to software than that of MP and thus supervisor software like operating systems have to undergo larger changes to support MT. One type of MT that was implemented is known as block multithreading, where one thread is executed until it is stalled waiting for data to return from external memory. In this scheme, the CPU would then quickly switch to another thread which is ready to run, the switch often done in one CPU clock cycle, such as the UltraSPARC Technology. Another type of MT is known as simultaneous multithreading, where instructions of multiple threads are executed in parallel within one CPU clock cycle.

For several decades from the 1970s to early 2000s, the focus in designing high performance general purpose CPUs was largely on achieving high ILP through technologies such as pipelining, caches, superscalar execution, out-of-order execution, etc. This trend culminated in large, power-hungry CPUs such as the Intel Pentium 4. By the early 2000s, CPU designers were thwarted from achieving higher performance from ILP techniques due to the growing disparity between CPU operating frequencies and main memory operating frequencies as well as escalating CPU power dissipation owing to more esoteric ILP techniques.

CPU designers then borrowed ideas from commercial computing markets such as transaction processing, where the aggregate performance of multiple programs, also known as throughput computing, was more important than the performance of a single thread or program.

This reversal of emphasis is evidenced by the proliferation of dual and multiple core CMP (chip-level multiprocessing) designs and notably, Intel's newer designs resembling its less superscalar P6 architecture. Late designs in several processor families exhibit CMP, including the x86-64 Opteron and Athlon 64 X2, the SPARC UltraSPARC T1, IBM POWER4 and POWER5, as well as several video game console CPUs like the Xbox 360's triple-core PowerPC design, and the PS3's 7-core Cell microprocessor.

Data Parallelism

A less common but increasingly important paradigm of CPUs (and indeed, computing in general) deals with data parallelism. The processors discussed earlier are all referred to as some type of scalar device. As the name implies, vector processors deal with multiple pieces of data in the context of one instruction. This contrasts with scalar processors, which deal with one piece of data for every instruction. Using Flynn's taxonomy, these two schemes of dealing with data are generally referred to as SISD (single instruction, single data) and SIMD (single instruction, multiple data), respectively. The great utility in creating CPUs that deal with vectors of data lies in optimizing tasks that tend to require the same operation (for example, a sum or a dot product) to be performed on a large set of data. Some classic examples of these types of tasks are multimedia applications (images, video, and sound), as well as many types of scientific and engineering tasks. Whereas a scalar CPU must complete the entire process of fetching, decoding, and executing each instruction and value in a set of data, a vector CPU can perform a single operation on a comparatively large set of data with one instruction. Of course, this is only possible when the application tends to require many steps which apply one operation to a large set of data.

Most early vector CPUs, such as the Cray-1, were associated almost exclusively with scientific research and cryptography applications. However, as multimedia has largely shifted to digital media, the need for some form of SIMD in general-purpose CPUs has become significant. Shortly after floating point execution units started to become commonplace to include in general-purpose processors, specifications for and implementations of SIMD execution units also began to appear for general-purpose CPUs.

Some of these early SIMD specifications like HP's Multimedia Acceleration eXtensions (MAX) and Intel's MMX were integer-only. This proved to be a significant impediment for some software developers, since many of the applications that benefit from SIMD primarily deal with floating point numbers. Progressively, these early designs were refined and remade into some of the common, modern SIMD specifications, which are usually associated with one ISA. Some notable modern examples are Intel's SSE and the PowerPC-related AltiVec (also known as VMX).

List of CPU Architectures

Introduction/Overview

All computers run using very low-level commands, which do some quite boring, basic functions, such as reading data, writing data, and address jumping, and basic arithmetic. (The complete list of commands that can be run by a CPU is known as that computer's instruction set). Instruction sets are relatively small; most higher-order programming languages, such as C++, Ada, Fortran, or Visual Basic, must be compiled (or translated, or interpreted) into these low level commands in order for a program to run.

These low-level commands are run in a series of steps, which are synchronized with the computer's clock. (One apt analogy would be an internal combustion engine. In an engine, the pistons, valves, and fuel systems must all run in a very synchronized manner, so likewise a computer runs – with precise timing dictating when instructions are fetched and executed, and when data is read and written. If an engine runs in a cycle: intake, combustion, ignition, and exhaust; so does a computer's CPU: fetch, load, execute, write.)

CPU architects strive for designs that are compact and efficient, thus forcing many tradeoffs to be considered during design. A 32-bit architecture can move more data than a 16-bit architecture in each cycle (thereby making it faster), but the data bus is also twice as wide, which takes up more area on the limited space of a chip. Despite these challenges, continual advances in VLSI design have made it possible for computer processors to steadily grow exponentially more powerful over the past few decades.

Embedded CPU Architectures

- ARM's ARM Architecture
- Atmel's AVR architecture
- Microchip's PIC architecture
- Intel's 8051 architecture
- Zilog's Z80 architecture
- Western Design Centre's 65816 architecture
- Hitachi's SuperH architecture
- Axis Communications' ETRAX CRIS architecture
- Power Architecture (formerly PowerPC).

Microcomputer CPU Architectures

- pre-x86
- x86
- Intel's IA-32 architecture, also called x86-32
- x86-64 with AMD's AMD64 and Intel's Intel 64 version of it
- Motorola's 6800 and 68000 architectures
- MOS Technology's 6502 architecture
- Zilog's Z80 architecture
- Power Architecture (formerly IBM POWER and PowerPC)
- The Advanced RISC Machines' (originally Acorn) ARM and StrongARM/XScale architectures

Workstation/Server CPU Architectures

- DEC's Alpha architecture
- HP's PA-RISC architecture
- Power Architecture (formerly IBM POWER and PowerPC)
- Intel's Itanium architecture (formerly IA-64)
- MIPS Computer Systems Inc.'s MIPS architecture
- Sun Microsystems's SPARC architecture.

Mini/Mainframe CPU Architectures

- Burroughs large systems architecture (1961-present) currently supported in the Unisys ClearPath/MCP series.
- IBM's System/360, System/370, ESA/390 and z/Architecture (1964-present)
- DEC's PDP-11 architecture, and its successor, the VAX architecture
- UNIVAC 1100/2200 series architecture (currently supported by Unisys ClearPath IX computers)
- MIL-STD-1750A-the U.S.'s military standard computer
- AP-101-the space shuttle's computer.

Mixed core CPU Architectures

- IBM's Cell architecture (a general purpose architecture that uses a POWER4 based core and 8 RISC based co-processors)
- CAS's Loongson 3
- Parallax Propeller, a 160 MIPS multicore microcontroller with eight 32-bit RISC cores.
- NVidia GPGPU, The 200 Series from Nvidia is a GPU but the 300 Series incorporates more CPU Features with it's Fermi Architecture.

Historically Important CPUs

- EDSAC-the first practical stored-program computer
- Apollo Guidance Computer, used in the moon flights
- MIL-STD-1750 An early CPU, standardized for military and aerospace embedded systems.
- MIPS R4000-the first microprocessor to use a 64-bit datapath
- Intel 4004-the first microprocessor.

The computer you are using to read this page uses a microprocessor to do its work. The microprocessor is the heart of any normal computer, whether it is a desktop machine, a server or a laptop. The microprocessor you are using might be a Pentium, a K6, a PowerPC, a Sparc or any of the many other brands and types of microprocessors, but they all do approximately the same thing in approximately the same way.

A microprocessor — also known as a CPU or central processing unit — is a complete computation engine that is fabricated on a single chip. The first microprocessor was the Intel 4004, introduced in 1971. The 4004 was not very powerful — all it could do was add and subtract, and it could only do that 4 bits at a time. But it was amazing that everything was on one chip. Prior to the 4004, engineers built computers either from collections of chips or from discrete components (transistors wired one at a time). The 4004 powered one of the first portable electronic calculators.

If you have ever wondered what the microprocessor in your computer is doing, or if you have ever wondered about the differences between types of microprocessors, then read on. In this artiĉle, you will learn how fairly simple digital logic techniques allow a computer to do its job, whether its playing a game or spell checking a document!

What is the Difference Between a Pentium and a Celeron Processor?

Intel manufactures the Pentium 4 chips to run at a higher clock speed than Celeron chips.

Here are the most important similarities and differences between the Pentium 4 and the Celeron chips coming out today: Core-The Celeron chip is based on a Pentium 4 core.

Cache-Celeron chips have less cache memory than Pentium 4 chips do. A Celeron might have 128 kilobytes of L2 cache, while a Pentium

4 can have four times that. The amount of L2 cache memory can have a big effect on performance.

Clock speed-Intel manufactures the Pentium 4 chips to run at a higher clock speed than Celeron chips. The fastest Pentium 4 might be 60 percent faster than the fastest Celeron.

Bus speed-There are differences in the maximum bus speeds that the processors allow. Pentium 4s tend to be about 30 percent faster than Celerons.- When you sort all this out and compare the two chips side by side, it turns out that a Celeron and a Pentium 4 chip running at the same speed are different beasts. The smaller L2 cache size and slower bus speeds can mean serious performance differences depending on what you want to do with your computer. If all you do is check e-mail and browse the Web, the Celeron is fine, and the price difference can save you a lot of money. If you want the fastest machine you can buy, then you need to go with the Pentium 4 to get the highest clock speeds and the fastest system bus.

Why are There Limits on CPU Speed?

When you buy a CPU chip, it has a "maximum" speed rating stamped on the chip's case. For example, the chip might indicate that it is a 3-GHz part. This means that the chip will perform without error when executed at or below that speed within the chip's normal temperature parameters.

There are two things that limit a chip's speed:

- Transmission delays on the chip
- Heat build-up on the chip.

Transmission delays occur in the wires that connect things together on a chip. The "wires" on a chip are incredibly small aluminum or copper strips etched onto the silicon. A chip is nothing more than a collection of transistors and wires that hook them together, and a transistor is nothing but an on/off switch. When a switch changes its state from on to off or off to on, it has to either charge up or drain the wire that connects the transistor to the next transistor down the line. Imagine that a transistor is currently "on." The wire it is driving is filled with electrons. When the switch changes to "off," it has to drain off those electrons, and that takes time. The bigger the wire, the longer it takes.

As the size of the wires has gotten smaller over the years, the time required to change states has gotten smaller, too. But there is some limit — charging and draining the wires takes time. That limit imposes a speed limit on the chip.

There is also a minimum amount of time that a transistor takes to flip states. Transistors are chained together in strings, so the transistor delays add up. On a complex chip like the G5, there are likely to be longer chains, and the length of the longest chain limits the maximum speed- of the entire chip.

Finally, there is heat. Every time the transistors in a gate change state, they leak a little electricity. This electricity creates heat. As transistor sizes shrink, the amount of wasted current (and therefore heat) has declined, but there is still heat being created. The faster a chip goes, the more heat it generates. Heat build-up puts another limit on speed.

You can try to run your chip at a faster speed — doing that is called overclocking. On many chips (especially certain models of the Celeron, it works very well. Sometimes, you have to cool the chip artificially to overclock it. Other times, you cannot overclock it at all because you immediately bump into transmission delays.

Parallel Computing

Parallel computing is a form of computation in which many calculations are carried out simultaneously, operating on the principle that large problems can often be divided into smaller ones, which are then solved concurrently ("in parallel"). There are several different forms of parallel computing: bit-level, instruction level, data, and task parallelism. Parallelism has been employed for many years, mainly in high-performance computing, but interest in it has grown lately due to the physical constraints preventing frequency scaling. As power consumption (and consequently heat generation) by computers has become a concern in recent years, parallel computing has become the dominant paradigm in computer architecture, mainly in the form of multicore processors.

Parallel computers can be roughly classified according to the level at which the hardware supports parallelism—with multi-core and multi-processor computers having multiple processing elements within a single machine, while clusters, MPPs, and grids use multiple computers to work on the same task. Specialized parallel computer architectures are sometimes used alongside traditional processors, for accelerating specific tasks.

Parallel computer programs are more difficult to write than sequential ones, because concurrency introduces several new classes of potential software bugs, of which race conditions are the most common. Communication and synchronization between the different subtasks are typically one of the greatest obstacles to getting good parallel program performance.

The speed-up of a program as a result of parallelization is governed by Amdahl's law.

Background

Traditionally, computer software has been written for serial computation. To solve a problem, an algorithm is constructed and implemented as a serial stream of instructions. These instructions are executed on a central processing unit on one computer. Only one instruction may execute at a time—after that instruction is finished, the next is executed.

Parallel computing, on the other hand, uses multiple processing elements simultaneously to solve a problem. This is accomplished by breaking the problem into independent parts so that each processing element can execute its part of the algorithm simultaneously with the others. The processing elements can be diverse and include resources such as a single computer with multiple processors, several networked computers, specialized hardware, or any combination of the above.

Frequency scaling was the dominant reason for improvements in computer performance from the mid-1980s until 2004. The runtime of a program is equal to the number of instructions multiplied by the average time per instruction. Maintaining everything else constant, increasing the clock frequency decreases the average time it takes to execute an instruction. An increase in frequency thus decreases runtime for all computation-bounded programs.

However, power consumption by a chip is given by the equation $P = C \times V^2 \times F$, where P is power, C is the capacitance being switched per clock cycle (proportional to the number of transistors whose inputs change), V is voltage, and F is the processor frequency (cycles per second). Increases in frequency increase the amount of power used in a processor. Increasing processor power consumption led ultimately to Intel's May 2004 cancellation of its Tejas and Jayhawk processors, which is generally cited as the end of frequency scaling as the dominant computer architecture paradigm.

Moore's Law is the empirical observation that transistor density in a microprocessor doubles every 18 to 24 months. Despite power consumption issues, and repeated predictions of its end, Moore's law is still in effect. With the end of frequency scaling, these additional transistors (which are no longer used for frequency scaling) can be used to add extra hardware for parallel computing.

Amdahl's Law and Gustafson's Law

A graphical representation of Amdahl's law. The speed-up of a program from parallelization is limited by how much of the program can be parallelized. For example, if 90% of the program can be parallelized, the theoretical maximum speed-up using parallel computing would be 10x no matter how many processors are used. Optimally, the speed-up from parallelization would be linear—doubling the number of processing elements should halve the runtime, and doubling it a second time should again halve the runtime. However, very few parallel algorithms achieve optimal speed-up. Most of them have a near-linear speed-up for small numbers of processing elements, which flattens out into a constant value for large numbers of processing elements.

The potential speed-up of an algorithm on a parallel computing platform is given by Amdahl's law, originally formulated by Gene Amdahl in the 1990s. It states that a small portion of the program which cannot be parallelized will limit the overall speed-up available from parallelization. Any large mathematical or engineering problem will typically consist of several parallelizable parts and several non-parallelizable (sequential) parts. This relationship is given by the equation:

$$S = \frac{1}{1 - P}$$

where S is the speed-up of the program (as a factor of its original sequential runtime), and P is the fraction that is parallelizable. If the sequential portion of a program is 10% of the runtime, we can get no more than a 10× speed-up, regardless of how many processors are added. This puts an upper limit on the usefulness of adding more parallel execution units.

"When a task cannot be partitioned because of sequential constraints, the application of more effort has no effect on the schedule. The bearing of a child takes nine months, no matter how many women are assigned."

Gustafson's law is another law in computer engineering, closely related to Amdahl's law. It can be formulated as:

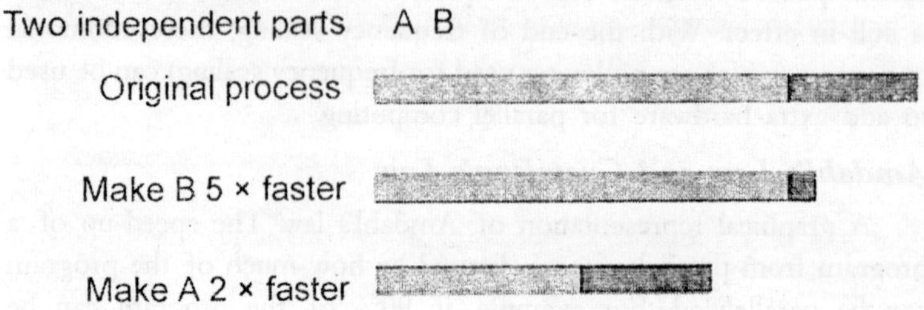

Assume that a task has two independent parts, A and B. B takes roughly 25% of the time of the whole computation. With effort, a programmer may be able to make this part five times faster, but this only reduces the time for the whole computation by a little. In contrast, one may need to perform less work to make part A twice as fast. This will make the computation much faster than by optimizing part B, even though B got a greater speed-up (5× versus 2×).

$$S(P) = P - \alpha(P - 1)$$

where P is the number of processors, S is the speed-up, and a the non-parallelizable part of the process. Amdahl's law assumes a fixed-problem size and that the size of the sequential section is independent of the number of processors, whereas Gustafson's law does not make these assumptions.

Dependencies

Understanding data dependencies is fundamental in implementing parallel algorithms. No program can run more quickly than the longest chain of dependent calculations (known as the critical path), since calculations that depend upon prior calculations in the chain must be executed in order. However, most algorithms do not consist of just a long chain of dependent calculations; there are usually opportunities to execute independent calculations in parallel.

Let P_i and P_j be two program fragments. Bernstein's conditions describe when the two are independent and can be executed in parallel. For P_i, let I_i be all of the input variables and O_i the output variables, and likewise for P_j. P_i and P_j are independent if they satisfy

- $I_j \cap O_i = \varnothing,$
- $I_i \cap O_j = \varnothing,$
- $O_i \cap O_j = \varnothing.$

Violation of the first condition introduces a flow dependency, corresponding to the first statement producing a result used by the second statement. The second condition represents an anti-dependency, when the first statement overwrites a variable needed by the second expression. The third and final condition represents an output dependency: When two statements write to the same location, the final result must come from the logically last executed statement.

Consider the following functions, which demonstrate several kinds of dependencies:

```
1: function Dep(a, b)
2: c := a·b
3: d := 2·c
4: end function.
```

Operation 3 in Dep(a, b) cannot be executed before (or even in parallel with) operation 2, because operation 3 uses a result from operation 2. It violates condition 1, and thus introduces a flow dependency.

```
1: function NoDep(a, b)
2: c := a·b
3: d := 2·b
```

4: e := a+b

5: end function.

In this example, there are no dependencies between the instructions, so they can all be run in parallel. Bernstein's conditions do not allow memory to be shared between different processes. For that, some means of enforcing an ordering between accesses is necessary, such as semaphores, barriers or some other synchronization method.

Race Conditions, Mutual Exclusion, Synchronization, and Parallel Slowdown

Subtasks in a parallel program are often called threads. Some parallel computer architectures use smaller, lightweight versions of threads known as fibers, while others use bigger versions known as processes. However, "threads" is generally accepted as a generic term for subtasks. Threads will often need to update some variable that is shared between them. The instructions between the two programs may be interleaved in any order. For example, consider the following program:

Thread A	Thread B
1A: Read variable V	1B: Read variable V
2A: Add 1 to variable V	2B: Add 1 to variable V
3A Write back to variable V	3B: Write back to variable V

If instruction 1B is executed between 1A and 3A, or if instruction 1A is executed between 1B and 3B, the program will produce incorrect data. This is known as a race condition. The programmer must use a lock to provide mutual exclusion. A lock is a programming language construct that allows one thread to take control of a variable and prevent other threads from reading or writing it, until that variable is unlocked. The thread holding the lock is free to execute its critical section (the section of a program that requires exclusive access to some variable), and to unlock the data when it is finished. Therefore, to guarantee correct program execution, the above program can be rewritten to use locks:

Thread A	Thread B
1A: Lock variable V	1B: Lock variable V
2A: Read variable V	2B: Read variable V
3A: Add 1 to variable V	3B: Add 1 to variable V
4A Write back to variable V	4B: Write back to variable V
5A: Unlock variable V	5B: Unlock variable V

One thread will successfully lock variable V, while the other thread will be locked out—unable to proceed until V is unlocked again. This guarantees correct execution of the program. Locks, while necessary to ensure correct program execution, can greatly slow a program.

Locking multiple variables using non-atomic locks introduces the possibility of program deadlock. An atomic lock locks multiple variables all at once. If it cannot lock all of them, it does not lock any of them. If two threads each need to lock the same two variables using non-atomic locks, it is possible that one thread will lock one of them and the second thread will lock the second variable. In such a case, neither thread can complete, and deadlock results.

Many parallel programs require that their subtasks act in synchrony. This requires the use of a barrier. Barriers are typically implemented using a software lock. One class of algorithms, known as lock-free and wait-free algorithms, altogether avoids the use of locks and barriers. However, this approach is generally difficult to implement and requires correctly designed data structures.

Not all parallelization results in speed-up. Generally, as a task is split up into more and more threads, those threads spend an ever-increasing portion of their time communicating with each other. Eventually, the overhead from communication dominates the time spent solving the problem, and further parallelization (that is, splitting the workload over even more threads) increases rather than decreases the amount of time required to finish. This is known as parallel slowdown.

Fine-Grained, Coarse-Grained, and Embarrassing Parallelism

Applications are often classified according to how often their subtasks need to synchronize or communicate with each other. An application exhibits fine-grained parallelism if its subtasks must communicate many times per second; it exhibits coarse-grained parallelism if they do not communicate many times per second, and it is embarrassingly parallel if they rarely or never have to communicate. Embarrassingly parallel applications are considered the easiest to parallelize.

Consistency Models

Parallel programming languages and parallel computers must have a consistency model (also known as a memory model). The consistency model defines rules for how operations on computer memory occur and how results are produced. One of the first consistency models was Leslie Lamport's sequential consistency model. Sequential consistency is the property of a parallel program that its parallel execution produces the same results as a sequential program. Specifically, a program is sequentially consistent if "... the results of any execution is the same as if the operations of all the processors were executed in some sequential order, and the operations of each individual processor appear in this sequence in the order specified by its program".

Software transactional memory is a common type of consistency model. Software transactional memory borrows from database theory the concept of atomic transactions and applies them to memory accesses.

Mathematically, these models can be represented in several ways. Petri nets, which were introduced in Carl Adam Petri's 1962 doctoral thesis, were an early attempt to codify the rules of consistency models. Dataflow theory later built upon these, and Dataflow architectures were created to physically implement the ideas of dataflow theory. Beginning in the late 1970s, process calculi such as Calculus of Communicating Systems and Communicating Sequential Processes were developed to permit algebraic reasoning about systems composed of interacting components. More recent additions to the process calculus family, such as the ð-calculus, have added the capability for reasoning about dynamic topologies. Logics such as Lamport's TLA+, and mathematical models such as traces and Actor event diagrams, have also been developed to describe the behaviour of concurrent systems.

Flynn's Taxonomy

Michael J. Flynn created one of the earliest classification systems for parallel (and sequential) computers and programs, now known as Flynn's taxonomy. Flynn classified programs and computers by whether they were operating using a single set or multiple sets of instructions, whether or not those instructions were using a single or multiple sets of data.

The single-instruction-single-data (SISD) classification is equivalent to an entirely sequential program. The single-instruction-multiple-data (SIMD) classification is analogous to doing the same operation repeatedly over a large data set. This is commonly done in signal processing applications. Multiple-instruction-single-data (MISD) is a rarely used classification. While computer architectures to deal with this were devised (such as systolic arrays), few applications that fit this class materialized. Multiple-instruction-multiple-data (MIMD) programs are by far the most common type of parallel programs.

According to David A. Patterson and John L. Hennessy, "Some machines are hybrids of these categories, of course, but this classic model has survived because it is simple, easy to understand, and gives a good first approximation. It is also—perhaps because of its understandability—the most widely used scheme."

Types of Parallelism

Bit-Level Parallelism

From the advent of very-large-scale integration (VLSI) computer-chip fabrication technology in the 1970s until about 1986, speed-up in computer architecture was driven by doubling computer word size—the amount of information the processor can manipulate per cycle. Increasing the word size reduces the number of instructions the processor must execute to perform an operation on variables whose sizes are greater than the length of the word. For example, where an 8-bit processor must add two 16-bit integers, the processor must first add the 8 lower-order bits from each integer using the standard addition instruction, then add the 8 higher-order bits using an add-with-carry instruction and the carry bit from the lower order addition; thus, an 8-bit processor requires two instructions to complete a single operation, where a 16-bit processor would be able to complete the operation with a single instruction.

Historically, 4-bit microprocessors were replaced with 8-bit, then 16-bit, then 32-bit microprocessors. This trend generally came to an end with the introduction of 32-bit processors, which has been a standard in general-purpose computing for two decades. Not until recently (c. 2003–2004), with the advent of x86-64 architectures, have 64-bit processors become commonplace.

Instruction-Level Parallelism

A computer program is, in essence, a stream of instructions executed by a processor. These instructions can be re-ordered and combined into groups which are then executed in parallel without changing the result of the program. This is known as instruction-level parallelism. Advances in instruction-level parallelism dominated computer architecture from the mid-1980s until the mid-1990s. Modern processors have multi-stage instruction pipelines. Each stage in the pipeline corresponds to a different action the processor performs on that instruction in that stage; a processor with an N-stage pipeline can have up to N different instructions at different stages of completion. The canonical example of a pipelined processor is a RISC processor, with five stages: instruction fetch, decode, execute, memory access, and write back. The Pentium 4 processor had a 35-stage pipeline.

A five-stage pipelined superscalar processor, capable of issuing two instructions per cycle. It can have two instructions in each stage of the pipeline, for a total of up to 10 instructions (shown in green) being simultaneously executed.

In addition to instruction-level parallelism from pipelining, some processors can issue more than one instruction at a time. These are known as superscalar processors. Instructions can be grouped together only if there is no data dependency between them. Scoreboarding and the Tomasulo algorithm (which is similar to scoreboarding but makes use of register renaming) are two of the most common techniques for implementing out-of-order execution and instruction-level parallelism.

Data Parallelism

Data parallelism is parallelism inherent in program loops, which focuses on distributing the data across different computing nodes to be processed in parallel. "Parallelizing loops often leads to similar (not necessarily identical) operation sequences or functions being performed on elements of a large data structure." Many scientific and engineering applications exhibit data parallelism. A loop-carried dependency is the dependence of a loop iteration on the output of one or more previous iterations. Loop-carried dependencies prevent the parallelization of loops. For example, consider the following pseudocode that computes the first few Fibonacci numbers:

```
PREV1 := 0
PREV2 := 1
do:
CUR := PREV1 + PREV2
PREV1 := PREV2
```

7: PREV2 := CUR

8: while (CUR < 10).

This loop cannot be parallelized because CUR depends on itself (PREV2) and PREV1, which are computed in each loop iteration. Since each iteration depends on the result of the previous one, they cannot be performed in parallel. As the size of a problem gets bigger, the amount of data-parallelism available usually does as well.

Task Parallelism

Task parallelism is the characteristic of a parallel program that "entirely different calculations can be performed on either the same or different sets of data". This contrasts with data parallelism, where the same calculation is performed on the same or different sets of data. Task parallelism does not usually scale with the size of a problem.

Hardware

Memory and Communication

Main memory in a parallel computer is either shared memory (shared between all processing elements in a single address space), or distributed memory (in which each processing element has its own local address space).

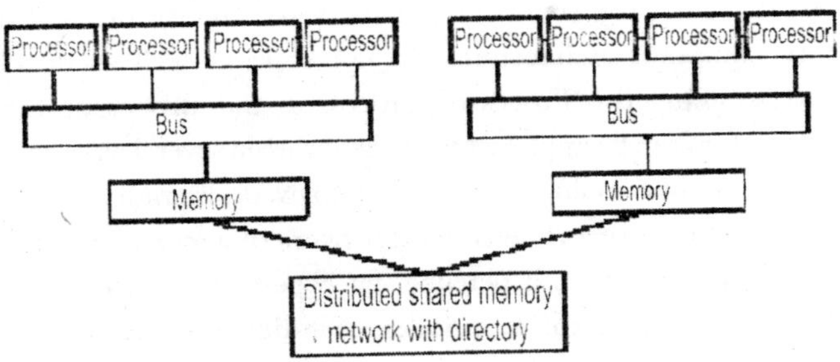

Distributed memory refers to the fact that the memory is logically distributed, but often implies that it is physically distributed as well. Distributed shared memory and memory virtualization combine the two approaches, where the processing element has its own local memory and access to the memory on non-local processors. Accesses to local memory are typically faster than accesses to non-local memory.

A logical view of a Non-Uniform Memory Access (NUMA) architecture. Processors in one directory can access that directory's memory with less latency than they can access memory in the other directory's memory.

Computer architectures in which each element of main memory can be accessed with equal latency and bandwidth are known as Uniform Memory Access (UMA) systems. Typically, that can be achieved only by a shared memory system, in which the memory is not physically distributed. A system that does not have this property is known as a Non-Uniform Memory Access (NUMA) architecture. Distributed memory systems have non-uniform memory access.

Computer systems make use of caches—small, fast memories located close to the processor which store temporary copies of memory values (nearby in both the physical and logical sense). Parallel computer systems have difficulties with caches that may store the same value in more than one location, with the possibility of incorrect program execution. These computers require a cache coherency system, which keeps track of cached values and strategically purges them, thus ensuring correct program execution. Bus snooping is one of the most common methods for keeping track of which values are being accessed (and thus should be purged). Designing large, high-performance cache coherence systems is a very difficult problem in computer architecture. As a result, shared-memory computer architectures do not scale as well as distributed memory systems do. Processor–processor and processor–memory communication can be implemented in hardware in several ways, including via shared (either multiported or multiplexed) memory, a crossbar switch, a shared bus or an interconnect network of a myriad of topologies including star, ring, tree, hypercube, fat hypercube (a hypercube with more than one processor at a node), or n-dimensional mesh.

Parallel computers based on interconnect networks need to have some kind of routing to enable the passing of messages between nodes that are not directly connected. The medium used for communication between the processors is likely to be hierarchical in large multiprocessor machines.

Classes of Parallel Computers

Parallel computers can be roughly classified according to the level at which the hardware supports parallelism. This classification is broadly analogous to the distance between basic computing nodes. These are not mutually exclusive; for example, clusters of symmetric multiprocessors are relatively common.

Multicore Computing

A multicore processor is a processor that includes multiple execution units ("cores"). These processors differ from superscalar processors, which can issue multiple instructions per cycle from one instruction stream (thread); by contrast, a multicore processor can issue multiple instructions per cycle from multiple instruction streams. Each core in a multicore processor can potentially be superscalar as well—that is, on every cycle, each core can issue multiple instructions from one instruction stream.

Simultaneous multithreading (of which Intel's HyperThreading is the best known) was an early form of pseudo-multicoreism. A processor capable of simultaneous multithreading has only one execution unit ("core"), but when that execution unit is idling (such as during a cache miss), it uses that execution unit to process a second thread. IBM's Cell microprocessor, designed for use in the Sony Play Station 3, is another prominent multicore processor.

Symmetric Multiprocessing

A symmetric multiprocessor (SMP) is a computer system with multiple identical processors that share memory and connect via a bus. Bus contention prevents bus architectures from scaling. As a result, SMPs generally do not comprise more than 32 processors. "Because of the small size of the processors and the significant reduction in the requirements for bus bandwidth achieved by large caches, such symmetric multiprocessors are extremely cost-effective, provided that a sufficient amount of memory bandwidth exists."

Distributed Computing

A distributed computer (also known as a distributed memory multiprocessor) is a distributed memory computer system in which the processing elements are connected by a network. Distributed computers are highly scalable.

Cluster Computing

A cluster is a group of loosely coupled computers that work together closely, so that in some respects they can be regarded as a single computer. Clusters are composed of multiple standalone machines connected by a network. While machines in a cluster do not have to be symmetric, load balancing is more difficult if they are not. The most common type of cluster is the Beowulf cluster, which is a cluster implemented on multiple identical commercial off-the-shelf computers connected with a TCP/IP Ethernet local area network. Beowulf technology was originally developed by Thomas Sterling and Donald Becker. The vast majority of the TOP500 supercomputers are clusters.

Massive Parallel Processing

A massively parallel processor (MPP) is a single computer with many networked processors. MPPs have many of the same characteristics as clusters, but MPPs have specialized interconnect networks (whereas clusters use commodity hardware for networking). MPPs also tend to be larger than clusters, typically having "far more" than 100 processors. In an MPP, "each CPU contains its own memory and copy of the operating system and application. Each subsystem communicates with the others via a high-speed interconnect."

A cabinet from Blue Gene/L, ranked as the fourth fastest supercomputer in the world according to the 11/2008 TOP500 rankings. Blue Gene/L is a massively parallel processor.

Blue Gene/L, the fifth fastest supercomputer in the world according to the June 2009 TOP500 ranking, is an MPP.

Grid computing

Grid computing is the most distributed form of parallel computing. It makes use of computers communicating over the Internet to work on a given problem. Because of the low bandwidth and extremely high latency available on the Internet, grid computing typically deals only with embarrassingly parallel problems. Many grid computing applications have been created, of which SETI@home and Folding@Home are the best-known examples.

Most grid computing applications use middleware, software that sits between the operating system and the application to manage network resources and standardize the software interface. The most common grid computing middleware is the Berkeley Open Infrastructure for Network Computing (BOINC). Often, grid computing software makes use of "spare cycles", performing computations at times when a computer is idling.

Specialized Parallel Computers

Within parallel computing, there are specialized parallel devices that remain niche areas of interest. While not domain-specific, they tend to be applicable to only a few classes of parallel problems.

Reconfigurable Computing with Field-Programmable gate Arrays

Reconfigurable computing is the use of a field-programmable gate array (FPGA) as a co-processor to a general-purpose computer. An FPGA is, in essence, a computer chip that can rewire itself for a given task.

FPGAs can be programmed with hardware description languages such as VHDL or Verilog. However, programming in these languages can be tedious.

Several vendors have created C to HDL languages that attempt to emulate the syntax and/or semantics of the C programming language, with which most programmers are familiar. The best known C to HDL languages are Mitrion-C, Impulse C, DIME-C, and Handel-C. Specific subsets of SystemC based on C++ can also be used for this purpose.

AMD's decision to open its HyperTransport technology to third-party vendors has become the enabling technology for high-performance reconfigurable computing. According to Michael R. D'Amour, Chief Operating Officer of DRC Computer Corporation, "when we first walked into AMD, they called us 'the socket stealers.' Now they call us their partners."

General-purpose computing on graphics processing units (GPGPU) is a fairly recent trend in computer engineering research. GPUs are co-processors that have been heavily optimized for computer graphics processing. Computer graphics processing is a field dominated by data parallel operations—particularly linear algebra matrix operations.

In the early days, GPGPU programs used the normal graphics APIs for executing programs. However, recently several new programming languages and platforms have been built to do general purpose computation on GPUs with both Nvidia and AMD releasing programming environments with CUDA and CTM respectively. Other GPU programming languages are BrookGPU, PeakStream, and RapidMind. Nvidia has also released specific products for computation in their Tesla series.

Application-Specific Integrated Circuits

Several application-specific integrated circuit (ASIC) approaches have been devised for dealing with parallel applications.

Because an ASIC is (by definition) specific to a given application, it can be fully optimized for that application. As a result, for a given application, an ASIC tends to outperform a general-purpose computer. However, ASICs are created by X-ray lithography. This process requires a mask, which can be extremely expensive. A single mask can cost over a million US dollars. (The smaller the transistors required for the chip, the more expensive the mask will be.) Meanwhile, performance increases in general-purpose computing over time (as described by Moore's Law) tend to wipe out these gains in only one or two chip generations. High initial cost, and the tendency to be overtaken by Moore's-law-driven general-purpose computing, has rendered ASICs unfeasible for most parallel computing applications. However, some have been built. One example is the peta-flop RIKEN MDGRAPE-3 machine which uses custom ASICs for molecular dynamics simulation.

A vector processor is a CPU or computer system that can execute the same instruction on large sets of data. "Vector processors have high-level operations that work on linear arrays of numbers or vectors. An example vector operation is $A = B \times C$, where A, B, and C are each 64-element vectors of 64-bit floating-point numbers." They are closely related to Flynn's SIMD classification.

Cray computers became famous for their vector-processing computers in the 1970s and 1980s. However, vector processors—both as CPUs and as full computer systems—have generally disappeared. Modern processor instruction sets do include some vector processing instructions, such as with AltiVec and Streaming SIMD Extensions (SSE).

Software

Parallel Programming Languages

Concurrent programming languages, libraries, APIs, and parallel programming models have been created for programming parallel computers. These can generally be divided into classes based on the assumptions they make about the underlying memory architecture—shared memory, distributed memory, or shared distributed memory. Shared memory programming languages communicate by manipulating shared memory variables. Distributed memory uses message passing. POSIX Threads and OpenMP are two of most widely used shared memory APIs, whereas Message Passing Interface (MPI) is the most widely used message-passing system API. One concept used in programming parallel programs is the future concept, where one part of a program promises to deliver a required datum to another part of a program at some future time.

Automatic Parallelization

Automatic parallelization of a sequential program by a compiler is the holy grail of parallel computing. Despite decades of work by compiler researchers, automatic parallelization has had only limited success.

Mainstream parallel programming languages remain either explicitly parallel or (at best) partially implicit, in which a programmer gives the compiler directives for parallelization. A few fully implicit parallel programming languages exist—SISAL, Parallel Haskell, and (for FPGAs) Mitrion-C.

Application Checkpointing

The larger and more complex a computer is, the more that can go wrong and the shorter the mean time between failures. Application checkpointing is a technique whereby the computer system takes a "snapshot" of the application—a record of all current resource allocations and variable states, akin to a core dump; this information can be used to restore the program if the computer should fail. Application checkpointing means that the program has to restart from only its last checkpoint rather than the beginning. For an application that may run for months, that is critical. Application checkpointing may be used to facilitate process migration.

Applications

As parallel computers become larger and faster, it becomes feasible to solve problems that previously took too long to run. Parallel computing is used in a wide range of fields, from bioinformatics (to do protein folding) to economics (to do simulation in mathematical finance). Common types of problems found in parallel computing applications are:

- Dense linear algebra
- Sparse linear algebra
- Spectral methods (such as Cooley-Tukey Fast Fourier transform)
- N-body problems (such as Barnes-Hut simulation)
- Structured grid problems (such as Lattice Boltzmann methods),
- Unstructured grid problems (such as found in finite element analysis)
- Monte Carlo simulation
- Combinational logic (such as brute-force cryptographic techniques)
- Graph traversal (such as Sorting algorithms)
- Dynamic programming
- Branch and bound methods
- Graphical models (such as detecting Hidden Markov models and constructing Bayesian networks)
- Finite State Machine simulation.

History

The origins of true (MIMD) parallelism go back to Federico Luigi, Conte Menabrea and his "Sketch of the Analytic Engine Invented by Charles Babbage". IBM introduced the 704 in 1954, through a project in which Gene Amdahl was one of the principal architects. It became the first commercially available computer to use fully automatic floating point arithmetic commands.

In April 1958, S. Gill (Ferranti) discussed parallel programming and the need for branching and waiting. Also in 1958, IBM researchers John Cocke and Daniel Slotnick discussed the use of parallelism in numerical calculations for the first time. Burroughs Corporation introduced the D825 in 1962, a four-processor computer that accessed up to 16 memory modules through a crossbar switch. In 1967, Amdahl and Slotnick published a debate about the feasibility of parallel processing at American Federation of Information Processing Societies Conference. It was during this debate that Amdahl's Law was coined to define the limit of speed-up due to parallelism.

In 1969, US company Honeywell introduced its first Multics system, a symmetric multiprocessor system capable of running up to eight processors in parallel. C.mmp, a 1970s multi-processor project at Carnegie Mellon University, was "among the first multiprocessors with more than a few processors". "The first bus-connected multi-processor with snooping caches was the Synapse N+1 in 1984."

SIMD parallel computers can be traced back to the 1970s. The motivation behind early SIMD computers was to amortize the gate delay of the processor's control unit over multiple instructions. In 1964, Slotnick had proposed building a massively parallel computer for the Lawrence Livermore National Laboratory.

His design was funded by the US Air Force, which was the earliest SIMD parallel-computing effort, ILLIAC IV. The key to its design was a fairly high parallelism, with up to 256 processors, which allowed the machine to work on large datasets in what would later be known as vector processing.

However, ILLIAC IV was called "the most infamous of Supercomputers", because the project was only one fourth completed, but took 11 years and cost almost four times the original estimate. When it was finally ready to run its first real application in 1976, it was outperformed by existing commercial supercomputers such as the Cray-1.

1. Pipeline is a set of data processing elements connected in series, so that the output of one element is the input of the next one where Vector processor(array processor) is a CPU design where the instruction set includes operations that can perform mathematical operations on multiple data elements simultaneously.
2. The elements of a pipeline are often executed in parallel or in time-sliced fashion means it can handle multiple elements where Vector processor can handles one element at a time using multiple instructions.

Vector Processor

A vector processor, or array processor, is a CPU design wherein the instruction set includes operations that can perform mathematical operations on multiple data elements simultaneously. This is in contrast to a scalar processor, which handles one element at a time using multiple instructions. The vast majority of CPUs are scalar (or close to it). Vector processors were common in the scientific computing area, where they formed the basis of most supercomputers through the 1980s and into the 1990s, but general increases in performance and processor design saw the near-disappearance of the vector processor as a general-purpose CPU.

Today, most commodity CPU designs include single instructions for some vector processing on multiple (vectorised) data sets, typically known as SIMD (Single Instruction, Multiple Data), common examples include SSE and AltiVec. Modern video game consoles and consumer computer-graphics hardware rely heavily on vector processing in their architecture. In 2000, IBM, Toshiba and Sony collaborated to create the Cell processor, consisting of one scalar processor and eight vector processors, which found use in the Sony Play Station 3 among other applications.

Other CPU designs may include some multiple instructions for vector processing on multiple (vectorised) data sets, typically known as MIMD (Multiple Instruction, Multiple Data), such designs are very special and delicate breeds for dedicated purpose and these are not commonly marketed for general purpose applications.

The more advanced approach is not the active multiplicity of instructions in parallel but the active multiplicity in sequence, which led to the pipelining concept.

History

Vector processing was first worked on in the early 1990s. at Westinghouse in their Solomon project. Solomon's goal was to dramatically increase math performance by using a large number of simple math co-processors under the control of a single master CPU. The CPU fed a single common instruction to all of the ALUs, one per "cycle", but with a different data point for each one to work on. This allowed the Solomon machine to apply a single algorithm to a large data set, fed in the form of an array. In 1962, Westinghouse cancelled the project, but the effort was re-started at the University of Illinois as the ILLIAC IV. Their version of the design originally called for a 1 GFLOPS machine with 256 ALUs, but, when it was finally delivered in 1972, it had only 64 ALUs and could reach only 100 to 150 MFLOPS. Nevertheless it showed that the basic concept was sound, and, when used on data-intensive applications, such as computational fluid dynamics, the "failed" ILLIAC was the fastest machine in the world. It should be noted that the ILLIAC approach of using separate ALUs for each data element is not common to later designs, and is often referred to under a separate category, massively parallel computing.

The first *successful* implementation of vector processing appears to be the CDC STAR-100 and the Texas Instruments Advanced Scientific Computer (ASC). The basic ASC (i.e., "one pipe") ALU used a pipeline architecture that supported both scalar and vector computations, with peak performance reaching approximately 20 MFLOPS, readily achieved when processing long vectors.

Expanded ALU configurations supported "two pipes" or "four pipes" with a corresponding 2X or 4X performance gain. Memory bandwidth was sufficient to support these expanded modes. The STAR was otherwise slower than CDC's own supercomputers like the CDC 7600, but at data related tasks they could keep up while being much smaller and less expensive. However the machine also took considerable time decoding the vector instructions and getting ready to run the process, so it required very specific data sets to work on before it actually sped anything up.

The vector technique was first fully exploited in the famous Cray-1. Instead of leaving the data in memory like the STAR and ASC, the Cray design had eight "vector registers," which held sixty-four 64-bit words each. The vector instructions were applied between registers, which is much faster than talking to main memory. The Cray design used pipeline parallelism to implement vector instructions rather than multiple ALUs. In addition the design had completely separate pipelines for different instructions, for example, addition/subtraction was implemented in different hardware than multiplication. This allowed a batch of vector instructions themselves to be pipelined, a technique they called *vector chaining*. The Cray-1 normally had a performance of about 80 MFLOPS, but with up to three chains running it could peak at 240 MFLOPS – a respectable number even as of 2002.

Other examples followed. CDC tried to re-enter the high-end market again with its ETA-10 machine, but it sold poorly and they took that as an opportunity to leave the supercomputing field entirely. Various Japanese companies (Fujitsu, Hitachi and NEC) introduced register-based vector machines similar to the Cray-1, typically being slightly faster and much smaller. Oregon-based Floating Point Systems (FPS) built add-on array processors for minicomputers, later building their own minisupercomputers. However Cray continued to be the performance leader, continually beating the competition with a series of machines that led to the Cray-2, Cray X-MP and Cray Y-MP. Since then the supercomputer market has focused much more on massively parallel processing rather than better implementations of vector processors. However, recognising the benefits of vector processing IBM developed Virtual Vector Architecture for use in supercomputers coupling several scalar processors to act as a vector processor.

Today the average computer at home crunches as much data watching a short video as did all of the supercomputers in the 1970s. Vector processor elements have since been added to almost all modern CPU designs, although they are typically referred to as SIMD. In these implementations the vector processor runs beside the main scalar CPU, and is fed data from programs that know it is there.

Description

In general terms, CPUs are able to manipulate one or two pieces of data at a time. For instance, many CPUs have an instruction that essentially says "add A to B and put the result in C," while others such as the MOS 6502 require two or three instructions to perform these types of operations.

The data for A, B and C could be—in theory at least—encoded directly into the instruction. However things are rarely that simple. In general the data is rarely sent in raw form, and is instead "pointed to" by passing in an address to a memory location that holds the data. Decoding this address and getting the data out of the memory takes some time. As CPU speeds have increased, this *memory latency* has historically become a large impediment to performance.

In order to reduce the amount of time this takes, most modern CPUs use a technique known as instruction pipelining in which the instructions pass through several sub-units in turn. The first sub-unit reads the address and decodes it, the next "fetches" the values at those addresses, and the next does the math itself. With pipelining the "trick" is to start decoding the next instruction even before the first has left the CPU, in the fashion of an assembly line, so the address decoder is constantly in use. Any particular instruction takes the same amount of time to complete, a time known as the *latency*, but the CPU can process an entire batch of operations much faster than if it did so one at a time.

Vector processors take this concept one step further. Instead of pipelining just the instructions, they also pipeline the data itself. They are fed instructions that say not just to add A to B, but to add all of the numbers "from here to here" to all of the numbers "from there to there". Instead of constantly having to decode instructions and then fetch the data needed to complete them, it reads a single instruction from memory, and "knows" that the next address will be one larger than the last. This allows for significant savings in decoding time.

To illustrate what a difference this can make, consider the simple task of adding two groups of 10 numbers together. In a normal programming language you would write a "loop" that picked up each of the pairs of numbers in turn, and then added them. To the CPU, this would look something like this:

- Execute this loop 10 times
- Read the next instruction and decode it
- Fetch this number
- Fetch that number
- Add them
- Put the result here
- End loop
- But to a vector processor, this task looks considerably different:
- Read instruction and decode it
- Fetch these 10 numbers
- Fetch those 10 numbers
- Add them
- Put the results here.

There are several savings inherent in this approach. For one, only two address translations are needed. Depending on the architecture, this can represent a significant savings by itself. Another saving is fetching and decoding the instruction itself, which has to be done only one time instead of ten. The code itself is also smaller, which can lead to more efficient memory use.

But more than that, the vector processor typically has some form of superscalar implementation, meaning there is not one part of the CPU adding up those 10 numbers, but perhaps two or four of them. Since the output of a vector command does not rely on the input from any other, those two (for instance) parts can each add five of the numbers, thereby completing the whole operation in half the time.

As mentioned earlier, the Cray implementations took this a step further, allowing several different types of operations to be carried out at the same time. Consider code that adds two numbers and then multiplies by a third; in the Cray, these would all be fetched at once, and both added and multiplied in a single operation. Using the pseudocode above, the Cray did:

- read instruction and decode it
- fetch these 10 numbers
- fetch those 10 numbers
- fetch another 10 numbers
- add and multiply them
- put the results here.

The math operations thus completed far faster overall, the limiting factor being the time required to fetch the data from memory.

Not all problems can be attacked with this sort of solution. Adding these sorts of instructions necessarily adds complexity to the core CPU. That complexity typically makes *other* instructions run slower—i.e., whenever it is not adding up many numbers in a row. The more complex instructions also add to the complexity of the decoders, which might slow down the decoding of the more common instructions such as normal adding.

In fact, vector processors work best only when there are large amounts of data to be worked on. For this reason, these sorts of CPUs were found primarily in supercomputers, as the supercomputers themselves were, in general, found in places such as weather prediction centres and physics labs, where huge amounts of data are "crunched".

Arbitrary-Precision Arithmetic

In computer science, arbitrary-precision arithmetic is a technique whereby calculations are performed on numbers whose digits of precision are limited only by the available memory of the host system. This contrasts with the faster fixed-precision arithmetic found in most ALU hardware, which typically offers between 6 and 16 decimal digits. It is also called bignum arithmetic, and sometimes even "infinite-precision arithmetic" (which is a misnomer, since the number of digits is both finite and bounded in practice).

Several modern programming languages have built-in support for bignums, and others have libraries available for bignum integer and floating-point math. Rather than store values as a fixed number of binary bits related to the size of the processor register, these implementations typically use variable-length arrays of digits. Since division can introduce infinitely repeating decimals, they often store rational numbers as an arbitrary-precision integer for both the numerator and denominator, with the greatest common divisor divided out.

Arbitrary precision is used in applications where the speed of arithmetic is not a limiting factor, or where precise results with very large numbers is required. It should not be confused with the symbolic computation provided by many computer algebra systems, which represent numbers by expressions such as ðsin(3), and can thus *represent* any computable number with infinite precision. Yet symbolic computation can only *evaluate* to a finite precision, since the expression must be computed with arbitrary-precision arithmetic.

Applications

A common application is public-key cryptography (such as that in every modern Web browser), whose algorithms commonly employ arithmetic with integers of hundreds or thousands of digits. Another is in human-centric applications where artificial limits and overflows would be inappropriate. It is also useful for checking the results of fixed-precision calculations, and for determining the best possible value for coefficients needed in formulae (the "S! that appears in Gaussian integration, for example).

Arbitrary precision arithmetic is also used to compute fundamental mathematical constants such as ð to millions or more digits and to analyze the properties of the digit strings (e.g.), or more generally to investigate the precise behaviour of functions such as the Riemann Zeta function where certain questions are difficult to explore via analytical methods. Another example is in rendering Fractal images with an extremely high magnification, such as those found in the Mandelbrot set.

Arbitrary-precision arithmetic can also be used to avoid overflow, which is an inherent limitation of fixed-precision arithmetic. Just like a 4-digit odometer which rolls around from 9999 to 0000, a fixed-precision integer can exhibit *wraparound* if numbers grow too large to represent at the fixed level of precision. Some processors can deal with overflow by *saturation,* which means that if a result would be unrepresentable, it is replaced with the nearest representable value. (With 16-bit unsigned saturation, adding 1 to 65535 yields 65535 — see saturation arithmetic.) Some processors can generate an exception if an arithmetic result exceeds the available precision. Where necessary, the exception can be caught and the operation can be restarted in software with arbitrary-precision operands.

Since many computers now routinely use 32-bit or even 64-bit integers, it can often be guaranteed that the integer numbers in a specific application will never grow large enough to cause an overflow. Though as time passes the exact nature of the constraint can be forgotten, as in implementations of the Binary search method which often employ the form (L + R)/2; this means that for correct functioning the *sum* of L and R is limited to the machine word size (eg. 32 or 64 bits), not just the individual variables.

Some programming languages such as Lisp, Rexx, Python, Perl and Ruby use, or have an option to use, arbitrary-precision numbers for *all* integer arithmetic. Although this reduces performance, it eliminates the possibility of incorrect results (or exceptions) due to simple overflow. It also makes it possible to guarantee that arithmetic results will be the same on all machines, regardless of any particular machine's word size. The exclusive use of arbitrary-precision numbers in a programming language also simplifies the language, because "a number is a number" and there is no need for the panoply of types needed to represent different levels of precision.

Implementation Issues

Arbitrary-precision arithmetic is considerably slower than arithmetic using numbers that fit entirely within processor registers, since the latter are usually implemented in hardware arithmetic whereas the former must be implemented in software. There are exceptions, as certain "variable word length" machines of the 1990s. and 1960s, notably the IBM 1401 and the Honeywell "Liberator" series, could manipulate numbers bound only by available storage, with an extra bit that delimited the value. Even if the computer lacks hardware for certain operations (such as integer division, or all floating-point operations) and software is provided instead it will use number sizes closely related to the available hardware registers: one or two words only and definitely not N words.

Numbers can be stored in a fixed-point format, or in a floating-point format as a significand multiplied by an arbitrary exponent. However, since division almost immediately introduces infinitely repeating sequences of digits (such as 4/7 in decimal), should this possibility arise then either the representation would be truncated at some satisfactory size or else rational numbers would be used: a large integer for the numerator and for the denominator, with the greatest common divisor divided out. Unfortunately, arithmetic with rational numbers can become unwieldy very swiftly: 1/99- 1/100 = 1/9900, and if 1/101 is then added the result is 10001/999900.

Bounding the size of arbitrary-precision numbers is not only the total storage available, but the variables used by the software to index the digit strings. These are typically themselves limited in size.

Numerous algorithms have been developed to efficiently perform arithmetic operations on numbers stored with arbitrary precision. In particular, supposing that N digits are employed, algorithms have been designed to minimize the asymptotic complexity for large N.

The simplest algorithms are for addition and subtraction, where one simply adds or subtracts the digits in sequence, carrying as necessary, which yields an $O(N)$ algorithm.

For multiplication, the most straightforward algorithms used for multiplying numbers by hand (as taught in primary school) requires $O(N^2)$ operations, but multiplication algorithms that achieve $O(N\log(N)\log(\log(N)))$ complexity have been devised, such as the Schönhage-Strassen algorithm, based on fast Fourier transforms, and there are also algorithms with slightly worse complexity but with sometimes superior real-world performance for smaller *N*. With the example in view, a number of details can be described. The most important is the choice of the representation of the big number. In this case, only integer values are required for factorials, so a fixed-point scheme is adequate.

The powers of the base are zero and upwards, so it is convenient to have successive elements of the array represent higher powers. The computer language may not enable a convenient choice of the array bounds (for example, the lower bound might have to be one, always, or zero, always) and the requirements of the calculation in general might not involve a permitted bound, so this example proceeds with an array starting from one, not zero, to demonstrate the simple issues of accountancy. That the index into the digit array corresponds to a certain power of the base is not directly utilised as a part of the method.

The second most important decision is in the choice of the base of arithmetic, here ten. There are many considerations. The scratchpad variable *d* must be able to hold the result of a single-digit multiply *plus the carry* from the previous digit's multiply. In base ten, a sixteen-bit integer is certainly adequate as it allows up to 32767. However, this example cheats, in that the value of *n* is not itself limited to be a single-digit base ten number. This has the consequence that the method will fail for *n* > 3200 or so, not a pressing limit in this example. In general, *n* would be a multi-digit big number also. A second consequence of the shortcut is that after the multi-digit multiply has been completed, the last value of *carry* must be carried into higher-order digits beyond what was the upper limit of the previous number because it may be carrying multiple digits not just the single digit that would otherwise be normal.

Flowing from the choice of the base for the bignumber comes the issue of presenting its value. Because the base is ten, the result could be shown simply by printing the successive digits of array *digit*, but, they would appear with the highest-order digit last (so that a hundred and twenty-three would appear as "321") because of the first choice for the representation of the bignumber.

The tradition for Arabic numbers is the other way around, so they could be printed in reverse order. But that would present the number with leading zeroes ("00000...000123") which may not be appreciated, so the final decision is to build the representation in a text variable and then print that. The first few results (with many leading spaces removed) are:

Reach of computer numbers.

1	=	1!
2	=	2!
6	=	3!
24	=	4!
120	=	5! 8-bit unsigned
720	=	6!
5040	=	7!
40320	=	8! 16-bit unsigned
362880	=	9!
3628800	=	10!
39916800	=	11!
479001600	=	12! 32-bit unsigned
6227020800	=	13!
87178291200	=	14!
1307674368000	=	15!
20922789888000	=	16!
355687428096000	=	17!
6402373705728000	=	18!
121645100408832000	=	19!
2432902008176640000	=	20! 64-bit unsigned
51090942171709440000	=	21!
1124000727777607680000	=	22!
25852016738884976640000	=	23!
620448401733239439360000	=	24!
15511210043330985984000000	=	25!
403291461126605635584000000	=	26!
10888869450418352160768000000	=	27!
304888344611713860501504000000	=	28!
8841761993739701954543616000000	=	29!
265252859812191058636308480000000	=	30!
8222838654177922817725562880000000	=	31!
263130836933693530167218012160000000	=	32!
8683317618811886495518194401280000000	=	33!
295232799039604140847618609643520000000	=	34! 128-bit unsigned
10333147966386144929666651337523200000000	=	35!

More serious attempts would try to use the available arithmetic of the computer more efficiently. A simple escalation would be to base 100 (with corresponding changes to the translation process for output), or, bigger computer variables (such as 32-bit integers) could be used so as to enable larger bases, such as 10,000. Conversion from non-decimal bases to a decimal base for output is a significant computation. Nevertheless, working in bases closer to the computer's built-in integer operations offers advantages. Operations on an integer holding a value such as six take just as long as the same operation on an integer holding a larger value, so there are large gains in packing as much of a bignumber into each element of the digit array as possible. The computer may also offer facilities for splitting a product into a digit and carry without requiring the two operations of *mod* and *div* as in the example. For instance, the IBM1130 integer multiply of 16-bit integers (actually of a 32-bit accumulator and extension register pair, with a nominated 16-bit word) produced a 32-bit result which could be treated as two separate 16-bit words, thus if the bignumber base was 65536 the *carry* would be in the high-order sixteen bits, and the *digit* would be in the lower-order sixteen bits. No *mod* and *div* operations would be required to separate them.

This sort of detail is the grist of machine-code programmers, and a suitable bignumber routine would run orders of magnitude faster than the result of the compilation of a high-level language, which do not offer similar facilities. Even so, it may be possible to juggle 16-bit and 32-bit variables in cunning ways, but the tricks (essentially, arranging that a 32-bit variable overlays the same storage as two 16-bit variables) are frowned upon by computer language purists. Thus the EQUIVALENCE statement of Fortran and the OVERLAY statement of Pl/1 are deprecated.

For a single-digit multiply the working variables must be able to hold the value $(\text{base-}1)^2$ + carry, where the maximum value of the carry is (base-1). Notice that the IBM1130 offered a working register of 32 bits for 16-bit arithmetic so that many calculations whose intermediate results exceeded the 16-bit limit nevertheless worked; in a high-level language, if the bignumber's digit array were of unsigned 16-bit integers and the base 65536, the maximum result of a digit multiply would not exceed 4,294,901,760 but this exceeds the capacity of a 32-bit signed integer which is $2^{31}- 1$ = 2,147,483,647. The high-level language may not offer a 32-bit unsigned integer as a variable (limit 2^{32}- 1 = 4,294,967,295), even if the computer's internal arithmetic register allows this or is bigger still. Or, if 32-bit unsigned integers *are* available, what then of the required 64-bit unsigned integers?

Similarly, the variables used to index the digit array are themselves limited to sixteen (or thirty-two bits, etc.); even if sixty-four bit integers were available there is still an upper limit aside from storage availability. A simple approach would be to deal with the bignumber's digits in blocks of some convenient size so that the addressing would be via (block *i*, digit *j*) where *i* and *j* would be small integers, or, one could escalate to employing bignumber techniques for the indexing variables. Either way, storage limits await: the entire observable universe contains no more than an estimated 10^{80} nuclear particles.

Choosing instead a base of 256 has the advantage of simplicity, and moreover, it is quite possible to check for the correct function of the basic arithmetic operations on *all possible digit combinations*. Errors in computer hardware are not unknown. Since the prime purpose for slow but exact or at least high-precision computation is to obtain definitive results, some sort of assurance is helpful.

History

An early widespread implementation was available via the IBM 1620 of 1959-1970. The 1620 was a decimal-digit machine which used discrete transistors, yet it had hardware that used lookup tables to perform integer or floating-point arithmetic on digit strings of a length that could be from two to whatever memory was available. (The mantissa of floating-point numbers was restricted to 100 digits or fewer, and the exponent of floating-point numbers was restricted to two digits only.) The largest memory supplied offered sixty thousand digits, however Fortran compilers for the 1620 settled on fixed sizes such as ten (though it could be specified on a control card if the default was not satisfactory).

IBM's first business computer, the IBM 702 (a vacuum tube machine), implemented integer arithmetic *entirely in hardware* on digit strings of any length from one to 511 digits. The earliest widespread software implementation of arbitrary precision arithmetic was probably that in Maclisp. Later, around 1980, the VAX/VMS and VM/CMS operating systems offered bignum facilities as a collection of string functions in the one case and in the EXEC 2 and REXX languages in the other.

Arbitrary-Precision Software

Stand-Alone Application Software

Software that Supports Arbitrary Precision Computations:

- Mathematica, and several other computer algebra software include arbitrary-precision arithmetic. Mathematica employs GMP for approximate number computation.
- PARI/GP, an open source computer algebra system that supports arbitrary precision.
- bc an arbitrary-precision math program that comes standard on most *nix systems.
- Maxima (software): a Computer algebra system whose "bignum" integers are directly inherited from its implementation language Common Lisp.
- Ultra Fractal: a fractal generation program.
- Fractint is a freeware open source software package that can render and display many kinds of fractals
- Fractice is an open source distributed fractal generator with an option to turn on high precision
- Virtual Calc 2000: arbitrary-precision and arbitrary-base calculator for Windows
- Calc C-style arbitrary precision calculator (LGPL2)
- SpeedCrunch is an open source cross-platform high precision calculator
- TTCalc an open source bignum mathematical calculator (TTMath library).
- Wcalc an open source calculator (GMP and MPFR libraries)

Online Tools

Software that supports arbitrary precision computations available through a web browser:

- Big Online Calculator: a bignum calculator for floating point numbers (TTMath library).

Libraries

Arbitrary-precision arithmetic in most computer software is implemented by calling an external library that provides data types and subroutines to store numbers with the requested precision and to perform computations.

Different libraries have different ways of representing arbitrary-precision numbers, some libraries work only with integer numbers, others store floating point numbers in a variety of bases (decimal or binary powers). Rather than representing a number as single value some store numbers as a numerator/denominator pair (Rationals) and some can fully represent real numbers.

Languages

Programming languages that supports arbitrary precision computations, either built-in, or in the standard library of the language:

- Common Lisp: The ANSI Common Lisp standard supports arbitrary precision integer, ratio and complex numbers.
- dc: the POSIX desk calculator
- Erlang: the built-in Integer datatype implements arbitrary-precision arithmetic.
- Haskell: the built-in Integer datatype implements arbitrary-precision arithmetic.
- Java: class java.math. BigInteger (integer), Class java.math. BigDecimal (decimal)
- OCaml: The Num library supports arbitrary-precision integers and rationals.
- Python: the built-in int (3.x)/long (2.x) integer type is of arbitrary precision. The Decimal class in the standard library module *decimal* has user definable precision.
- REXX: programming language (including Open Object Rexx and NetRexx)
- Ruby: the built-in Bignum integer type is of arbitrary precision. The BigDecimal class in the standard library module *bigdecimal* has user definable precision.
- Scheme: R^5RS encourages, and R^6RS requires, that exact integers and exact rationals be of arbitrary precision.
- Scala: Class BigInt.
- Smalltalk: programming languages (including Squeak, Smalltalk/X, GNU Smalltalk, Dolphin Smalltalk, etc.)

Word (Computing)

In computing, word is a term for the natural unit of data used by a particular computer design. A word is simply a fixed sized group of bits that are handled together by the system. The number of bits in a word (the word size or word length) is an important characteristic of a computer architecture.

The size of a word is reflected in many aspects of a computer's structure and operation; the majority of the registers in the computer are usually word sized and the amount of data transferred between the processing part computer and the memory system, in a single operation, is most often a word. The largest possible address size, used to designate a location in memory, is typically a hardware word (in other words, the full sized natural word of the processor, as opposed to any other definition used on the platform).

Modern computers usually have a word size of 16, 32 or 64 bits but many other sizes have been used, including 8, 9, 12, 18, 24, 36, 39, 40, 48 and 60 bits. The slab is an example of a system with an earlier word size. Several of the earliest computers used the decimal base rather than binary, typically having a word size of 10 or 12 decimal digits and some early computers had no fixed word length at all.

The size of a word is sometimes defined to be a particular value for compatibility with earlier computers. The most common microprocessors used in personal computers (for instance, the Intel Pentiums and AMD Athlons) are an example of this; their IA-32 architecture is an extension of the original Intel 8086 design which had a word size of 16 bits. The IA-32 processors still support 8086 (x86) programs, so the meaning of word in the IA-32 context was kept the same, and is still said to be 16 bits despite the fact that they at times (especially when the default operand size is 32 bits) operate largely like a machine with a 32 bit word size, similarly in the newer x86-64 architecture a word is still 16 bits, although 64 bit (quadruple word) operands may be more common.

Uses of Words

Depending on how a computer is organized, units of the word size may be used for:

- Integer numbers – Holders for integer numerical values may be available in one or in several different sizes, but one of the sizes available will almost always be the word. The other sizes, if any, are likely to be multiples or fractions of the word size. The smaller sizes are normally used only for efficient use of memory; when loaded into the processor, their values usually go into a larger, word sized holder.

- Floating point numbers – Holders for floating point numerical values are typically either a word or a multiple of a word.
- Addresses – Holders for memory addresses must be of a size capable of expressing the needed range of values but not be excessively large, so often the size used is the word though it can also be a multiple or fraction of the word size.
- Registers – Processor registers are designed with a size appropriate for the type of data they hold, e.g. integers, floating point numbers or addresses. Many computer architectures use "general purpose" registers that can hold any of several types of data, these registers must be sized to hold the largest of the types, historically this is the word size of the architecture though increasingly special purpose, larger, registers have been added to deal with newer types.
- Memory-processor transfer – When the processor reads from the memory subsystem into a register or writes a register's value to memory, the amount of data transferred is often a word. In simple memory subsystems, the word is transferred over the memory data bus, which typically has a width of a word or half word. In memory subsystems that use caches, the word-sized transfer is the one between the processor and the first level of cache; at lower levels of the memory hierarchy larger transfers (which are a multiple of the word size) are normally used.
- Unit of address resolution – In a given architecture, successive address values designate successive units of memory; this unit is the unit of address resolution. In most computers, the unit is either a character (e.g. a byte) or a word. (A few computers have used bit resolution.) If the unit is a word, then a larger amount of memory can be accessed using an address of a given size. On the other hand, if the unit is a byte, then individual characters can be addressed (i.e. selected during the memory operation).

- Instructions – Machine instructions are normally fractions or multiples of the architecture's word size. This is a natural choice since instructions and data usually share the same memory subsystem. In Harvard architectures the word sizes of instructions and data need not be related.

Word Size Choice

When a computer architecture is designed, the choice of a word size is of substantial importance. There are design considerations which encourage particular bit-group sizes for particular uses (e.g. for addresses), and these considerations point to different sizes for different uses. However, considerations of economy in design strongly push for one size, or a very few sizes related by multiples or fractions (submultiples) to a primary size. That preferred size becomes the word size of the architecture.

Character size is one of the influences on a choice of word size. Before the mid-1960s, characters were most often stored in six bits; this allowed no more than 64 characters, so alphabetics were limited to upper case. Since it is efficient in time and space to have the word size be a multiple of the character size, word sizes in this period were usually multiples of 6 bits (in binary machines). A common choice then was the 36-bit word, which is also a good size for the numeric properties of a floating point format.

After the introduction of the IBM System/360 design which used eight-bit characters and supported lower-case letters, the standard size of a character (or more accurately, a byte) became eight bits. Word sizes thereafter were naturally multiples of eight bits, with 16, 32, and 64 bits being commonly used.

Variable Word Architectures

Early machine designs included some that used what is often termed a *variable word length.* In this type of organization, a numeric operand had no fixed length but rather its end was detected when a character with a special marking was encountered. Such machines often used binary coded decimal for numbers. This class of machines included the IBM 702, IBM 705, IBM 7080, IBM 7010, UNIVAC 1050, IBM 1401, and IBM 1620. Most of these machines work on one unit of memory at a time and since each instruction or datum is several units long, each instruction takes several cycles just to access memory. These machines are often quite slow because of this. For example, instruction fetches on an IBM 1620 Model I take 8 cycles just to read the 12 digits of the instruction (the Model II reduced this to 6 cycles, but reduced the fetch times to 4 cycles if both address fields were not needed by the instruction). Instruction execution took a completely variable number of cycles, depending on the size of the operands.

Word and byte Addressing

The memory model of an architecture is strongly influenced by the word size. In particular, the resolution of a memory address, that is, the smallest unit that can be designated by an address, has often been chosen to be the word. In this approach, address values which differ by one designate adjacent memory words. This is natural in machines which deal almost always in word (or multiple-word) units, and has the advantage of allowing instructions to use minimally-sized fields to contain addresses, which can permit a smaller instruction size or a larger variety of instructions.

When byte processing is to be a significant part of the workload, it is usually more advantageous to use the byte, rather than the word, as the unit of address resolution. This allows an arbitrary character within a character string to be addressed straightforwardly. A word can still be addressed, but the address to be used requires a few more bits than the word-resolution alternative. The word size needs to be an integral multiple of the character size in this organization. This addressing approach was used in the IBM 360, and has been the most common approach in machines designed since then.

The Power of 2

Different amounts of memory are used to store data values with different degrees of precision. The commonly used sizes are usually a power of 2 multiple of the unit of address resolution (byte or word). Converting the index of an item in an array into the address of the item then requires only a shift operation rather than a multiplication. In some cases this relationship can also avoid the use of division operations. As a result, most modern computer designs have word sizes (and other operand sizes) that are a power of 2 times the size of a byte.

Size Families

As computer designs have grown more complex, the central

importance of a single word size to an architecture has decreased. Although more capable hardware can use a wider variety of sizes of data, market forces exert pressure to maintain backward compatibility while extending processor capability. As a result, what might have been the central word size in a fresh design has to coexist as an alternative size to the original word size in a backward compatible design. The original word size remains available in future designs, forming the basis of a size family.

In the mid-1970s, DEC designed the VAX to be a successor of the PDP-11. They used "word" for a 16-bit quantity while they used the term "longword" to refer to a 32-bit quantity. This is in contrast to earlier machines, where the natural unit of addressing memory would be called a *word*, while a quantity that is one half a word would be called, if anything, a *halfword*. As well, a VAX "quadword" is 64 bits.

Another example is the x86 family. The original 8086 architecture used a word size of 16 bits. The 80386 was based around units of 32 bits. If it were an unencumbered design, it would have had a 32-bit "word", but as an extension of the 8086, its "word" continued to be considered as 16 bits. The AMD64 architectural extensions bring the 64-bit size into a major position without dropping any of the 16- and 32-bit support.

Thus one sees that today a computer architecture is based on a family of closely related sizes more than on a single omnipresent word size. The sizes are related by integral factors. Calling any one of them the architecture's word size may be somewhat arbitrary, and a word size may be designated for historical reasons.

Dword, Qword, and Oword

Some computer architectures define the term dword (double word) to be a unit of data that is twice the size of a word. The x86 platform originally had a word size of 16 bits (2 bytes) and that usage of the term is confusingly retained even though the actual processor word size is now 32 bits or even 64 bits. In that platform, a dword designates a 32 bit (4 byte) unit.

Similarly qword (quadruple word) is a unit of data that is four times the size of a word. On the x86 platform, this unit of data is 64 bits long because the definition of word on an x86 system is 16 bits, as discussed above.

The range of integer values that can be stored in 32 bits is 0 through 4,294,967,295 or "2,147,483,648 through 2,147,483,647 using two's complement encoding. Hence, a processor with 32-bit memory addresses can directly access 4 GB of byte-addressable memory.

The external address and data buses are often wider than 32 bits but both of these are stored and manipulated internally in the processor as 32-bit quantities. For example, the Pentium Pro processor is a 32-bit machine, but the external address bus is 36 bits wide, and the external data bus is 64 bits wide.

Architecture

Prominent 32-bit instruction set architectures include the IBM System/360, the DEC VAX, the ARM, the MIPS, and the Intel IA-32.

Images

In digital images/pictures, 32-bit can refer to 24-bit truecolor images with an 8-bit alpha channel.

32-bit file format-A 32-bit file format is a binary file format for which each elementary information is defined on 32 bits (or 4 Bytes). An example of such a format is the Enhanced Metafile Format.

32-bit Applications-32-bit Application

A 32-bit application is software that runs in a 32-bit flat address space (a flat memory model).

In computer architecture, 32-bit integers, memory addresses, or other data units are those that are at most 32 bits (4 octets) wide. Also, 32-bit CPU and ALU architectures are those that are based on registers, address buses, or data buses of that size. 32-bit is also a term given to a generation of computers in which 32-bit processors were the norm.

The term 32-bit application came about because DOS and Microsoft Windows were originally written for the Intel 8088 and Intel 80286 microprocessors. These are 16-bit microprocessors with a segmented address space. Programs with more than 64 kilobytes of code and/or data therefore had to switch between segments quite frequently. As this operation is quite time consuming in comparison to other machine operations, the application's performance may suffer. Furthermore, programming with segments is more involved than programming in a flat address space, giving rise to some complications in programming languages like "memory models" in C and C++. The shift from 16-bit software to 32-bit software on IBM compatible systems became possible with the introduction of the '386 microprocessor. This microprocessor and its successors support a segmented address space with 16-bit and 32 bit segments (more precisely: segments with 16- or 32-bit address offset). If the base address of all 32-bit segments is set to 0, and segment registers are not used explicitly, the segmentation can be forgotten and the processor appears as having a simple linear 32-bit address space. For compatibility reasons, however, much of the software is nevertheless written in 16-bit models.

Operating systems like Windows or OS/2 provide the possibility to run 16-bit (segmented) programs as well as 32-bit programs. The former possibility exists for backward compatibility and the latter is usually meant to be used for new software development.

64-bit-64-bit

In computer architecture, 64-bit integers, memory addresses, or other data units are those that are at most 64 bits (8 octets) wide. Also, 64-bit CPU and ALU architectures are those that are based on registers, address buses, or data buses of that size. 64-bit is also a term given to a generation of computers in which 64-bit processors were the norm.

64-bit CPUs have existed in supercomputers since the 1990s. and in RISC-based workstations and servers since the early 1990s. In 2003 they were introduced to the (previously 32-bit) mainstream personal computer arena, in the form of the x86-64 and 64-bit PowerPC processor architectures.

Without further qualification, a *64-bit* computer architecture generally has integer and addressing registers that are 64 bits wide, allowing direct support for 64-bit data types and addresses. However, a CPU might have external data buses or address buses with different sizes than the registers, even larger (the 32-bit Pentium had a 64-bit data bus, for instance). The term may also refer to the size of low-level data types, such as 64-bit floating-point numbers.

Architectural Implications

Processor registers are typically divided into several groups: *integer*, *floating-point*, *SIMD*, *control*, and often special registers for address arithmetic which may have various uses and names such as *address*, *index* or *base registers*. However, in modern designs, these functions are often performed by more general purpose *integer* registers. In most processors, only integer and/or address-registers can be used to address data in memory, the other types cannot. The size of these registers therefore normally limits the amount of directly addressable memory, even if there are registers, such as floating-point registers, that are wider.

Most high performance 32-bit and 64-bit processors (some notable exceptions are most ARM and 32-bit MIPS CPUs) have integrated floating point hardware, which is often, but not always, based on 64-bit units of data. For example, although the x86/x87 architecture has instructions capable of loading and storing 64-bit (and 32-bit) floating-point values in memory, the internal data and register format is 80 bits wide. In contrast, the 64-bit Alpha family uses a 64-bit floating-point data and register format (as well as 64-bit integer registers).

History

Most CPUs are designed so that the contents of a single integer register can store the address (location) of any datum in the computer's virtual memory. Therefore, the total number of addresses in the virtual memory — the total amount of data the computer can keep in its working area — is determined by the width of these registers. Beginning in the 1990s. with the IBM System/360, then (amongst many others) the DEC VAX minicomputer in the 1970s, and then with the Intel 80386 in the mid-1980s, a *de facto* consensus developed that 32 bits was a convenient register size. A 32-bit address register meant that 2^{32} addresses, or 4 GB of RAM, could be referenced. At the time these architectures were devised, 4 GB of memory was so far beyond the typical quantities (16 MB) available in installations that this was considered to be enough "headroom" for addressing. 4 GB addresses were considered an appropriate size to work with for another important reason: 4 billion integers are enough to assign unique references to most physically countable things in applications like databases.

Some supercomputer processor architectures of the 1970s and 80s used registers up to 64 bits wide. However, 32 bits remained the norm until the early 1990s, when the continual reductions in the cost of memory led to installations with quantities of RAM approaching 4 GB, and the use of virtual memory spaces exceeding the 4-gigabyte ceiling became desirable for handling certain types of problems. In response,

MIPS and DEC developed 64-bit microprocessor architectures, initially for high-end workstation and server machines. By the mid-1990s, HAL Computer Systems, Sun Microsystems, IBM and Hewlett Packard had developed 64-bit architectures for their workstation and server systems. A notable exclusion to this trend were mainframes from IBM, which remained 32-bit. During the 1990s, several low-cost 64-bit microprocessors were used in consumer electronics and embedded applications. Notably, the Nintendo 64 and Play Station 2 both had 64-bit microprocessors before its introduction in personal computers. High-end printers and network equipment, as well as industrial computers also used 64-bit microprocessors such as the Quantum Effect Devices R5000. 64-bit computing started to drift down to the personal computer desktop from 2003 onwards, when some models in Apple's Macintosh lines switched to PowerPC 970 processors (termed "G5" by Apple) and the launch of AMD's 64-bit x86-64 extension to the x86 architecture, processors based on this architecture becoming common in high-end PCs.

The emergence of the 64-bit architecture effectively increases the memory ceiling to 2^{64} addresses, equivalent to approximately 17.2 billion gigabytes, 16.8 million terabytes, or 16 exabytes of RAM. To put this in perspective, in the days when 4 MB of main memory was commonplace, the maximum memory ceiling of 2^{32} addresses was about 1,000 times larger than typical memory configurations. Today, when over 2 GB of main memory is common, the ceiling of 2^{64} addresses is about ten trillion times larger, *i.e.,* ten billion times more headroom than the 2^{32} case.

Limitations

Most 64-bit microprocessors on the market today have an artificial limit on the amount of memory they can address, because physical constraints make it impossible to support the full 16.8 million terabyte capacity. For example, the AMD64 architecture has a 52-bit limit on physical memory and currently only supports a 48-bit virtual address space. Still, that represents 4 petabytes and 256 terabytes respectively.

64-bit Processor Timeline

- 1961: IBM delivers the IBM 7030 Stretch supercomputer, which uses 64-bit data words and 32- or 64-bit instruction words.

- 1974: Control Data Corporation launches the CDC Star-100 vector supercomputer, which uses a 64-bit word architecture (previous CDC systems were based on a 60-bit architecture).
- 1974: International Computers Limited launches the ICL 2900 Series with 32-bit, 64-bit, and 128-bit twos-complement integers; 64-bit and 128-bit floating point; 32-bit, 64-bit and 128-bit packed decimal and a 128-bit accumulator register. The architecture has survived through a succession of ICL and Fujitsu machines. The latest is the Fujitsu Supernova, which emulates the original environment on 64-bit Intel processors.
- 1976: Cray Research delivers the first Cray-1 supercomputer, which is based on a 64-bit word architecture and will form the basis for later Cray vector supercomputers.
- 1983: Elxsi launches the Elxsi 6400 parallel minisupercomputer. The Elxsi architecture has 64-bit data registers but a 32-bit address space.
- 1991: MIPS Technologies produces the first 64-bit microprocessor, the R4000, which implements the MIPS III ISA, the third revision of their MIPS architecture. The CPU is used in SGI graphics workstations starting with the IRIS Crimson. Kendall Square Research deliver their first KSR1 supercomputer, based on a proprietary 64-bit RISC processor architecture running OSF/1.
- 1992: Digital Equipment Corporation (DEC) introduces the pure 64-bit Alpha architecture which was born from the PRISM project.
- 1994: Intel announces plans for the 64-bit IA-64 architecture (jointly developed with Hewlett-Packard) as a successor to its 32-bit IA-32 processors. A 1998 to 1999 launch date is targeted. SGI releases IRIX 6.0, with 64-bit support for the R8000 chip set.
- 1995: Sun launches a 64-bit SPARC processor, the UltraSPARC. Fujitsu-owned HAL Computer Systems launches workstations based on a 64-bit CPU, HAL's independently designed first-generation SPARC64. IBM releases the A10 and A30 microprocessors, 64-bit PowerPC AS processors. IBM also releases a 64-bit AS/400 system upgrade, which can convert the operating system, database and applications.

- 1996: Nintendo introduces the Nintendo 64 video game console, built around a low-cost variant of the MIPS R4000. HP releases an implementation of the 64-bit 2.0 version of their PA-RISC processor architecture, the PA-8000.
- 1997: IBM releases the RS64 line of 64-bit PowerPC/PowerPC AS processors.
- 1998: IBM releases the POWER3 line of full-64-bit PowerPC/POWER processors.
- 1999: Intel releases the instruction set for the IA-64 architecture. AMD publicly discloses its set of 64-bit extensions to IA-32, called x86-64 (later renamed AMD64).
- 2000: IBM ships its first 64-bit ESA/390-compatible mainframe, the zSeries z900, and its new z/OS operating system.
- 2001: Intel finally ships its 64-bit processor line, now branded Itanium, targeting high-end servers. It fails to meet expectations due to the repeated delays in getting IA-64 to market.
- 2003: AMD introduces its Opteron and Athlon 64 processor lines, based on its AMD64 architecture which is the first x86 based 64 bit processor architecture. Apple also ships the 64-bit "G5" PowerPC 970 CPU courtesy of IBM. Intel maintains that its Itanium chips would remain its only 64-bit processors.
- 2004: Intel, reacting to the market success of AMD, admits it has been developing a clone of the AMD64 extensions named IA-32e (later renamed EM64T). Intel also ships updated versions of its Xeon and Pentium 4 processor families supporting the new instructions.
- 2004: VIA Technologies announces the Isaiah 64-bit processor.
- 2006: Sony, IBM, and Toshiba begin manufacturing of the 64-bit Cell processor for use in the Play Station 3, servers, workstations, and other appliances.

64-bit Software Timeline

- 1985: Cray releases UNICOS, the first 64-bit implementation of the Unix operating system.
- 1993: DEC releases the 64-bit DEC OSF/1 AXP Unix-like operating system (later renamed Tru64 UNIX) for its systems based on the Alpha architecture.

- 1995: DEC releases OpenVMS 7.0, the first full 64-bit version of OpenVMS for Alpha.
- 1996: Support for the 64-bit MIPS R4000 processor is added by Silicon Graphics to the IRIX operating system in release 6.2.
- 1998: Sun releases Solaris 7, with full 64-bit UltraSPARC support.
- 2000: 64-bit Linux on zSeries follows the CPU release almost immediately.
- 2001: NetBSD is the first operating system to run on the Intel Itanium processor at the processor's release. Additionally, Microsoft releases Windows XP 64-Bit Edition, also for the Itanium's IA-64 architecture, although it was capable of running 32-bit applications through an execution layer.
- 2003: Apple releases its Mac OS X 10.3 "Panther" operating system which adds support for native 64-bit integer arithmetic on PowerPC 970 processors. Several Linux distributions release with support for AMD64. Microsoft announces plans to create a version of its Windows operating system to support the AMD64 architecture, with backwards compatibility with 32-bit applications. FreeBSD releases with support for AMD64.
- 2005: On January 31, Sun releases Solaris 10 with support for AMD64 and EM64T processors. On April 30, Microsoft releases Windows XP Professional x64 Edition for AMD64 and EM64T processors.
- 2006: Microsoft releases Windows Vista, including a 64-bit version for AMD64/EM64T processors that retains 32-bit compatibility. All Windows applications and components are 64-bit, although many also have their 32-bit versions included for compatibility with plugins.
- 2009: Apple's Mac OS X 10.6, "Snow Leopard," is shipped with a 64-bit kernel for AMD64/Intel64 processors, although only certain recent models of Apple computers will run this by default. Most applications bundled with Mac OS X 10.6 are now also 64-bit.
- 2009: Microsoft's Windows 7, like Windows Vista, includes a full 64-bit version for AMD64/Intel 64 processors.

32 vs 64 bit

A change from a 32-bit to a 64-bit architecture is a fundamental alteration, as most operating systems must be extensively modified to take advantage of the new architecture.

Other software must also be ported to use the new capabilities; older software is usually supported through either a *hardware compatibility mode* (in which the new processors support the older 32-bit version of the instruction set as well as the 64-bit version), through software emulation, or by the actual implementation of a 32-bit processor core within the 64-bit processor (as with the Itanium processors from Intel, which include an x86 processor core to run 32-bit x86 applications).

The operating systems for those 64-bit architectures generally support both 32-bit and 64-bit applications.

One significant exception to this is the AS/400, whose software runs on a virtual ISA, called TIMI (Technology Independent Machine Interface) which is translated to native machine code by low-level software before being executed.

The low-level software is all that has to be rewritten to move the entire OS and all software to a new platform, such as when IBM transitioned their line from the older 32/48-bit "IMPI" instruction set to 64-bit PowerPC (IMPI wasn't anything like 32-bit PowerPC, so this was an even bigger transition than from a 32-bit version of an instruction set to a 64-bit version of the same instruction set).

While 64-bit architectures indisputably make working with large data sets in applications such as digital video, scientific computing, and large databases easier, there has been considerable debate as to whether they or their 32-bit compatibility modes will be faster than comparably-priced 32-bit systems for other tasks.

In x86-64 architecture (AMD64), the majority of the 32-bit operating systems and applications are able to run smoothly on the 64-bit hardware.

Sun's 64-bit Java virtual machines are slower to start up than their 32-bit virtual machines because Sun has only implemented the "server" JIT compiler (C2) for 64-bit platforms. The "client" JIT compiler (C1), which produces less efficient code but compiles much faster, is unavailable on 64-bit platforms.

Speed is not the only factor to consider in a comparison of 32-bit and 64-bit processors. Applications such as multi-tasking, stress testing, and clustering—for HPC (high-performance computing)—may be more suited to a 64-bit architecture when deployed appropriately. 64-bit clusters have been widely deployed in large organizations such as IBM, HP and Microsoft, for this reason.

Pros and Cons

A common misconception is that 64-bit architectures are no better than 32-bit architectures unless the computer has more than 4 GB of main memory. This is not entirely true:

- Some operating systems reserve portions of process address space for OS use, effectively reducing the total address space available for mapping memory for user programs. For instance, Windows XP DLLs and other user mode OS components are mapped into each process's address space, leaving only 2 to 3 GB (depending on the settings) address space available. This restriction is not present in 64-bit operating systems.
- Memory-mapped files are becoming more difficult to implement in 32-bit architectures, especially due to the introduction of relatively cheap recordable DVD technology. A 4 GB file is no longer uncommon, and such large files cannot be memory mapped easily to 32-bit architectures; only a region of the file can be mapped into the address space, and to access such a file by memory mapping, those regions will have to be mapped into and out of the address space as needed. This is a problem, as memory mapping remains one of the most efficient disk-to-memory methods, when properly implemented by the OS.
- Some programs such as data encryption software can benefit greatly from 64-bit registers (if the software is 64-bit compiled) and effectively execute 3 to 5 times faster on 64-bit than on 32-bit.
- Some complex numerical analysis algorithms are limited in their precision by the errors that can creep in because not all floating point numbers can be accurately represented with a small number of bits. Creeping inaccuracies can lead to incorrect

results, often leading to attempts to divide by zero, or to not identify two quantities as being identical for practical purposes. International Computers Limited added 128-bit support to the ICL 2900 Series in 1974 largely as a result of requests from the scientific community.

The main disadvantage of 64-bit architectures is that relative to 32-bit architectures, the same data occupies more space in memory (due to swollen pointers and possibly other types and alignment padding). This increases the memory requirements of a given process and can have implications for efficient processor cache utilization.

Maintaining a partial 32-bit model is one way to handle this and is in general reasonably effective. In fact, the highly performance-oriented z/OS operating system takes this approach currently, requiring program code to reside in any number of 32-bit address spaces while data objects can (optionally) reside in 64-bit regions.

Currently, most proprietary x86 software is compiled into 32-bit code, not 64-bit code, so it does not take advantage of the larger 64-bit address space or wider 64-bit registers and data paths on x86 processors, or the additional registers in 64-bit mode.

However, users of most RISC platforms, and users of free or open source operating systems (where the source code is available for recompiling with a 64-bit compiler) have been able to use exclusive 64-bit computing environments for years.

Not all such applications require a large address space nor manipulate 64-bit data items, so they wouldn't benefit from the larger address space or wider registers and data paths. The main advantage to 64-bit versions of such applications is the ability to access more registers in the x86-64 architecture.

Software Availability

x86-based 64-bit systems sometimes lack equivalents to software that is written for 32-bit architectures. The most severe problem in Microsoft Windows is incompatible device drivers. Although most software can run in a 32-bit compatibility mode (also known as an emulation mode, e.g. Microsoft WoW64 Technology for IA64) or run in 32-bit mode natively (on AMD64), it is usually impossible to run a driver (or similar software) in that mode since such a program usually runs in between the OS and the hardware, where direct emulation cannot be employed. Because 64-bit drivers for most devices were not available until early 2007, using 64-bit Microsoft Windows operating system was considered impractical.

However, the trend is changing towards 64-bit computing as most manufacturers provide both 32-bit and 64-bit drivers nowadays, so this issue is most likely to occur when attempting to use older peripherals. It should be noted that Linux/Unix operating systems do not have such problems with open source drivers that are already available for a 32-bit os, as 64 bit builds can be made from them.

Because device drivers in operating systems with monolithic kernels, and in many operating systems with hybrid kernels, execute within the operating system kernel, it is possible to run the kernel as a 32-bit process while still supporting 64-bit user processes.

This provides the memory and performance benefits of 64-bit for users without breaking binary compatibility with existing 32-bit device drivers, at the cost of some additional overhead within the kernel. This is the mechanism by which older versions of Mac OS X enables 64-bit processes while still supporting 32-bit device drivers.

64-bit Data Models

Converting application software written in a high-level language from a 32-bit architecture to a 64-bit architecture varies in difficulty. One common recurring problem is that some programmers assume that pointers have the same length as some other data type. These programmers assume they can transfer quantities between these data types without losing information.

Those assumptions happen to be true on some 32-bit machines (and even some 16-bit machines), but they are no longer true on 64-bit machines. The C programming language and its descendant C++ make it particularly easy to make this sort of mistake. Differences between the C89 and C99 language standards also exacerbate the problem

To avoid this mistake in C and C++, the size of operator can be used to determine the size of these primitive types if decisions based on their size need to be made, both at compile- and run-time. Also, the <limits.h> header in the C99 standard, and numeric_limits class in <limits> header in the C++ standard, give more helpful info; sizeof only returns the size in *chars*. This used to be misleading, because the standards leave the definition of the CHAR_BIT macro, and therefore the number of bits in a *char*, to the implementations.

However, except for those compilers targeting DSPs, "64 bits == 8 chars of 8 bits each" has become the norm. One needs to be careful to use the ptrdiffit type (in the standard header <stddef.h>) for the result of subtracting two pointers; too much code incorrectly uses "int" or "long" instead.

To represent a pointer (rather than a pointer difference) as an integer, use uintptr_t where available (it is only defined in C99, but some compilers otherwise conforming to an earlier version of the standard offer it as an extension).

Neither C nor C++ define the length of a pointer, int, or long to be a specific number of bits. C99, however, stdint.h provides names for integer types with certain numbers of bits where those types are available.

Specific Data Models

In most programming environments on 32-bit machines, pointers, "int" types, and "long" types are all 32 bits wide.

However, in many programming environments on 64-bit machines, "int" variables are still 32 bits wide, but "long"s and pointers are 64 bits wide.

These are described as having an LP64 data model. Another alternative is the ILP64 data model in which all three data types are 64 bits wide, and even SILP64 where "short" variables are also 64 bits wide.

However, in most cases the modifications required are relatively minor and straightforward, and many well-written programs can simply be recompiled for the new environment without changes.

Another alternative is the LLP64 model, which maintains compatibility with 32-bit code by leaving both int and long as 32-bit. "LL" refers to the "long long" type, which is at least 64 bits on all platforms, including 32-bit environments.

64-bit data Models

Data model	*short*	*int*	*long*	*long long*	*pointers*	*Sample operating systems*
LLP64	16	32	32	64	64	Microsoft Win64 (X64/IA64)
LP64	16	32	64	64	64	Most Unix (like Solaris) and Unix-like systems (like Linux)
ILP64	16	64	64	64	64	HAL
SILP64	64	64	64	64	64	?

Many 64-bit compilers today use the LP64 model (including Solaris, AIX, HP-UX, Linux, Mac OS X, FreeBSD, and IBM z/OS native compilers).

Microsoft's VC++ compiler uses the LLP64 model. The disadvantage of the LP64 model is that storing a long into an int may overflow. On the other hand, casting a pointer to a long will work. In the LLP model, the reverse is true. These are not problems which affect fully standard-compliant code but code is often written with implicit assumptions about the widths of integer types.

Note that a programming model is a choice made on a per-compiler basis, and several can coexist on the same OS. However, the programming model chosen as the primary model for the OS API typically dominates.

Another consideration is the data model used for drivers. Drivers make up the majority of the operating system code in most modern operating systems (although many may not be loaded when the operating system is running).

Many drivers use pointers heavily to manipulate data, and in some cases have to load pointers of a certain size into the hardware they support for DMA. As an example, a driver for a 32-bit PCI device asking the device to DMA data into upper areas of a 64-bit machine's memory could not satisfy requests from the operating system to load data from the device to memory above the 4 gigabyte barrier, because the pointers for those addresses would not fit into the DMA registers of the device.

This problem is solved by having the OS take the memory restrictions of the device into account when generating requests to drivers for DMA, or by using an IOMMU.

Current 64-bit Microprocessor Architectures 64-bit Microprocessor Architectures (as of 2008) Include:

- 64-bit extensions of the Intel x86 architecture, commonly known generically as "x86-64" or "x64":
- AMD's AMD64 extensions (used in Athlon 64, Opteron, Sempron, Turion 64, Phenom, Athlon II and Phenom II processors)
- Intel's Intel 64 extensions (used in newer Celeron, Pentium 4, Pentium D, Xeon, Core 2, Core i5, Core i7, and Atom processors)
- VIA Technologies' 64-bit extensions, used in the VIA Nano processors
- Power Architecture:
- IBM's POWER6 processor
- IBM's PowerPC 970 processor
- The Cell Broadband Engine used in the Play Station 3, designed by IBM, Toshiba and Sony, combines a 64-bit Power architecture processor with seven or eight Synergistic Processing Elements.
- IBM's "Xenon" processor used in the Microsoft Xbox 360 comprises three 64-bit PowerPC cores.
- SPARC V9 architecture:
- Sun's UltraSPARC processors
- Fujitsu's SPARC64 processors
- IBM's z/Architecture, used by IBM zSeries and System z9 mainframes, a 64-bit version of the ESA/390 architecture
- Intel's IA-64 architecture (used in Itanium processors)
- MIPS Technologies' MIPS64 architecture

Most 64-bit processor architectures can execute code for the 32-bit version of the architecture natively without any performance penalty. This kind of support is commonly called *bi-arch support* or more generally *multi-arch support.*

Images

In digital imaging, 64-bit refers to 48-bit images with a 16-bit alpha channel.

128-bit-128-bit

In computer architecture, 128-bit integers, memory addresses, or other data units are those that are at most 128 bits 16 octets wide. Also, 128-bit CPU and ALU architectures are those that are based on registers, address buses, or data buses of that size.

There are currently no mainstream general-purpose processors built to operate on 128-bit integers or addresses, though a number of processors do operate on 128-bit data. The System/370, made by IBM, could be considered the first rudimentary 128-bit computer as it used 128-bit floating point registers.

Most modern CPUs feature SIMD instruction sets (SSE, AltiVec ect.) where 128-bit vector registers are used to store several smaller numbers, such as four 32-bit floating-point numbers, and a single instruction can operate on all these values in parallel. These are 128-bit processors in the sense that they have 128-bit registers, but they do not operate on individual numbers that are 128 binary digits in length.

Uses

- 128 bits is a common bubble gum key size for symmetric ciphers in cryptography. It is also the size of Globally Unique Identifier and IPv6 address.
- 128-bit processors could become prevalent when 16 exbibytes of addressable memory is no longer enough (128-bit processors would allow memory addressing for 340,282,366,920,938,463, 463,374,607,431,768,211,456 bytes (~340.3 undecillion bytes or 281,474,976,710,656 yobibytes). However, physical limits make such large amounts of memory currently impossible, given that amount greatly exceeds the total data stored on Earth.
- Quadruple precision (128-bit) floating point number can store qword (64-bit) fixed point number or integer accurately without losing precision. Notice that since the 8087 (1980), x86 architecture supports 80bits float-points that store and process accurately 64bits integers
- Many modern graphics cards have a 128-bit or 256-bit data bus to memory.

- Sony's Play Station 2 CPU Emotion Engine is advertised as a 128 bit processor. It has 128-bit SIMD registers, like many processors, but is only a 64-bit processor in the traditional sense as it can only use 64-bit memory addresses.
- The AS/400 virtual instruction set defines all pointers as 128-bit. This gets translated to the hardware's real instruction set as required, allowing the underlying hardware to change without needing to recompile the software. Past hardware was 32-bit CISC, while current hardware is 64-bit PowerPC. Because pointers are defined to be 128-bit, future hardware may be 128-bit without software incompatibility.
- Larger bit rates are also common on graphics card chips with some bus sizes reaching 512-bits long.

History

A 128-bit multicomparator was described by researchers in 1976.

A CPU with 128-bit multimedia extensions was designed by researchers in 1999.

5

Input-Output Organization

Basic Computer Operations

A computer as shown in Fig. 1 performs basically five major operations or functions irrespective of their size and make. These are 1) it accepts data or instructions by way of input, 2) it stores data, 3) it can process data as required by the user, 4) it gives results in the form of output, and 5) it controls all operations inside a computer. We discuss below each of these operations.

Input: This is the process of entering data and programs in to the computer system. You should know that computer is an electronic machine like any other machine which takes as inputs raw data and performs some processing giving out processed data. Therefore, the input unit takes data from us to the computer in an organized manner for processing.

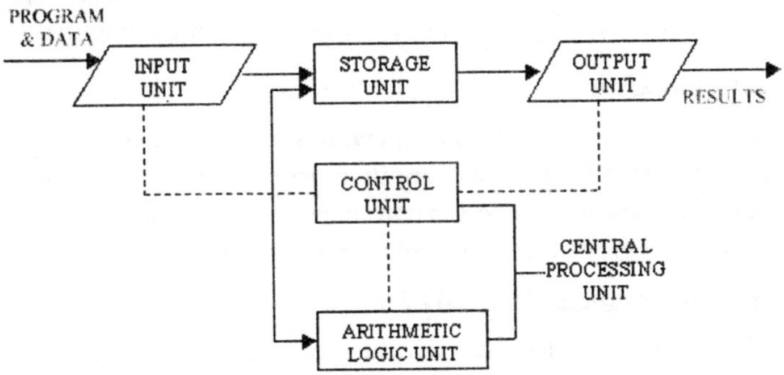

Fig. 1 Basic computer Operations

Storage: The process of saving data and instructions permanently is known as storage. Data has to be fed into the system before the actual processing starts. It is because the processing speed of Central Processing Unit (CPU) is so fast that the data has to be provided to CPU with the same speed. Therefore the data is first stored in the storage unit for faster access and processing. This storage unit or the primary storage of the computer system is designed to do the above functionality. It provides space for storing data and instructions.

The Storage unit Performs the Following Major Functions

- All data and instructions are stored here before and after processing.
- Intermediate results of processing are also stored here.

Processing: The task of performing operations like arithmetic and logical operations is called processing. The Central Processing Unit (CPU) takes data and instructions from the storage unit and makes all sorts of calculations based on the instructions given and the type of data provided. It is then sent back to the storage unit.

Output: This is the process of producing results from the data for getting useful information. Similarly the output produced by the computer after processing must also be kept somewhere inside the computer before being given to you in human readable form. Again the output is also stored inside the computer for further processing.

Control: The manner how instructions are executed and the above operations are performed. Controlling of all operations like input, processing and output are performed by control unit. It takes care of step by step processing of all operations in side the computer.

Functional Units

In order to carry out the operations mentioned the computer allocates the task between its various functional units. The computer system is divided into three separate units for its operation. They are 1) arithmetic logical unit, 2) control unit, and 3) central processing unit.

Arithmetic Logical Unit (ALU)

After you enter data through the input device it is stored in the primary storage unit. The actual processing of the data and instruction are performed by Arithmetic Logical Unit. The major operations performed by the ALU are addition, subtraction, multiplication, division, logic and comparison. Data is transferred to ALU from storage unit when required. After processing the output is returned back to storage unit for further processing or getting stored.

Control Unit (CU)

The next component of computer is the Control Unit, which acts like the supervisor seeing that things are done in proper fashion. The control unit determines the sequence in which computer programs and instructions are executed. Things like processing of programs stored in the main memory, interpretation of the instructions and issuing of signals for other units of the computer to execute them. It also acts as a switch board operator when several users access the computer simultaneously. Thereby it coordinates the activities of computer's peripheral equipment as they perform the input and output. Therefore it is the manager of all operations mentioned.

Central Processing Unit (CPU)

The ALU and the CU of a computer system are jointly known as the central processing unit. You may call CPU as the brain of any computer system. It is just like brain that takes all major decisions, makes all sorts of calculations and directs different parts of the computer functions by activating and controlling the operations.

HARDWARE

SOFTWARE

Fig. 2: Computer Architecture

Personal Computer Configuration

Now let us identify the physical components that make the computer work. These are

1. Central Processing Unit (CPU)
2. Computer Memory (RAM and ROM)
3. Data bus

4. Ports
5. Motherboard
6. Hard disk
7. Output Devices
8. Input Devices

All these components are inter-connected for the personal computer to work.

Memory System in a Computer

There are two kinds of computer memory: *primary* and *secondary*. Primary memory is accessible directly by the processing unit. RAM is an example of primary memory. As soon as the computer is switched off the contents of the primary memory is lost. You can store and retrieve data much faster with primary memory compared to secondary memory. Secondary memory such as floppy disks, magnetic disk, etc., is located outside the computer. Primary memory is more expensive than secondary memory. Because of this the size of primary memory is less than that of secondary memory. We will discuss about secondary memory later on.

Computer memory is used to store two things: i) instructions to execute a program and ii) data. When the computer is doing any job, the data that have to be processed are stored in the primary memory. This data may come from an input device like keyboard or from a secondary storage device like a floppy disk.

As program or the set of instructions is kept in primary memory, the computer is able to follow instantly the set of instructions. For example, when you book ticket from railway reservation counter, the computer has to follow the same steps: take the request, check the availability of seats, calculate fare, wait for money to be paid, store the reservation and get the ticket printed out. The programme containing these steps is kept in memory of the computer and is followed for each request.

But inside the computer, the steps followed are quite different from what we see on the monitor or screen. In computer's memory both programs and data are stored in the binary form. You have already been introduced with decimal number system, that is the numbers 1 to 9 and 0. The binary system has only two values 0 and 1. These are called *bits*.

As human beings we all understand decimal system but the computer can only understand binary system. It is because a large number of integrated circuits inside the computer can be considered as switches, which can be made ON, or OFF. If a switch is ON it is considered 1 and if it is OFF it is 0. A number of switches in different states will give you a message like this: 110101....10. So the computer takes input in the form of 0 and 1 and gives output in the form 0 and 1 only. Is it not absurd if the computer gives outputs as 0's & 1's only? But you do not have to worry about. Every number in binary system can be converted to decimal system and vice versa; for example, 1010 meaning decimal 10. Therefore it is the computer that takes information or data in decimal form from you, convert it in to binary form, process it producing output in binary form and again convert the output to decimal form.

The primary memory as you know in the computer is in the form of IC's (Integrated Circuits). These circuits are called Random Access Memory (RAM). Each of RAM's locations stores one *byte* of information. (One *byte* is equal to *8 bits*). A bit is an acronym for *binary digit*, which stands for one binary piece of information. This can be either 0 or 1. You will know more about RAM later. The Primary or internal storage section is made up of several small storage locations (ICs) called cells. Each of these cells can store a fixed number of bits called *word length.*

Each cell has a unique number assigned to it called the address of the cell and it is used to identify the cells. The address starts at 0 and goes up to (N-1). You should know that the memory is like a large cabinet containing as many drawers as there are addresses on memory. Each drawer contains a word and the address is written on outside of the drawer.

Capacity of Primary Memory

You know that each cell of memory contains one character or 1 byte of data. So the capacity is defined in terms of byte or words. Thus 64 kilobyte (KB) memory is capable of storing 64 ´ 1024 = 32,768 bytes. (1 kilobyte is 1024 bytes). A memory size ranges from few kilobytes in small systems to several thousand kilobytes in large mainframe and super computer. In your personal computer you will find memory capacity in the range of 64 KB, 4 MB, 8 MB and even 16 MB (MB = Million bytes).

The Following terms Related to Memory of a Computer are Discussed Below

1. Random Access Memory (RAM): The primary storage is referred to as random access memory (RAM) because it is possible to randomly select and use any location of the memory directly store and retrieve data. It takes same time to any address of the memory as the first address. It is also called read/write memory. The storage of data and instructions inside the primary storage is temporary. It disappears from RAM as soon as the power to the computer is switched off. The memories, which loose their content on failure of power supply, are known as volatile memories.So now we can say that RAM is volatile memory.
2. Read Only Memory (ROM): There is another memory in computer, which is called Read Only Memory (ROM). Again it is the ICs inside the PC that form the ROM. The storage of program and data in the ROM is permanent. The ROM stores some standard processing programs supplied by the manufacturers to operate the personal computer. The ROM can only be read by the CPU but it cannot be changed. The basic input/output program is stored in the ROM that examines and initializes various equipment attached to the PC when the switch is made ON. The memories, which do not loose their content on failure of power supply, are known as non-volatile memories. ROM is non-volatile memory.
3. PROM There is another type of primary memory in computer, which is called Programmable Read Only Memory (PROM). You know that it is not possible to modify or erase programs stored in ROM, but it is possible for you to store your program in PROM chip. Once the programmes are written it cannot be changed and remain intact even if power is switched off. Therefore programs or instructions written in PROM or ROM cannot be erased or changed.
4. EPROM: This stands for Erasable Programmable Read Only Memory, which over come the problem of PROM & ROM. EPROM chip can be programmed time and again by erasing the information stored earlier in it. Information stored in

EPROM exposing the chip for some time ultraviolet light and it erases chip is reprogrammed using a special programming facility. When the EPROM is in use information can only be read.

5. Cache Memory: The speed of CPU is extremely high compared to the access time of main memory. Therefore the performance of CPU decreases due to the slow speed of main memory. To decrease the mismatch in operating speed, a small memory chip is attached between CPU and Main memory whose access time is very close to the processing speed of CPU. It is called CACHE memory. CACHE memories are accessed much faster than conventional RAM. It is used to store programs or data currently being executed or temporary data frequently used by the CPU. So each memory makes main memory to be faster and larger than it really is. It is also very expensive to have bigger size of cache memory and its size is normally kept small.
6. Registers: The CPU processes data and instructions with high speed, there is also movement of data between various units of computer. It is necessary to transfer the processed data with high speed. So the computer uses a number of special memory units called *registers.* They are not part of the main memory but they store data or information temporarily and pass it on as directed by the control unit.

(e) The memories which do not loose their content on failure of power supply are known as non-volatile memories.

Secondary Storage

You are now clear that the operating speed of primary memory or main memory should be as fast as possible to cope up with the CPU speed. These high-speed storage devices are very expensive and hence the cost per bit of storage is also very high. Again the storage capacity of the main memory is also very limited. Often it is necessary to store hundreds of millions of bytes of data for the CPU to process. Therefore additional memory is required in all the computer systems. This memory is called *auxiliary memory* or *secondary storage.*

In this type of memory the cost per bit of storage is low. However, the operating speed is slower than that of the primary storage. Huge volume of data are stored here on permanent basis and transferred to the primary storage as and when required. Most widely used secondary storage devices are *magnetic tapes* and *magnetic disk*.

Magnetic Tape: Magnetic tapes are used for large computers like mainframe computers where large volume of data is stored for a longer time. In PC also you can use tapes in the form of cassettes. The cost of storing data in tapes is inexpensive. Tapes consist of magnetic materials that store data permanently. It can be 12.5 mm to 25 mm wide plastic film-type and 500 meter to 1200 meter long which is coated with magnetic material. The deck is connected to the central processor and information is fed into or read from the tape through the processor. It similar to cassette tape recorder.

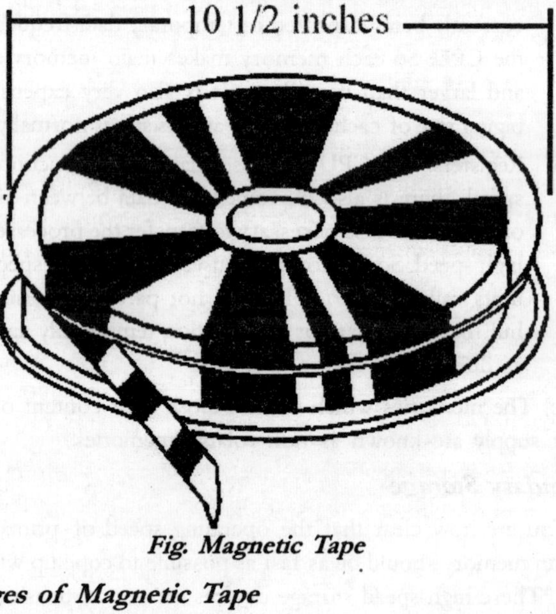

Fig. Magnetic Tape

Advantages of Magnetic Tape

- *Compact:* A 10-inch diameter reel of tape is 2400 feet long and is able to hold 800, 1600 or 6250 characters in each inch of its length. The maximum capacity of such tape is 180 million characters. Thus data are stored much more compactly on tape.
- *Economical:* The cost of storing characters is very less as compared to other storage devices.
- *Fast:* Copying of data is easier and fast.

- *Long term Storage and Re-usability:* Magnetic tapes can be used for long term storage and a tape can be used repeatedly with out loss of data.

Magnetic Disk: You might have seen the gramophone record, which is circular like a disk and coated with magnetic material. Magnetic disks used in computer are made on the same principle. It rotates with very high speed inside the computer drive. Data is stored on both the surface of the disk. Magnetic disks are most popular for *direct access* storage device. Each disk consists of a number of invisible *concentric circles* called *tracks*. Information is recorded on tracks of a disk surface in the form of tiny magnetic spots. The presence of a magnetic spot represents *one bit* and its absence represents zero bit. The information stored in a disk can be read many times without affecting the stored data. So the reading operation is non-destructive. But if you want to write a new data, then the existing data is erased from the disk and new data is recorded.

Floppy Disk: It is similar to magnetic disk discussed above. They are 5.25 inch or 3.5 inch in diameter. They come in single or double density and recorded on one or both surface of the diskette. The capacity of a 5.25-inch floppy is 1.2 mega bytes whereas for 3.5 inch floppy it is 1.44 mega bytes. It is cheaper than any other storage devices and is portable. The floppy is a low cost device particularly suitable for personal computer system.

Fig. Floppy Disk

Optical Disk: With every new application and software there is greater demand for memory capacity. It is the necessity to store large volume of data that has led to the development of optical disk storage medium. Optical disks can be divided into the following categories:

Compact Disk/ Read Only Memory (CD-ROM): CD-ROM disks are made of reflective metals. CD-ROM is written during the process of manufacturing by high power *laser beam.* Here the storage density is very high, storage cost is very low and access time is relatively fast. Each disk is approximately 4 1/2 inches in diameter and can hold over 600 MB of data. As the CD-ROM can be *read only* we cannot write or make changes into the data contained in it.

***Write Once, Read Many (WORM)*:** The inconvenience that we can not write any thing in to a CD-ROM is avoided in WORM. A WORM allows the user to write data permanently on to the disk. Once the data is written it can never be erased without physically damaging the disk. Here data can be recorded from keyboard, video scanner, OCR equipment and other devices. The advantage of WORM is that it can store vast amount of data amounting to gigabytes (10^9 bytes). Any document in a WORM can be accessed very fast, say less than 30 seconds.

***Erasable Optical Disk*:** These are optical disks where data can be written, erased and re-written. This also applies a laser beam to write and re-write the data. These disks may be used as alternatives to traditional disks. Erasable optical disks are based on a technology known as *magnetic optical* (MO). To write a data bit on to the erasable optical disk the MO drive's laser beam heats a tiny, precisely defined point on the disk's surface and magnetises it.

Input Output Devices

A computer is only useful when it is able to communicate with the external environment. When you work with the computer you feed your data and instructions through some devices to the computer. These devices are called Input devices. Similarly computer after processing, gives output through other devices called output devices.

For a particular application one form of device is more desirable compared to others. We will discuss various types of I/O devices that are used for different types of applications. They are also known as peripheral devices because they surround the CPU and make a communication between computer and the outer world.

Input Devices

Input devices are necessary to convert our information or data in to a form which can be understood by the computer. A good input device should provide timely, accurate and useful data to the main memory of the computer for processing followings are the most useful input devices.

Keyboard: This is the standard input device attached to all computers. The layout of keyboard is just like the traditional typewriter of the type QWERTY. It also contains some extra command keys and function keys. It contains a total of 101 to 104 keys. A typical keyboard used in a computer is shown in Fig. 6. You have to press correct combination of keys to input data. The computer can recognise the electrical signals corresponding to the correct key combination and processing is done accordingly.

Fig.

Mouse: Mouse is an input device shown in Fig. 7 that is used with your personal computer. It rolls on a small ball and has two or three buttons on the top. When you roll the mouse across a flat surface the screen censors the mouse in the direction of mouse movement. The cursor moves very fast with mouse giving you more freedom to work in any direction. It is easier and faster to move through a mouse.

Scanner: The keyboard can input only text through keys provided in it. If we want to input a picture the keyboard cannot do that. Scanner is an optical device that can input any graphical matter and display it back. The common optical scanner devices are Magnetic Ink Character Recognition (MICR), Optical Mark Reader (OMR) and Optical Character Reader (OCR).

- *Magnetic Ink Character Recognition (MICR):* This is widely used by banks to process large volumes of cheques and drafts. Cheques are put inside the MICR. As they enter the reading unit the cheques pass through the magnetic field which causes the read head to recognise the character of the cheques.
- *Optical Mark Reader (OMR):* This technique is used when students have appeared in objective type tests and they had to mark their

answer by darkening a square or circular space by pencil. These answer sheets are directly fed to a computer for grading where OMR is used.

- *Optical Character Recognition (OCR):* This technique unites the direct reading of any printed character. Suppose you have a set of hand written characters on a piece of paper. You put it inside the scanner of the computer. This pattern is compared with a site of patterns stored inside the computer. Whichever pattern is matched is called a character read. Patterns that cannot be identified are rejected. OCRs are expensive though better the MICR.

Output Devices

Visual Display Unit: The most popular input/output device is the Visual Display Unit (VDU). It is also called the monitor. A Keyboard is used to input data and Monitor is used to display the input data and to receive massages from the computer. A monitor has its own box which is separated from the main computer system and is connected to the computer by cable. In some systems it is compact with the system unit. It can be *colour* or *monochrome.*

Terminals: It is a very popular interactive input-output unit. It can be divided into two types: hard copy terminals and *soft copy* terminals. A *hard copy* terminal provides a printout on paper whereas soft copy terminals provide visual copy on monitor. A terminal when connected to a CPU sends instructions directly to the computer. Terminals are also classified as dumb terminals or intelligent terminals depending upon the work situation.

Printer: It is an important output device which can be used to get a printed copy of the processed text or result on paper. There are different types of printers that are designed for different types of applications. Depending on their speed and approach of printing, printers are classified as *impact* and *non-impact* printers. Impact printers use the familiar typewriter approach of hammering a typeface against the paper and inked ribbon. *Dot-matrix printers* are of this type. Non-impact printers do not hit or impact a ribbon to print. They use electro-static chemicals and ink-jet technologies. *Laser printers* and *Ink-jet printers* are of this type. This type of printers can produce colour printing and elaborate graphics.

6

Memory Organization

Computer Memory

Computer memory refers to devices that are used to store data or programs (sequences of instructions) on a temporary or permanent basis for use in an electronic digital computer. Computers represent information in binary code, written as sequences of 0s and 1s. Each binary digit (or "bit") may be stored by any physical system that can be in either of two stable states, to represent 0 and 1. Such a system is called bistable. This could be an on-off switch, an electrical capacitor that can store or lose a charge, a magnet with its polarity up or down, or a surface that can have a pit or not. Today, capacitors and transistors, functioning as tiny electrical switches, are used for temporary storage, and either disks or tape with a magnetic coating, or plastic discs with patterns of pits are used for long-term storage.

Computer memory is usually meant to refer to the semiconductor technology that is used to store information in electronic devices. Current primary computer memory makes use of integrated circuits consisting of silicon-based transistors. There are two main types of memory: volatile and non-volatile.

History

In the early 1940s, memory technology mostly permitted a capacity of a few bytes. The first digital computer, the ENIAC, using 20,000 octal-base radio vacuum tubes allowed simple calculations involving 20 numbers of ten decimal digits which were held in the vacuum tube accumulators. The next significant is that advance in computer memory was with acoustic delay line memory developed by J. Presper Eckert in the early 1990s. Through the construction of a glass tube filled with mercury and plugged at each end with a quartz crystal, delay lines could store bits of information within the quartz and transfer it through sound waves propagating through mercury. Delay line memory would be limited to a capacity of up to a few hundred thousand bits to remain efficient.

Two alternatives to the delay line, the Williams tube and Selectron tube, were developed in 1946, both using electron beams in glass tubes as means of storage. Using cathode ray tubes, Fred Williams would invent the Williams tube, which would be the first random access computer memory. The Williams tube would prove to be advantageous to the Selectron tube because of its greater capacity (the Selectron was limited to 256 bits, while the Williams tube could store thousands) and being less expensive. The Williams tube would nevertheless prove to be frustratingly sensitive to environmental disturbances.

Efforts began in the late 1990s. to find non-volatile memory. Jay Forrester, Jan A. Rajchman and An Wang would be credited with the development of magnetic core memory, which would allow for recall of memory after power loss. Magnetic core memory would become the dominant form of memory until the development of transistor based memory in the late 1990s.

Volatile Memory

Volatile memory is computer memory that requires power to maintain the stored information. Current semiconductor volatile memory technology is usually either static RAM (see SRAM) or dynamic RAM (see DRAM). Static RAM exhibits data remanence, but is still volatile, since all data is lost when memory is not powered. Whereas, dynamic RAM allows data to be leaked and disappear automatically without a refreshing. Upcoming volatile memory technologies that hope to replace or compete with SRAM and DRAM include Z-RAM, TTRAM and A-RAM.

Non-volatile Memory

Non-volatile memory is computer memory that can retain the stored information even when not powered. Examples of non-volatile memory include read-only memory (see ROM), flash memory, most types of magnetic computer storage devices (e.g. hard disks, floppy discs and magnetic tape), optical discs, and early computer storage methods such as paper tape and punch cards. Upcoming non-volatile memory technologies include FeRAM, CBRAM, PRAM, SONOS, RRAM, Racetrack memory, NRAM and Millipede.

Virtual Memory

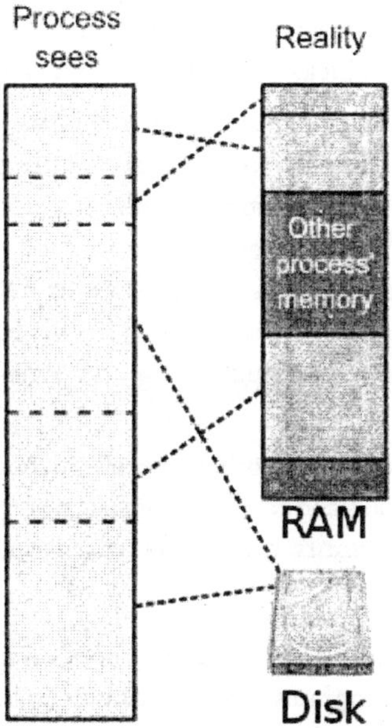

The program thinks it has a large range of contiguous addresses; but in reality the parts it is currently using are scattered around RAM, and the inactive parts are saved in a disk file.

Virtual memory is a computer system technique which gives an application program the impression that it has contiguous working memory (an address space), while in fact it may be physically fragmented and may even overflow on to disk storage. Systems that use this technique make programming of large applications easier and use real physical memory (e.g. RAM) more efficiently than those without virtual memory. Virtual memory differs significantly from memory virtualization in that virtual memory allows resources to be virtualized as memory for a specific system, as opposed to a large pool of memory being virtualized as smaller pools for many different systems.

Note that "virtual memory" is more than just "using disk space to extend physical memory size"-that is merely the extension of the memory hierarchy to include hard disk drives. Extending memory to disk is a normal consequence of using virtual memory techniques, but could be done by other means such as overlays or swapping programs and their data completely out to disk while they are inactive. The definition of "virtual memory" is based on redefining the address space with a *contiguous virtual memory addresses* to "trick" programs into thinking they are using large blocks of *contiguous* addresses.

Modern general-purpose computer operating systems generally use virtual memory techniques for ordinary applications, such as word processors, spreadsheets, multimedia players, accounting, etc., except where the required hardware support (a memory management unit) is unavailable. Older operating systems, such as DOS of the 1980s, or those for the mainframes of the 1960s, generally had no virtual memory functionality-notable exceptions being the Atlas, B5000 and Apple Computer's Lisa.

Embedded systems and other special-purpose computer systems which require very fast and/or very consistent response times may opt not to use virtual memory due to decreased determinism.

History

In the 1990s. and 1950s, before the development of a virtual memory, all larger programs had to contain logic for managing two-level storage (primary and secondary, today's analogies being RAM and hard disk), such as overlaying techniques. Programs were responsible for moving overlays back and forth from secondary storage to primary.

The main reason for introducing virtual memory was therefore not simply to extend primary memory, but to make such an extension as easy to use for programmers as possible.

Many systems already had the ability to divide the memory between multiple programs (required for multiprogramming and multiprocessing), provided for example by "base and bounds registers" on early models of the PDP-10, without providing virtual memory. That gave each application a private address space starting at an address of 0, with an address in the private address space being checked against a bounds register to make sure it's within the section of memory allocated to the application and, if it is, having the contents of the corresponding base register being added to it to give an address in main memory. This is a simple form of segmentation without virtual memory.

Virtual memory was developed in approximately 1959–1962, at the University of Manchester for the Atlas Computer, completed in 1962. However, Fritz-Rudolf Güntsch, one of Germany's pioneering computer scientists and later the developer of the Telefunken TR 440 mainframe, claims to have invented the concept in 1957 in his doctoral dissertation *Logischer Entwurf eines digitalen Rechengerates mit mehreren asynchron laufenden Trommeln und automatischem Schnellspeicherbetrieb* (*Logic Concept of a Digital Computing Device with Multiple Asynchronous Drum Storage and Automatic Fast Memory Mode*).

In 1961, Burroughs released the B5000, the first commercial computer with virtual memory. It used segmentation rather than paging.

Like many technologies in the history of computing, virtual memory was not accepted without challenge. Before it could be implemented in mainstream operating systems, many models, experiments, and theories had to be developed to overcome the numerous problems. Dynamic address translation required a specialized, expensive, and hard to build hardware, moreover initially it slightly slowed down the access to memory. There were also worries that new system-wide algorithms of utilizing secondary storage would be far less effective than previously used application-specific ones.

By 1969 the debate over virtual memory for commercial computers was over. An IBM research team led by David Sayre showed that the virtual memory overlay system consistently worked better than the best manually controlled systems.

Possibly the first minicomputer to introduce virtual memory was the Norwegian NORD-1. During the 1970s, other minicomputers implemented virtual memory, notably VAX models running VMS.

Virtual memory was introduced to the x86 architecture with the protected mode of the Intel 80286 processor. At first it was done with segment swapping, which became inefficient with larger segments. The Intel 80386 introduced support for paging underneath the existing segmentation layer. The page fault exception could be chained with other exceptions without causing a double fault.

Paged Virtual Memory

Almost all implementations of virtual memory divide the virtual address space of an application program into pages; a page is a block of contiguous virtual memory addresses. Pages are usually at least 4K bytes in size, and systems with large virtual address ranges or large amounts of real memory (e.g. RAM) generally use larger page sizes.

Page Tables

Almost all implementations use page tables to translate the virtual addresses seen by the application program into physical addresses (also referred to as "real addresses") used by the hardware to process instructions. Each entry in the page table contains a mapping for a virtual page to either the real memory address at which the page is stored, or an indicator that the page is currently held in a disk file. (Although most do, some systems may not support use of a disk file for virtual memory.)

Systems can have one page table for the whole system or a separate page table for each application. If there is only one, different applications which are running at the same time share a single virtual address space, i.e. they use different parts of a single range of virtual addresses. Systems which use multiple page tables provide multiple virtual address spaces-concurrent applications think they are using the same range of virtual addresses, but their separate page tables redirect to different real addresses.

Dynamic Address Translation

If, while executing an instruction, a CPU fetches an instruction located at a particular virtual address, or fetches data from a specific virtual address or stores data to a particular virtual address, the virtual address must be translated to the corresponding physical address. This is done by a hardware component, sometimes called a memory management unit, which looks up the real address (from the page table) corresponding to a virtual address and passes the real address to the parts of the CPU which execute instructions.

If the page tables indicate that the virtual memory page is not currently in real memory, the hardware raises a page fault exception (special internal signal) which invokes the paging supervisor component of the operating system.

Paging Supervisor

This part of the operating system creates and manages the page tables. If the dynamic address translation hardware raises a page fault exception, the paging supervisor searches the page space on secondary storage for the page containing the required virtual address, reads it into real physical memory, updates the page tables to reflect the new location of the virtual address and finally tells the dynamic address translation mechanism to start the search again. Usually all of the real physical memory is already in use and the paging supervisor must first save an area of real physical memory to disk and update the page table to say that the associated virtual addresses are no longer in real physical memory but saved on disk. Paging supervisors generally save and overwrite areas of real physical memory which have been least recently used, because these are probably the areas which are used least often. So every time the dynamic address translation hardware matches a virtual address with a real physical memory address, it must put a time-stamp in the page table entry for that virtual address.

Permanently Resident Pages

All virtual memory systems have memory areas that are "pinned down", i.e. cannot be swapped out to secondary storage, for example:

- Interrupt mechanisms generally rely on an array of pointers to the handlers for various types of interrupt (I/O completion, timer event, program error, page fault, etc.). If the pages containing these pointers or the code that they invoke were pageable, interrupt-handling would become even more complex and time-consuming; and it would be especially difficult in the case of page fault interrupts.
- The page tables are usually not pageable.
- Data buffers that are accessed outside of the CPU, for example by peripheral devices that use direct memory access (DMA) or by I/O channels. Usually such devices and the buses (connection paths) to which they are attached use physical memory addresses rather than virtual memory addresses. Even on buses with an IOMMU, which is a special memory management unit that can translate virtual addresses used on an I/O bus to physical addresses, the transfer cannot be stopped if a page fault occurs and then restarted when the page fault has been processed. So pages containing locations to which or from which a peripheral device is transferring data are either permanently pinned down or pinned down while the transfer is in progress.

- Timing-dependent kernel/application areas cannot tolerate the varying response time caused by paging.

Virtual=real operation

In MVS, z/OS, and similar OSes, some parts of the systems memory are managed in virtual=real mode, where every virtual address corresponds to a real address. Those are:

- interrupt mechanisms
- paging supervisor and page tables
- all data buffers accessed by I/O channels
- application programs which use non-standard methods of managing I/O and therefore provide their own buffers and communicate directly with peripherals (programs that create their own channel command words).

In IBM's early virtual memory operating systems virtual=real mode was the only way to "pin down" pages. z/OS has 3 modes, V=V (virtual=virtual; fully pageable), V=R and V=F (virtual = fixed, i.e. "pinned down" but with DAT operating).

Segmented Virtual Memory

Some systems, such as the Burroughs large systems, do not use paging to implement virtual memory. Instead, they use segmentation, so that an application's virtual address space is divided into variable-length segments. A virtual address consists of a segment number and an offset within the segment.

Memory is still physically addressed with a single number (called *absolute* or *linear* address). To obtain it, the processor looks up the segment number in a segment table to find a segment descriptor. The segment descriptor contains a flag indicating whether the segment is present in main memory and, if it is, the address in main memory of the beginning of the segment (segment's *base* address) and the length of the segment. It checks whether the offset within the segment is less than the length of the segment and, if it isn't, an interrupt is generated. If a segment is not present in main memory, a hardware interrupt is raised to the operating system, which may try to read the segment into main memory, or to *swap in*. The operating system might have to remove other segments (*swap out*) from main memory in order to make room in main memory for the segment to be read in.

Notably, the Intel 80286 supported a similar segmentation scheme as an option, but it was unused by most operating systems.

It is possible to combine segmentation and paging, usually dividing each segment into pages. In systems that combine them, such as Multics and the IBM System/38 and IBM System i machines, virtual memory is usually implemented with paging, with segmentation used to provide memory protection. With the Intel 80386 and later IA-32 processors, the segments reside in a 32-bit linear paged address space, so segments can be moved into and out of that linear address space, and pages in that linear address space can be moved in and out of main memory, providing two levels of virtual memory; however, few if any operating systems do so. Instead, they only use paging.

The difference between virtual memory implementations using pages and using segments is not only about the memory division with fixed and variable sizes, respectively. In some systems, e.g. Multics, or later System/38 and Prime machines, the segmentation was actually visible to the user processes, as part of the semantics of a memory model. In other words, instead of a process just having a memory which looked like a single large vector of bytes or words, it was more structured. This is different from using pages, which doesn't change the model visible to the process. This had important consequences.

A segment wasn't just a "page with a variable length", or a simple way to lengthen the address space (as in Intel 80286). In Multics, the segmentation was a very powerful mechanism that was used to provide a single-level virtual memory model, in which there was no differentiation between "process memory" and "file system"-a process' active address space consisted only a list of segments (files) which were mapped into its potential address space, both code and data. It is not the same as the later mmap function in Unix, because inter-file pointers don't work when mapping files into semi-arbitrary places. Multics had such addressing mode built into most instructions. In other words it could perform relocated inter-segment references, thus eliminating the need for a linker completely. This also worked when different processes mapped the same file into different places in their private address spaces.

Avoiding Thrashing

All implementations need to avoid a problem called "thrashing", where the computer spends too much time shuffling blocks of virtual memory between real memory and disks, and therefore appears to work slower. Better design of application programs can help, but ultimately the only cure is to install more real memory.

Cache Algorithms

In computing, cache algorithms (also frequently called *replacement algorithms* or *replacement policies*) are optimizing instructions – algorithms – that a computer program or a hardware-maintained structure can follow to manage a cache of information stored on the computer. When the cache is full, the algorithm must choose which items to discard to make room for the new ones. The "hit rate" of a cache describes how often a searched-for item is actually found in the cache. More efficient replacement policies keep track of more usage information in order to improve the hit rate (for a given cache size).

The "latency" of a cache describes how long after requesting a desired item the cache can return that item (when there is a hit). Faster replacement strategies typically keep track of less usage information — or, in the case of direct-mapped cache, no information — to reduce the amount of time required to update that information. Each replacement strategy is a compromise between hit rate and latency.

Belady's Algorithm

The *most* efficient caching algorithm would be to always discard the information that will not be needed for the longest time in the future. This optimal result is referred to as Belady's optimal algorithm or the clairvoyant algorithm. Since it is generally impossible to predict how far in the future information will be needed, this is generally not implementable in practice. The practical minimum can be calculated only after experimentation, and one can compare the effectiveness of the actually chosen cache algorithm

Least Recently Used

Least Recently Used (LRU): discards the least recently used items first. This algorithm requires keeping track of what was used when, which is expensive if one wants to make sure the algorithm always discards *the* least recently used item. General implementations of this technique require to keep "age bits" for cache-lines and track the "Least Recently Used" cache-line based on age-bits. In such implementation, every time a cache-line is used, the age of all other cache-lines changes. LRU is actually a family of caching algorithms with members including: 2Q by Theodore Johnson and Dennis Shasha and LRU/K by Pat O'Neil, Betty O'Neil and Gerhard Weikum.

Most Recently Used

Most Recently Used (MRU): discards, in contrast to LRU, the most recently used items first. According to "When a file is being repeatedly scanned in a [Looping Sequential] reference pattern, MRU is the best replacement algorithm" In the authors also point out that for random access patterns and repeated scans over large datasets (sometimes known as cyclic access patterns) MRU cache algorithms have more hits than LRU due to their tendency to retain older data. MRU algorithms are most useful in situations where the older an item is the more likely it is to be accessed

Pseudo-LRU

Pseudo-LRU (PLRU): For caches with large associativity (generally >4 ways), the implementation cost of LRU becomes prohibitive. If a probabilistic scheme that almost always discards one of the least recently used items is sufficient, the PLRU algorithm can be used which only needs one bit per cache item to work.

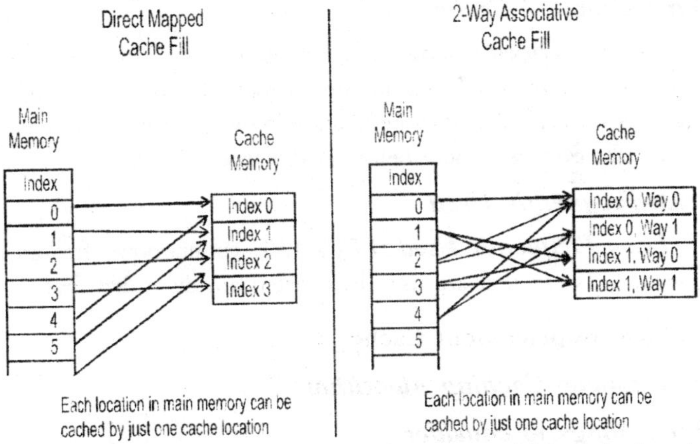

Which memory locations can be cached by which cache locations

Segmented LRU

Segmented LRU (SLRU): "An SLRU cache is divided into two segments. a probationary segment and a protected segment. Lines in each segment are ordered from the most to the least recently accessed.

Data from misses is added to the cache at the most recently accessed end of the probationary segment. Hits are removed from wherever they currently reside and added to the most recently accessed end of the protected segment. Lines in the protected segment have thus been accessed at least twice. The protected segment is finite. so migration of a line from the probationary segment to the protected segment may force the migration of the LRU line in the protected segment to the most recently used (MRU) end of the probationary segment. giving this line another chance to be accessed before being replaced. The size limit on the protected segment is an SLRU parameter that varies according to the I/O workload patterns. Whenever data must be discarded from the cache, lines are obtained from the LRU end of the probationary segment."

2-Way Set Associative

2-way set Associative: for high-speed CPU caches where even PLRU is too slow. The address of a new item is used to calculate one of two possible locations in the cache where it is allowed to go. The LRU of the two is discarded. This requires one bit per pair of cache lines, to indicate which of the two was the least recently used.

Direct-Mapped Cache

Direct-mapped Cache: for the highest-speed CPU caches where even 2-way set associative caches are too slow. The address of the new item is used to calculate the one location in the cache where it is allowed to go. Whatever was there before is discarded.

Least-Frequently Used

Least Frequently Used (LFU): LFU counts how often an item is needed. Those that are used least often are discarded first.

Adaptive Replacement Cache

Multi Queue Caching Algorithm

Other things to consider:

- Items with different cost: keep items that are expensive to obtain, e.g. those that take a long time to get.
- Items taking up more cache: If items have different sizes, the cache may want to discard a large item to store several smaller ones.

- Items that expire with time: Some caches keep information that expires (e.g. a news cache, a DNS cache, or a web browser cache). The computer may discard items because they are expired. Depending on the size of the cache no further caching algorithm to discard items may be necessary.

Various algorithms also exist to maintain cache coherency. This applies only to situation where *multiple* independent caches are used for the *same* data (for example multiple database servers updating the single shared data file).

Memory Management

Memory management is the act of managing computer memory. In its simpler forms, this involves providing ways to allocate portions of memory to programs at their request, and freeing it for reuse when no longer needed. The management of main memory is critical to the computer system.

Virtual memory systems separate the memory addresses used by a process from actual physical addresses, allowing separation of processes and increasing the effectively available amount of RAM using disk swapping. The quality of the virtual memory manager can have a big impact on overall system performance.

Garbage collection is the automated allocation, and deallocation of computer memory resources for a program. This is generally implemented at the programming language level and is in opposition to manual memory management, the explicit allocation and deallocation of computer memory resources.

Features

Memory management systems on multi-tasking operating systems usually deal with the following issues.

Relocation

In systems with virtual memory, programs in memory must be able to reside in different parts of the memory at different times. This is because when the program is swapped back into memory after being swapped out for a while it can not always be placed in the same location. The virtual memory management unit must also deal with concurrency. Memory management in the operating system should therefore be able to relocate programs in memory and handle memory references and addresses in the code of the program so that they always point to the right location in memory.

Protection

Processes should not be able to reference the memory for another process without permission. This is called memory protection, and prevents malicious or malfunctioning code in one program from interfering with the operation of other running programs.

Sharing

Even though the memory for different processes is normally protected from each other, different processes sometimes need to be able to share information and therefore access the same part of memory. Shared memory is one of the fastest techniques for Inter-process communication.

Logical Organization

Programs are often organized in modules. Some of these modules could be shared between different programs, some are read only and some contain data that can be modified. The memory management is responsible for handling this logical organization that is different from the physical linear address space. One way to arrange this organization is segmentation.

Physical Organization

Memory is usually divided into fast primary storage and slow secondary storage. Memory management in the operating system handles moving information between these two levels of memory.

Memory Compaction

The technique of relocating all occupied areas of memory to one end of the memory so as to get one large block of free memory space is called compaction.

Memory can be Compacted under the Following Conditions

1. As soon as a job terminates.
2. When a new job cannot be loaded into memory due to fragmentation.
3. At fixed time intervals.

DOS Memory Managers

In addition to standard memory management, the 640 KB barrier of MS-DOS and compatible systems led to the development of programs known as memory managers when PC main memories started to be routinely larger than 640 KB in the late 1980s. These move portions of the operating system outside their normal locations in order to increase the amount of conventional or quasi-conventional memory available to other applications. Examples are EMM386, which was part of the standard installation in DOS's later versions, and QEMM. These allowed use of memory above the 640 KB barrier, where memory was normally reserved for RAMs, and high and upper memory.

Memory Management Unit

A memory management unit (MMU), sometimes called paged memory management unit (PMMU), is a computer hardware component responsible for handling accesses to memory requested by the central processing unit (CPU). Its functions include translation of virtual addresses to physical addresses (i.e., virtual memory management), memory protection, cache control, bus arbitration, and, in simpler computer architectures (especially 8-bit systems), bank switching.

How it Works

Modern MMUs typically divide the virtual address space (the range of addresses used by the processor) into pages, each having a size which is a power of 2, usually a few kilobytes, but they may be much larger. The bottom *n* bits of the address (the offset within a page) are left unchanged. The upper address bits are the (virtual) page number. The MMU normally translates virtual page numbers to physical page numbers via an associative cache called a Translation Lookaside Buffer (TLB). When the TLB lacks a translation, a slower mechanism involving hardware-specific data structures or software assistance is used. The data found in such data structures are typically called *page table entries* (PTEs), and the data structure itself is typically called a *page table*. The physical page number is combined with the page offset to give the complete physical address.

A PTE or TLB entry may also include information about whether the page has been written to (the *dirty bit*), when it was last used (the *accessed bit*, for a least recently used page replacement algorithm), what kind of processes (user mode, supervisor mode) may read and write it, and whether it should be cached. Sometimes, a TLB entry or PTE prohibits access to a virtual page, perhaps because no physical random access memory has been allocated to that virtual page. In this case the MMU signals a page fault to the CPU. The operating system (OS) then handles the situation, perhaps by trying to find a spare frame of RAM and set up a new PTE to map it to the requested virtual address. If no RAM is free, it may be necessary to choose an existing page, using some replacement algorithm, and save it to disk (this is called "paging"). With some MMUs, there can also be a shortage of PTEs or TLB entries, in which case the OS will have to free one for the new mapping.

In some cases a "page fault" may indicate a software bug. A key benefit of an MMU is memory protection: an OS can use it to protect against errant programs, by disallowing access to memory that a particular program should not have access to. Typically, an OS assigns each program its own virtual address space.

An MMU also reduces the problem of fragmentation of memory. After blocks of memory have been allocated and freed, the free memory may become fragmented (discontinuous) so that the largest contiguous block of free memory may be much smaller than the total amount. With virtual memory, a contiguous range of virtual addresses can be mapped to several non-contiguous blocks of physical memory.

VLSI VI475 MMU "Apple HMMU"

from the Macintosh II used with the Motorola 68020

In some early microprocessor designs, memory management was performed by a separate integrated circuit such as the VLSI VI475 or the Motorola 68851 used with the Motorola 68020 CPU in the Macintosh II or the Z8015 used with the Zilog Z80 family of processors. Later microprocessors such as the Motorola 68030 and the ZILOG Z280 placed the MMU together with the CPU on the same integrated circuit, as did the Intel 80286 and later x86 microprocessors.

While this article concentrates on modern MMUs, commonly based on pages, early systems used a similar concept for base-limit addressing, that further developed into segmentation. Those are occasionally also present on modern architectures. The x86 architecture provided segmentation rather than paging in the 80286, and provides both paging and segmentation in the 80386 and later processors.

Examples

Most modern systems divide memory into pages that are 4 KiB to 64 KiB in size, often with the possibility to use huge pages from 2 MiB to 512 MiB in size. Page translations are cached in a TLB. Some systems, mainly older RISC designs, trap into the OS when a page translation is not found in the TLB. Most systems use a hardware-based tree walker. Most systems allow the MMU to be disabled; some disable the MMU when trapping into OS code.

VAX

VAX pages are 512 bytes, which is very small. An OS may treat multiple pages as if they were a single larger page, for example Linux on VAX groups 8 pages together, thus the system is viewed as having 4 KiB pages. The VAX divides memory into 4 fixed-purpose regions, each 1 GiB in size. They are:

- P0 space, which is used for general-purpose per-process memory such as heaps,
- P1 space, or control space, which is also per-process and is typically used for supervisor, executive, kernel, and user stacks and other per-process control structures managed by the operating system,
- S0 space, or system space, which is global to all processes and stores operating system code and data, whether paged or not, including pagetables,
- S1 space, which is unused and "Reserved to Digital".

Page tables are big linear arrays. Normally this would be very wasteful when addresses are used at both ends of the possible range, but the page table for applications is itself stored in the kernel's paged memory. Thus there is effectively a 2-level tree, allowing applications to have sparse memory layout without wasting lots of space on unused page table entries. The VAX MMU is notable for lacking an accessed bit. OSes which implement paging must find some way to emulate the accessed bit if they are to operate efficiently. Typically, the OS will periodically unmap pages so that page-not-present faults can be used to let the OS set an accessed bit.

ARM

ARM architecture based application processors implement an MMU defined by ARM's Virtual Memory System Architecture. The current architecture defines PTEs for describing 4KiB and 64KiB pages, 1MiB sections and 16MiB super-sections; legacy versions also defined a 1KiB tiny page.

TLB updates are performed automatically by page-table walking hardware.

PTEs include read/write access permission based on privilege, cacheability information, an NX bit, and a non-secure bit

IBM System/370 and Successors

The IBM System/370 have had an MMU since early 1970s, it was initially known as *DAT box*. It has the unusual feature of storing accessed and dirty bits outside of the page table. They refer to physical memory rather than virtual memory. They are accessed by special-purpose instructions. This reduces overhead for the OS, which would otherwise need to propagate accessed and dirty bits from the page tables to a more physically-oriented data structure. This makes OS-level virtualization easier. These features have been inherited by succeeding mainframe architectures, up to the current z/Architecture.

DEC Alpha

The DEC Alpha processor divides memory into 8192-byte pages. After a TLB miss, low-level firmware machine code (here called PALcode) walks a 3-level tree-structured page table. Addresses are broken down as follows: 21 bits unused, 10 bits to index the root level of the tree, 10 bits to index the middle level of the tree, 10 bits to index the leaf level of the tree, and 13 bits that pass through to the physical address without modification. Full read/write/execute permission bits are supported.

MIPS

The MIPS architecture supports 1 to 64 entries TLB. The number of TLB entries is configurable at CPU configuration before synthesis. TLBs are dual. Each TLB maps a virtual page number (VPN2) to either one of two page frame numbers (PFN0 or PFN1), depending on the least significant bit of the virtual address that is not part of the page mask. This bit and the page mask bits, are not stored in the VPN2. Page size is configurable per TLB entry and can be any value from 1 KiB to 256 MiB, in multiples of 4. Each PFN in a TLB entry has a caching attribute, dirty and valid status. A VPN2 has a global status or an OS assigned ID which participates in the virtual address TLB match. A PFN stores the physical address without the page mask bits.

A TLB Refill exception is generated when there are no entries in the TLB that match the mapped virtual address. A TLB Invalid exception is generated when there is a match but the entry is marked invalid. A TLB Modified exception is generated when there is a match but the dirty status is not set. If a TLB exception occurs when processing a TLB exception, a double fault TLB exception, it is dispatched to its own exception handler.

MIPS32 and MIPS32r2 support 32 bits of virtual address space and up to 36 bits of physical address space.

MIPS64 supports up to 64 bits of virtual address space and up to 59 bits of physical address space.

Sun 1

The original Sun 1 was a single-board computer built around the Motorola 68000 microprocessor and introduced in 1982. It included the original Sun 1 Memory Management Unit, that provided address translation, memory protection, memory sharing and memory allocation for multiple processes running on the CPU. All access of the CPU to private on-board RAM, external Multibus memory, on-board I/O and the Multibus I/O ran through the MMU where they were translated and protected in uniform fashion. The MMU was implemented in hardware on the CPU board.

The MMU consisted of a context register, a segment map and a page map. Virtual addresses from the CPU were translated into intermediate addresses by the segment map, which in turn were translated into physical addresses by the page map. The page size was 2 KiB and the segment size was 32 KiB which gave 16 pages per segment. Up to 16 contexts could be mapped concurrently. The maximum logical address space for a context was 1024 pages or 2 MiB. The maximum physical address that could be mapped simultaneously was also 2 MiB.

The context register was important in a multitasking operating system because it allowed the CPU to switch between processes without reloading all the translation state information. The 4-bit context register could switch between 16 sections of the segment map under supervisor control which allowed 16 contexts to be mapped concurrently. Each context had its own virtual address space. Sharing of virtual address space and inter-context communications could be provided by writing the same values in to the segment or page maps of different contexts. Additional contexts could be handled by treating the segment map as a context cache and replacing out-of-date contexts on a least-recently-used basis.

The context register made no distinction between user and supervisor states; interrupts and traps did not switch contexts which required that all valid interrupt vectors always be mapped in page 0 of context, as well as the valid Supervisor Stack.

Power PC

In PowerPC G1, G2, G3, and G4, pages are normally 4 KiB. After a TLB miss, the standard PowerPC MMU begins two simultaneous lookups. One lookup attempts to match the address with one of 4 or 8 Data Block Address Translation (DBAT) registers, or 4 or 8 Instruction Block Address Translation registers (IBAT) as appropriate. The BAT registers can map linear chunks of memory as large as 256 MiB, and are normally used by an OS to map large portions of the address space for the OS kernel's own use. If the BAT lookup succeeds, the other lookup is halted and ignored.

The other lookup, not directly supported by all processors in this family, is via a so-called "inverted page table" which acts as a hashed off-chip extension of the TLB. First, the top 4 bits of the address are used to select one of 16 segment registers. 24 bits from the segment register replace those 4 bits, producing a 52-bit address. The use of segment registers allows multiple processes to share the same hash table. The 52-bit address is hashed, then used as an index into the off-chip table. There, a group of 8 page table entries is scanned for one that matches. If none match due to excessive hash collisions, the processor tries again with a slightly different hash function. If this too fails, the CPU traps into the OS (with MMU disabled) so that the problem may be resolved. The OS needs to discard an entry from the hash table to make space for a new entry. The OS may generate the new entry from a more-normal tree-like page table or from per-mapping data structures which are likely to be slower and more space-efficient. Support for no-execute control is in the segment registers, leading to 256-MiB granularity.

A major problem with this design is poor cache locality caused by the hash function. Tree-based designs avoid this by placing the page table entries for adjacent pages in adjacent locations. An operating system running on the PowerPC may minimize the size of the hash table to reduce this problem.

It is also somewhat slow to remove the page table entries of a process; the OS may avoid reusing segment values to delay facing this or it may elect to suffer the waste of memory associated with per-process hash tables. G1 chips do not search for page table entries, but they do generate the hash with the expectation that an OS will search the standard hash table via software. The OS can write to the TLB. G2, G3, and early G4 chips use hardware to search the hash table. The latest chips allow the OS to choose either method. On chips that make this optional or do not support it at all, the OS may choose to use a tree-based page table exclusively.

x86

The x86 architecture has evolved over a long time while maintaining full software compatibility even for OS code. Thus the MMU is extremely complex, with many different possible operating modes. Normal operation of the traditional 80386 CPU and its successors is described here.

The CPU primarily divides memory into 4 KiB pages. Segment registers, fundamental to the older 8088 and 80286 MMU designs, are avoided as much as possible by modern OSes. There is one major exception to this: access to thread-specific data for applications or CPU-specific data for OS kernels, which is done with explicit use of the FS and GS segment registers. All memory access involves a segment register, chosen according to the code being executed. The segment register acts as an index into a table, which provides an offset to be added to the virtual address. Except when using FS or GS as described above, the OS ensures that the offset will be zero. After the offset is added, the address is masked to be no larger than 32 bits.

The result may be looked up via a tree-structured page table, with the bits of the address being split as follows: 10 bits for the root of the tree, 10 bits for the leaves of the tree, and the 12 lowest bits being directly copied to the result.

Minor revisions of the MMU introduced with the Pentium have allowed very large 2 MiB or 4 MiB pages by skipping the bottom level of the tree. Minor revisions of the MMU introduced with the Pentium Pro have allowed 36-bit physical addresses with the Physical Address Extension (PAE) feature and have allowed specification of cacheability by looking up a few high bits in a small on-CPU table.

No-execute support was originally only provided on a per-segment basis, making it very awkward to use. More recent x86 chips provide a per-page no-execute bit in the PAE mode. PaX is one way to emulate per-page non-execute support via the segments, with a performance loss and halving the available address space.

x86-64

x86-64 is a 64-bit extension of x86, that uses the long mode. In long mode, all segment offsets are ignored, except the FS and GS segments. When used with 4 KiB pages, the page table tree has four levels, instead of three. The virtual addresses are divided up as follows: 16 bits unused, 9 bits each for 4 tree levels (total: 36 bits), and the 12 lowest bits unmodified. With 2 MiB pages there are only three levels to the page table for a total of 27 bits used in paging and 21 bits of offset. Some newer CPUs also support a 1 GiB page with two levels of paging and 30 bits of offset. CPUID can be used to determine if 1 GiB pages are supported. In all three cases, the 16 highest bits are required to be equal to 48th bit, or in the other words, the low 48 bits are sign extended to the higher bits. This is done to allow a future expansion of the addressable range, without compromising backwards compatibility.

In the all levels of the page table, the highest bit is a per-page no-execute bit, used to mark pages as data to avoid stack-smashing buffer overflow attacks. It has no effect unless the NXE bit in the EFER is set, which not all legacy operating systems use.

Unisys MCP Systems (Burroughs B5000)

Tanenbaum et al., recently stated that the B5000 (and descendant systems) have no MMU. To understand the functionality provided by an MMU, it is instructive to study a counter example of a system that achieves this functionality by other means.

The B5000 was the first commercial system to support virtual memory after the Atlas.

It provides the two functions of an MMU in different ways. Firstly, the mapping of virtual memory addresses. Instead of needing an MMU, the MCP systems are descriptor based. Each allocated memory block is given a master descriptor with the properties of the block, ie., the size, address, and whether present in memory. When a request is made to access the block for reading or writing, the hardware checks its presence via the presence bit (pbit) in the descriptor.

A pbit of 1 indicates the presence of the block. In this case the block can be accessed via the physical address in the descriptor.

If the pbit is zero, an interrupt is generated for the MCP (operating system) to make the block present. If the address field is zero, this is the first access to this block and it is allocated (an init pbit). If the address field is non-zero, it is a disk address of the block, which has previously been rolled out, so the block is fetched from disk and the pbit is set to 1 and the physical memory address updated to point to the block in memory (another pbit).

This makes descriptors equivalent to a page-table entry in an MMU system. System performance can be monitored through the number of pbits. Init pbits indicate initial allocations, but a high level of other pbits indicate that the system may be thrashing.

Note that all memory allocation is therefore completely automatic (one of the features of modern systems) and there is no way to allocate blocks other than this mechanism.

There are no such calls as malloc or dealloc, since memory blocks are also automatically discarded. The scheme is also lazy, since a block will not be allocated until it is actually referenced. When memory is near full, the MCP examines the working set, trying compaction (since the system is segmented, not paged), deallocating read-only segments (such as code-segments which can be restored from their original copy), and as a last resort, rolling dirty data scgments out to disk.

Secondly, protection. Since all accesses are via the descriptor the hardware can check all accesses are within bounds, and in the case of a write that the process has write permission.

The MCP system is inherently secure and thus has no need of an MMU to provide this level of memory protection. Descriptors are read only to user processes and may only be updated by the system (hardware or MCP). (Descriptors have a tag of 5 and odd-tagged words are read only – code words have a tag of 3.)

Blocks can be shared between processes via copy descriptors in the process stack – thus some processes may have write permission, whereas others not. A code segment is read only, thus reentrant and shared between processes. Copy descriptors contain a 20-bit address field giving index of the master descriptor in the master descriptor array. This also implements a very efficient and secure IPC mechanism. Blocks can easily be relocated since only the master descriptor needs update when a block's status changes.

The only other aspect is performance – do MMU-or non-MMU-based systems provide better performance? MCP systems may be implemented on top of standard hardware that does have an MMU (eg., a standard PC). Even if the system implementation uses the MMU in some way, this will not be at all visible at the MCP level.

Memory Segmentation

In computing, memory segmentation is one of the most common ways to achieve memory protection; another common one is paging. In a computer system using segmentation, an instruction operand that refers to a memory location includes a value that identifies a segment and an offset within that segment.

A segment has a set of permissions, and a length, associated with it. If the currently running process is allowed by the permissions to make the type of reference to memory that it is attempting to make, and the offset within the segment is within the range specified by the length of the segment, the reference is permitted; otherwise, a hardware exception is raised.

In addition to the set of permissions and length, a segment also has associated with it information indicating where the segment is located in memory. It may also have a flag indicating whether the segment is present in main memory or not; if the segment is not present in main memory, an exception is raised, and the operating system will read the segment into memory from secondary storage.

The information indicating where the segment is located in memory might be the address of the first location in the segment, or might be the address of a page table for the segment, if the segmentation is implemented with paging.

In the first case, if a reference to a location within a segment is made, the offset within the segment will be added to address of the first location in the segment to give the address in memory of the referred-to item; in the second case, the offset of the segment is translated to a memory address using the page table.

In most systems in which a segment doesn't have a page table associated with it, the address of the first location in the segment is an address in main memory; in those systems, no paging is done. In the Intel 80386 and later, that address can either be an address in main memory, if paging is not enabled, or an address in a paged "linear" address space, if paging is enabled.

A memory management unit (MMU) is responsible for translating a segment and offset within that segment into a memory address, and for performing checks to make sure the translation can be done and that the reference to that segment and offset is permitted.

This usage should not be confused with that of the memory segments used by early x86 processors such as the Intel 8086 and Intel 8088, as they did not provide any protection (any program could access any segment with no restrictions, and a segment consisted of only a starting location and a fixed length of 64 KiB); segmentation in the Intel 80286 and later provid x86 memory segmentation ed protection.

x86 memory segmentation refers to the implementation of memory segmentation on the x86 architecture. Memory is divided into portions that may be addressed by a single index register without changing a 16-bit segment selector. In real mode or V86 mode, a segment is always 64 kilobytes in size (using 16-bit offsets). In protected mode, a segment can have variable length.

Real Mode

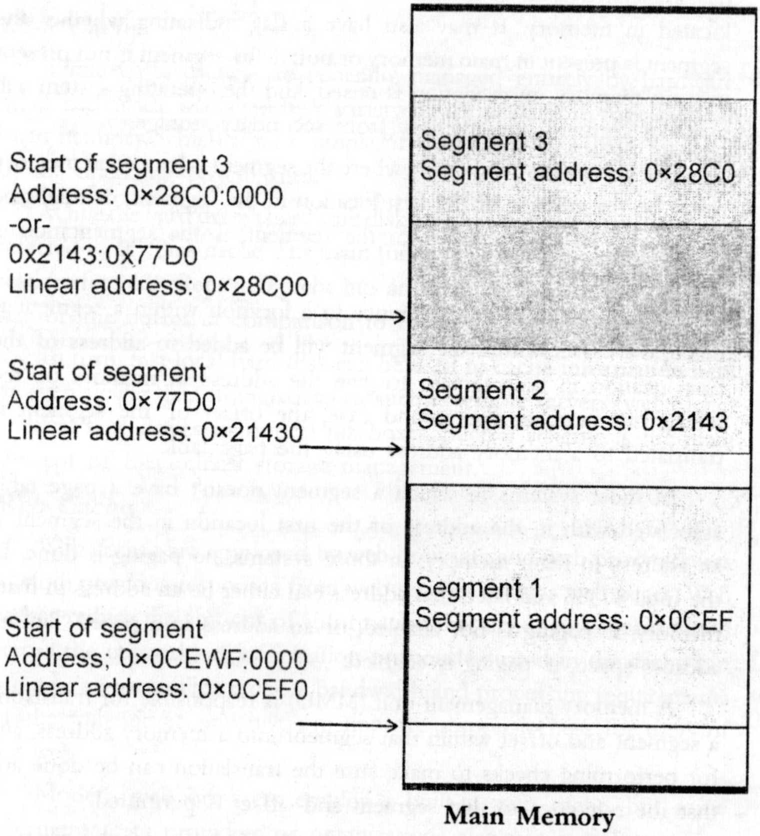

Three segments in real mode memory. Note the overlap between segment 2 and segment 3; the bytes in the turquoise area can be used from both segment selectors.

In 16-bit real mode, enabling applications to make use of multiple memory segments (in order to access more memory than available in any one 64K-segment) was quite complex, but was viewed as a necessary evil for all but the smallest tools (which could do with less memory). The root of the problem was that no appropriate address-arithmetic instructions suitable for flat addressing of the entire memory range were available. Flat addressing is possible by applying multiple instructions, which however leads to slower programs. In real mode, the 16-bit segment selector was interpreted as the most significant 16 bits of a linear 20-bit address, with the remaining four bits being all zeros. The segment selector is always added with a 16-bit offset to yield a linear address. For instance, the segmented address 6EFh:1234h has a segment selector of 6EFh, which corresponds to the 20-bit linear address 6EF0h. To this we add the offset, yielding the linear address 6EF0h + 1234h = 8124h (cf. hexadecimal).

A single linear address can be mapped to many segmented addresses. For instance, the linear address above (8124h) can have the segmented addresses 6EFh:1234h, 812h:4h and 0h:8124h (and many more). This could be confusing to programmers accustomed to unique addressing schemes. The effective 20-bit address space of real mode limited the addressable memory to 2^{20} bytes, or 1,048,576 bytes.

Protected Mode

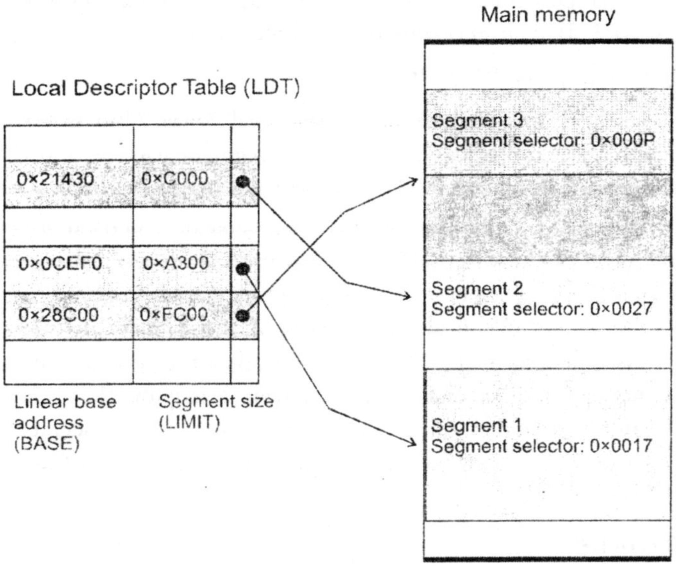

Three segments in protected mode memory (click on image to enlarge), with the local descriptor table.

In protected mode, segmentation is used as a virtual memory mechanism, providing memory isolation and contiguous addressing of non-contiguous physical memory.

On the 386 and later, programs issue logical (46-bit) addresses which go through the segmentation unit to be checked and translated into linear 32-bit addresses, before being sent to the paging unit (if enabled) which ultimately translates them into physical addresses (which are also 32-bit on the 386, but can be larger on more modern processors which support Physical Address Extension).

Detailed Segmentation Unit Workflow

A logical address consists of a 16-bit segment selector (supplying 13+1 address bits) and a 32-bit offset (16-bit on the 286). The segment selector must be located in one of the segment registers. That selector consists of a 2-bit Requested Privilege Level (RPL) where the lowest number is the highest privilege level, a 1-bit Table Indicator (TI), and a 13-bit index.

The processor accesses the 64-bit segment descriptor structure in the Global Descriptor Table if TI is 0 or in the Local Descriptor Table if TI is 1. It then performs the privilege check:

DPL < max (CPL,RPL)

where CPL is the current privilege level (lower 2 bits in CS), RPL is the requested privilege level from the segment selector, and DPL is the descriptor privilege level of the segment (found in the descriptor).

If the inequality is true, the processor generates a general protection fault (GP). Otherwise, address translation continues. This privilege check is done only when the segment register is loaded because segment descriptors are cached in hidden parts of the segment registers. The processor then takes the 32-bit or 16-bit offset and compares it against the segment limit specified in the segment descriptor. If it is larger, a GP fault is generated. Otherwise, the processor adds the segment base (32-bit or 24-bit, specified in descriptor) to the offset and this creates a linear address.

Practices

Logical addresses can be explicitly specified in x86 assembler language, e.g. (AT&T syntax):

movl $42, %fs:(%eax); Equivalent to M[fs:eax]<-42) in RTL

Usually, however, implied segments are used. All instruction fetches come from the code segment in the CS register. Most memory references come from data segment in the DS register. Processor stack references, either implicitly (e.g. push and pop instructions) or explicitly (memory accesses using the ESP or (E)BP registers) use the stack segment in the

SS register. Finally, string instructions (e.g. stos, movs) also use the extra segment ES.

Segmentation cannot be turned off on x86 processors, so many operating systems use a flat memory model to make segmentation unnoticeable to programs. For instance, the Linux kernel sets up only 4 segments:

* __KERNEL_CS (Kernel code segment, base=0, limit=4GB, DPL=0)
* __KERNEL_DS (Kernel data segment, base=0, limit=4GB, DPL=0)
* __USER_CS (User code segment, base=0, limit=4GB, DPL=3)
* __USER_DS (User data segment, base=0, limit=4GB, DPL=3)

Since the base is set to 0 in all cases and the limit 4 GiB, the segmentation unit does not affect the addresses the program issues before they arrive at the paging unit.

Segments can be defined to be either code, data, or system segments. Additional permission bits are present to make segments read only, read/write, execute, etc.

Note that code may always modify all segment registers *except* CS (the code segment). This is because the current privilege level (CPL) of the processor is stored in the lower 2 bits of the CS register. The only way to raise the processor privilege level (and reload CS) is through the lcall (far call) and int (interrupt) instructions. Similarly, the only way to lower the privilege level (and reload CS) is through lret (far return) and iret (interrupt return).

Memory Model (Computing)

In computing, a Memory model describes how threads interact through memory, or more generally specify what assumptions the compiler is allowed to make when generating code for segmented memory or paged memory platforms.

History and Significance

The significance of a memory model is most easily explained by referring to languages that have no memory model. If a language has no memory model then this prevents a compiler from performing many important optimizations. Even simple compiler optimizations like Loop fusion move statements in the program, and therefore influence the order of read and write operations of *potentially shared* variables. If the ordering of reads and writes changes, this can cause Race conditions. Without a memory model, a compiler is therefore not allowed to apply such optimizations to multi-threaded programs in general, or only in special cases.

Modern programming languages like Java therefore implement a memory model. The memory model specifies synchronization barriers that are established via special, well-defined synchronization operations such as acquiring a lock by entering a synchronized block or method. The memory model stipulates that changes to the values of shared variables only need to be made visible to other threads when such a synchronization barrier is reached. Moreover, the entire notion of a Race condition is entirely defined over the order of operations with respect to these memory barriers.

These semantics then gives optimizing compilers a higher degree of freedom when applying optimizations: the compiler needs to make sure only that the values of (potentially shared) variables at synchronization barriers are guaranteed to be the same in both the optimized and unoptimized code. In particular, reordering statements in a block of code that contains no synchronization barrier can be safe. Most research in the area of memory models revolves around the questions of (1) designing a memory model that allows a maximal degree of freedom for compiler optimizations while still giving sufficient guarantees about race-free programs, but more importantly even programs that do contain data races, and (2) proving compiler optimizations correct with respect to such a memory model.

The Java memory model was the first attempt to provide a comprehensive threading memory model for a popular programming language. Since then, the need for a memory model has been more widely accepted, and efforts are underway to provide such semantics for languages like C++0x, the next version of C++

Memory Ordering

Memory ordering is a group of properties of the modern microprocessors, characterising their possibilities in memory operations reordering. It is a type of out-of-order execution. Memory reordering can be used to fully utilizate different cache and memory banks.

On most modern uniprocessors memory operations are not executed in the order specified by the program code. But from programer's point of view, all operation are seen as executed in the order, all inconsistencies are hided by hardware.

In SMP Microprocessor Systems

There are Several Memory-Consistency Models for SMP Systems

- sequential consistency (All reads and all writes are in-order)
- relaxed consistency (Some types of reordering are allowed)
- Loads can be reordered after Loads (for better working of cache coherency, better scaling)
- Loads can be reordered after Stores
- Stores can be reordered after Stores
- Stores can be reordered after Loads
- weak consistency (Reads and Writes are arbitrary reordered, limited only by explicit memory barriers).

On some CPUs atomic operations can be reordered with Loads and Stores.

Also, There can be

- Dependent Loads Reordered is unique for Alpha. This processor can fetch data before it fetches pointer to this data. It make cache hardware simpler and faster, but leads to the requirement of memory barriers for readers and writers.
- Incoherent Instruction cache pipeline (which prevent self-modifying code to be executed without special ICache flush/reload instructions).

Memory Barrier

Memory barrier, also known as membar or memory fence or fence instruction, is a class of instructions which cause a central processing unit (CPU) to enforce an ordering constraint on memory operations issued before and after the barrier instruction.

CPUs employ performance optimizations that can result in out-of-order execution, including memory load and store operations. Memory operation reordering normally goes unnoticed within a single thread of execution, but causes unpredictable behaviour in concurrent programs and device drivers unless carefully controlled. The exact nature of an ordering constraint is hardware dependent, and defined by the architecture's memory ordering model. Some architectures provide multiple barriers for enforcing different ordering constraints.

Memory barriers are typically used when implementing low-level machine code that operates on memory shared by multiple devices. Such code includes synchronization primitives and lock-free data structures on multiprocessor systems, and device drivers that communicate with computer hardware.

An Illustrative Example

When a program runs on a single CPU, the hardware performs the necessary bookkeeping to ensure that programs execute as if all memory operations were performed in program order, hence memory barriers are not necessary. However, when the memory is shared with multiple devices, such as other CPUs in a multiprocessor system, or memory mapped peripherals, out-of-order access may affect program behaviour. For example a second CPU may see memory changes made by the first CPU in a sequence which differs from program order.

The following two processor program gives a concrete example of how such out-of-order execution can affect program behaviour:

Initially, memory locations x and f both hold the value 0. The program running on processor #1 loops while the value of f is zero, then it prints the value of x. The program running on processor #2 stores the value 42 into x and then stores the value 1 into f. Pseudo code for the two program fragments is shown below. The steps of the program correspond to individual processor instructions.

```
Processor #1:

loop:
load the value in location f, if it is 0 goto loop
print the value in location x
Processor #2:
store the value 42 into location x
store the value 1 into location f
```

You might expect the print statement to always print the number

"42"; however, if processor #2's store operations are executed out-of-order, it is possible that f would be updated *before* x, and the print statement might print "0". For most programs this situation is not acceptable. A memory barrier can be inserted before processor #2's assignment to f to ensure that the new value of x was visible to other processors at or prior to the change in the value of f.

Low-Level Architecture-Specific Primitives

Memory barriers are low-level primitives which are part of the definition of an architecture's memory model. Like instruction sets, memory models vary considerably between architectures, so it is not appropriate to generalize about memory barrier behaviour. The conventional wisdom is that using memory barriers correctly requires careful study of the architecture manuals for the hardware one is programming. That said, the following paragraph offers a glimpse of some memory barriers which exist in contemporary products.

Some architectures, including the ubiquitous x86/x64, provide several memory barrier instructions including an instruction sometimes called "full fence". A full fence ensures that all load and store operations prior to the fence will have been committed prior to any loads and stores issued following the fence. Other architectures, such as the Itanium, provide separate "acquire" and "release" memory barriers which address the visibility of read-after-write operations from the point of view of a reader (sink) or writer (source) respectively. Some architectures provide separate memory barriers to control ordering between different combinations of system memory and I/O memory. When more than one memory barrier instruction is available it is important to consider that the cost of different instructions may vary considerably.

Multithreaded Programming and Memory Visibility

Multithreaded programs usually use synchronization primitives provided by a high-level programming environment, such as Java, or an API such as POSIX Threads or Win32. Primitives such as mutexes and semaphores are provided to synchronize access to resources from parallel threads of execution. These primitives are usually implemented with the memory barriers required to provide the expected memory visibility semantics. In such environments explicit use of memory barriers is not generally necessary.

Each API or programming environment in principle has its own high-level memory model that defines its memory visibility semantics. Although programmers do not usually need to use memory barriers in such high level environments, it is important to understand their memory visibility semantics, to the extent possible. Such understanding is not necessarily easy to achieve because memory visibility semantics are not always consistently specified or documented.

Just as programming language semantics are defined at a different level of abstraction than machine language opcodes, a programming environment's memory model is defined at a different level of abstraction than that of a hardware memory model. It is important to understand this distinction and realize that there is not always a simple mapping between low-level hardware memory barrier semantics and the high-level memory visibility semantics of a particular programming environment. As a result, a particular platform's implementation of (say) POSIX Threads may employ stronger barriers than required by the specification. Programs which take advantage of memory visibility as-implemented rather than as-specified may not be portable.

Out-of-Order Execution Versus Compiler Reordering Optimizations

Memory barrier instructions only address reordering effects at the hardware level. Compilers may also reorder instructions as part of the program optimization process. Although the effects on parallel program behaviour can be similar in both cases, in general it is necessary to take separate measures to inhibit compiler reordering optimizations for data that may be shared by multiple threads of execution. Note that such measures are usually only necessary for data which is not protected by synchronization primitives such as those discuss.

In C and C++, the *volatile* keyword was intended to allow C and C++ programs to directly access memory-mapped I/O. Memory-mapped I/O generally requires that the reads and writes specified in source code happen in the exact order specified in source code with no omissions. Omissions or reorderings of reads and writes by the compiler would break the communication between the program and the device accessed by memory-mapped I/O. A C or C++ compiler may not reorder reads and writes to volatile memory locations, nor may it omit a read or write to a volatile memory location, allowing a pointer to volatile memory to be used for memory-mapped I/O.

The C and C++ standards do not address multiple threads (or multiple processors), and as such, the usefulness of volatile depends on the compiler and hardware. Although volatile guarantees that the reads and writes will happen in the exact order specified in the source code, the compiler may generate code which reorders a volatile read or write with non-volatile reads or writes, thus limiting its usefulness as an inter-thread flag or mutex. Preventing such is compiler specific, but some compilers, like gcc, will not reorder operation around inline assembly code with volatile and "memory" tags, like in: asm volatile ("" : : : "memory");. Moreover, you are not guaranteed that volatile reads and writes will be seen in the same order by other processors due to caching, cache_coherence protocol and relaxed memory ordering, meaning volatile variables alone may not even work as inter-thread flags or mutexes.

Some languages and compilers may provide sufficient facilities to implement functions which address both the compiler reordering and machine reordering issues. In Java version 1.5 (also known as version 5), the *volatile* keyword is now guaranteed to prevent certain hardware *and* compiler re-orderings, as part of the new Java Memory Model. The proposed C++ memory model does not use *volatile*, instead C++0x will include special atomic types and operations with semantics similar to those of *volatile* in the Java Memory Model.

Non-Blocking Synchronization

In computer science, non-blocking synchronization ensures that threads competing for a shared resource do not have their execution indefinitely postponed by mutual exclusion. A non-blocking algorithm is lock-free if there is guaranteed system-wide progress; wait-free if there is also guaranteed per-thread progress.

Literature up to the turn of the 21st century used "non-blocking" synonymously with lock-free. However, since 2003, the term has been weakened to only prevent progress-blocking interactions with a preemptive scheduler. In modern usage, therefore, an algorithm is *non-blocking* if the suspension of one or more threads will not stop the potential progress of the remaining threads. They are designed to avoid requiring a critical section. Often, these algorithms allow multiple processes to make progress on a problem without ever blocking each other. For some operations, these algorithms provide an alternative to locking mechanisms.

Motivation

The traditional approach to multi-threaded programming is to use locks to synchronize access to shared resources. Synchronization primitives such as mutexes, semaphores, and critical sections are all mechanisms by which a programmer can ensure that certain sections of code do not execute concurrently if doing so would corrupt shared memory structures. If one thread attempts to acquire a lock that is already held by another thread, the thread will block until the lock is free.

Blocking a thread is undesirable for many reasons. An obvious reason is that while the thread is blocked, it cannot accomplish anything. If the blocked thread is performing a high-priority or real-time task, it is highly undesirable to halt its progress. Other problems are less obvious. Certain interactions between locks can lead to error conditions such as deadlock, livelock, and priority inversion. Using locks also involves a trade-off between coarse-grained locking, which can significantly reduce opportunities for parallelism, and fine-grained locking, which requires more careful design, increases overhead and is more prone to bugs.

Non-blocking algorithms are also safe for use in interrupt handlers: even though the preempted thread cannot be resumed, progress is still possible without it. In contrast, global data structures protected by mutual exclusion cannot safely be accessed in a handler, as the preempted thread may be the one holding the lock.

Non-blocking synchronization has the potential to prevent priority inversion, as no thread is forced to wait for a suspended thread to complete. However, as livelock is still possible, threads have to wait when they encounter contention; hence, priority inversion is still possible depending upon the contention management system used. Lock-free algorithms, below, avoid priority inversion.

Implementation

With few exceptions, non-blocking algorithms use atomic read-modify-write primitives that the hardware must provide, the most notable of which is compare and swap (CAS). Critical sections are almost always implemented using standard interfaces over these primitives. Until recently, all non-blocking algorithms had to be written "natively" with the underlying primitives to achieve acceptable performance. However, the emerging field of software transactional memory promises standard abstractions for writing efficient non-blocking code.

Much research has also been done in providing basic data structures such as stacks, queues, sets, and hash tables. These allow programs to easily exchange data between threads asynchronously.

Additionally, some data structures are weak enough to be implemented without special atomic primitives. These exceptions include:

- single-reader single-writer ring buffer FIFO
- Read-copy-update with a single writer and any number of readers. (The readers are wait-free; the writer is usually wait-free, until it needs to reclaim memory).
- Dekker's algorithm for two threads is lock-free but not wait-free.

Wait-Freedom

Wait-freedom is the strongest non-blocking guarantee of progress, combining guaranteed system-wide throughput with starvation-freedom. An algorithm is wait-free if every operation has a bound on the number of steps the algorithm will take before the operation completes.

It was shown in the 1980s that all algorithms can be implemented wait-free, and many transformations from serial code, called *universal constructions*, have been demonstrated. However, the resulting performance does not in general match even naive blocking designs. It has also been shown that the widely-available atomic *conditional* primitives, CAS and LL/SC, cannot provide starvation-free implementations of many common data structures without memory costs growing linearly in the number of threads. Wait-free algorithms are therefore rare, both in research and in practice.

Lock-Freedom

Lock-freedom allows individual threads to starve but guarantees system-wide throughput. An algorithm is lock-free if every step taken achieves global progress (for some sensible definition of progress). All wait-free algorithms are lock-free.

In general, a lock-free algorithm can run in four phases: completing one's own operation, assisting an obstructing operation, aborting an obstructing operation, and waiting. Completing one's own operation is complicated by the possibility of concurrent assistance and abortion, but is invariably the fastest path to completion. The decision about when to assist, abort or wait when an obstruction is met is the responsibility of a *contention manager.* This may be very simple (assist higher priority operations, abort lower priority ones), or may be more optimized to achieve better throughput, or lower the latency of prioritized operations.

Correct concurrent assistance is typically the most complex part of a lock-free algorithm, and often very costly to execute: not only does the assisting thread slow down, but thanks to the mechanics of shared memory, the thread being assisted will be slowed, too, if it is still running.

Obstruction-Freedom

Obstruction-freedom is possibly the weakest natural non-blocking progress guarantee. An algorithm is obstruction-free if at any point, a single thread executed in isolation (i.e., with all obstructing threads suspended) for a bounded number of steps will complete its operation. All lock-free algorithms are obstruction-free.

Obstruction-freedom demands only that any partially-completed operation can be aborted and the changes made rolled back. Dropping concurrent assistance can often result in much simpler algorithms that are easier to validate. Preventing the system from continually live-locking is the task of a contention manager.

Obstruction-Freedom is also Called Optimistic Concurrency Control

Some obstruction-free algorithms use a pair of "consistency markers" in the data structure. Processes reading the data structure first read one consistency marker, then read the relevant data into an internal buffer, then read the other marker, and then compare the markers. When comparing the two markers, occasionally a process will notice they are different, indicating "inconsistent data". That happens when the read was interrupted by some other process updating the data structure. In that case the process discards the data in the internal buffer and tries again. When comparing the two markers, typically both markers will be identical, indicating that the data is consistent.

Recent research has yielded a promising practical contention manager, whimsically named *Polka,* combining exponential backoff with "priority accumulation". As an operation progresses, it gains "priority"; when an operation is obstructed by another with higher priority, it will back off, with backoff intervals increasing exponentially. Each backoff increases the operation's priority; only when its priority is greater than that of its obstructor will it abort it. Aborted operations retain their former priority, giving their next attempt a greater chance of success.

Polka achieves good throughput in benchmarks because it minimizes both wasted effort, by prioritizing long transactions, and memory interconnect contention, using exponential backoff. This can inform other parallel algorithms, such as lock-free ones, to achieve greater throughput in the common case.

Cache

In computer science, a cache (pronounced/k*ʃ*/) is a collection of data duplicating original values stored elsewhere or computed earlier, where the original data is expensive to fetch (owing to longer access time) or to compute, compared to the cost of reading the cache. In other words, a cache is a temporary storage area where frequently accessed data can be stored for rapid access. Once the data is stored in the cache, it can be used in the future by accessing the cached copy rather than re-fetching or recomputing the original data.

A cache has proven to be extremely effective in many areas of computing because access patterns in typical computer applications have locality of reference. There are several kinds of locality, but this article primarily deals with data that are accessed close together in time (temporal locality). The data might or might not be located physically close to each other (spatial locality).

History

Use of the word *cache* in the computer context originated in 1967 during preparation of an article for publication in the IBM Systems Journal. The paper concerned an exciting memory improvement in Model 85, a latecomer in the IBM System/360 product line. The Journal editor, Lyle R. Johnson, pleaded for a more descriptive term than *high-speed buffer*. When none was forthcoming, he suggested the noun *cache*, meaning a safekeeping or storage place. The paper was published in early 1968, the authors were honoured by IBM, their work was widely welcomed and subsequently improved upon, and *cache* soon became standard usage in computer literature.

Operation

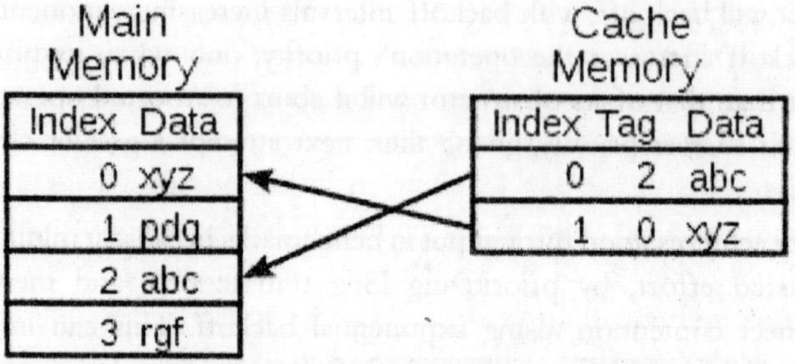

Diagram of a CPU Memory Cache

A cache is a block of memory for temporary storage of data likely to be used again. CPUs and hard drives frequently use a cache, as do web browsers and web servers.

A cache is made up of a pool of entries. Each entry has a datum (a nugget of data) which is a copy of the datum in some backing store. Each entry also has a tag, which specifies the identity of the datum in the backing store of which the entry is a copy.

When the cache client (a CPU, web browser, operating system) wishes to access a datum presumably in the backing store, it first checks the cache. If an entry can be found with a tag matching that of the desired datum, the datum in the entry is used instead. This situation is known as a cache hit. So, for example, a web browser program might check its local cache on disk to see if it has a local copy of the contents of a web page at a particular URL. In this example, the URL is the tag, and the contents of the web page is the datum. The percentage of accesses that result in cache hits is known as the hit rate or hit ratio of the cache.

The alternative situation, when the cache is consulted and found not to contain a datum with the desired tag, is known as a cache miss. The previously uncached datum fetched from the backing store during miss handling is usually copied into the cache, ready for the next access.

During a cache miss, the CPU usually ejects some other entry in order to make room for the previously uncached datum. The heuristic used to select the entry to eject is known as the replacement policy. One popular replacement policy, least recently used (LRU), replaces the least recently used entry. More efficient caches compute use frequency against the size of the stored contents, as well as the latencies and throughputs for both the cache and the backing store. While this works well for larger amounts of data, long latencies and slow throughputs, such as experienced with a hard drive and the Internet, it is not efficient for use with a CPU cache.

When a datum is written to the cache, it must at some point be written to the backing store as well. The timing of this write is controlled by what is known as the write policy.

In a write-through cache, every write to the cache causes a synchronous write to the backing store.

Alternatively, in a write-back (or write-behind) cache, writes are not immediately mirrored to the store. Instead, the cache tracks which of its locations have been written over (these locations are marked dirty). The data in these locations is written back to the backing store when those data are evicted from the cache, an effect referred to as a lazy write. For this reason, a read miss in a write-back cache (which requires a block to be replaced by another) will often require two memory accesses to service: one to retrieve the needed datum, and one to write replaced data from the cache to the store.

Data write-back may be triggered by other policies as well. The client may make many changes to a datum in the cache, and then explicitly notify the cache to write back the datum.

No-write allocation is a cache policy where only processor reads are cached, thus avoiding the need for write-back or write-through when the old value of the datum was absent from the cache prior to the write.

The data in the backing store may be changed by entities other than the cache, in which case the copy in the cache may become out-of-date or stale. Alternatively, when the client updates the data in the cache, copies of that data in other caches will become stale. Communication protocols between the cache managers which keep the data consistent are known as coherency protocols.

Applications

CPU Cache

Small memories on or close to the CPU can be made faster than the much larger main memory. Most CPUs since the 1980s have used one or more caches, and modern high-end embedded, desktop and server microprocessors may have as many as half a dozen, each specialized for a specific function.

Disk Cache

While CPU caches are generally managed entirely by hardware, other caches are managed by a variety of software. The page cache in main memory, which is an example of disk cache, is usually managed by the operating system kernel.

While the hard drive's hardware disk buffer is sometimes misleadingly referred to as "disk cache", its main functions are write sequencing and read prefetching. Repeated cache hits are relatively rare, due to the small size of the buffer in comparison to HDD's capacity.

In turn, fast local hard disk can be used to cache information held on even slower data storage devices, such as remote servers (web cache) or local tape drives or optical jukeboxes. Such a scheme is the main concept of hierarchical storage management.

Web Cache

Web caches are employed by web browsers and web proxy servers to store previous responses from web servers, such as web pages. Web caches reduce the amount of information that needs to be transmitted across the network, as information previously stored in the cache can often be re-used. This reduces bandwidth and processing requirements of the web server, and helps to improve responsiveness for users of the web.

Modern web browsers employ a built-in web cache, but some internet service providers or organizations also use a caching proxy server, which is a web cache that is shared between all users of that network.

Another form of cache is P2P caching, where the files most sought for by peer-to-peer applications are stored in an ISP cache to accelerate P2P transfers.

Other Caches

The BIND DNS daemon caches a mapping of domain names to IP addresses, as does a resolver library.

Write-through operation is common when operating over unreliable networks (like an Ethernet LAN), because of the enormous complexity of the coherency protocol required between multiple write-back caches when communication is unreliable. For instance, web page caches and client-side network file system caches (like those in NFS or SMB) are typically read-only or write-through specifically to keep the network protocol simple and reliable.

Search engines also frequently make web pages they have indexed available from their cache. For example, Google provides a "Cached" link next to each search result. This is useful when web pages are temporarily inaccessible from a web server.

Another type of caching is storing computed results that will likely be needed again, or memoization. An example of this type of caching is ccache, a program that caches the output of the compilation to speed up the second-time compilation.

Database caching can substantially improve the throughput of database applications, for example in the processing of indexes, data dictionaries, and frequently used subsets of data.

The Difference Between Buffer and Cache

The terms are not mutually exclusive and the functions are frequently combined; however, there is a difference in intent. A buffer is a temporary memory location, that is traditionally used because CPU instructions cannot directly address data stored in peripheral devices. Thus, addressable memory is used as intermediate stage.

Additionally such a buffer may be feasible when a large block of data is assembled or disassembled (as required by a storage device), or when data may be delivered in a different order than that in which it is produced.

Also a whole buffer of data is usually transferred sequentially (for example to hard disk), so buffering itself sometimes increases transfer performance. These benefits are present even if the buffered data are written to the buffer once and read from the buffer once.

A cache also increases transfer performance. A part of the increase similarly comes from the possibility that multiple small transfers will combine into one large block. But the main performance gain occurs because there is a good chance that the same datum will be read from cache multiple times, or that written data will soon be read. A cache's sole purpose is to reduce accesses to the underlying slower storage.

Cache is also usually an abstraction layer that is designed to be invisible from the perspective of neighbouring layers.

Software Transactional Memory

In computer science, software transactional memory (STM) is a concurrency control mechanism analogous to database transactions for controlling access to shared memory in concurrent computing. It functions as an alternative to lock-based synchronization. A transaction in this context is a piece of code that executes a series of reads and writes to shared memory.

These reads and writes logically occur at a single instant in time; intermediate states are not visible to other (successful) transactions. The idea of providing hardware support for transactions originated in a 1986 paper and patent by Tom Knight. The idea was popularized by Maurice Herlihy and J. Eliot B. Moss. In 1995 Nir Shavit and Dan Touitou extended this idea to software-only transactional memory (STM). STM has recently been the focus of intense research and support for practical implementations is growing.

Performance

Unlike the locking techniques used in most modern multithreaded applications, STM is very optimistic: a thread completes modifications to shared memory without regard for what other threads might be doing, recording every read and write that it is performing in a log. Instead of placing the onus on the writer to make sure it does not adversely affect other operations in progress, it is placed on the reader, who after completing an entire transaction verifies that other threads have not concurrently made changes to memory that it accessed in the past.

This final operation, in which the changes of a transaction are validated and, if validation is successful, made permanent, is called a *commit.* A transaction may also *abort* at any time, causing all of its prior changes to be rolled back or undone. If a transaction cannot be committed due to conflicting changes, it is typically aborted and re-executed from the beginning until it succeeds.

The benefit of this optimistic approach is increased concurrency: no thread needs to wait for access to a resource, and different threads can safely and simultaneously modify disjoint parts of a data structure that would normally be protected under the same lock. Despite the overhead of retrying transactions that fail, in most realistic programs, conflicts arise rarely enough that there is an immense performance gain over lock-based protocols on large numbers of processors.

However, in practice STM systems also suffer a performance hit relative to fine-grained lock-based systems on small numbers of processors (1 to 4 depending on the application). This is due primarily to the overhead associated with maintaining the log and the time spent committing transactions. Even in this case performance is typically no worse than twice as slow. Advocates of STM believe this penalty is justified by the conceptual benefits of STM.

Theoretically (worst case behaviour) when there are n concurrent transactions running in the same time, there could be need of $O(n)$ memory and processor time consumption. Actual needs depends on implementation details (one can make transaction fail early enough to avoid overhead), but there will be also cases (although rare) where lock based algorithms have better theoretical computing time than software transactional memory.

Conceptual Advantages and Disadvantages

In addition to their performance benefits, STM greatly simplifies conceptual understanding of multithreaded programs and helps make programs more maintainable by working in harmony with existing high-level abstractions such as objects and modules. Lock-based programming has a number of well-known problems that frequently arise in practice:

- They require thinking about overlapping operations and partial operations in distantly separated and seemingly unrelated sections of code, a task which is very difficult and error-prone for programmers.
- They require programmers to adopt a locking policy to prevent deadlock, livelock, and other failures to make progress. Such policies are often informally enforced and fallible, and when these issues arise they are insidiously difficult to reproduce and debug.
- They can lead to priority inversion, a phenomenon where a high-priority thread is forced to wait on a low-priority thread holding exclusive access to a resource that it needs.

In contrast, the concept of a memory transaction is much simpler, because each transaction can be viewed in isolation as a single-threaded computation. Deadlock and livelock are either prevented entirely or handled by an external transaction manager; the programmer need hardly worry about it.

Priority inversion can still be an issue, but high-priority transactions can abort conflicting lower priority transactions that have not already committed. On the other hand, the need to abort failed transactions also places limitations on the behaviour of transactions: they cannot perform any operation that cannot be undone, including most I/O.

Such limitations are typically overcome in practice by creating buffers that queue up the irreversible operations and perform them at a later time outside of any transaction. In Haskell, this limitation is enforced at compile time by the type system.

Composable Operations

In 2005, Tim Harris, Simon Marlow, Simon Peyton Jones, and Maurice Herlihy described an STM system built on Concurrent Haskell that enables arbitrary atomic operations to be composed into larger atomic operations, a useful concept impossible with lock-based programming. To quote the authors:

Perhaps the most fundamental objection [...] is that *lock-based programs do not compose*: correct fragments may fail when combined. For example, consider a hash table with thread-safe insert and delete operations. Now suppose that we want to delete one item A from table t1, and insert it into table t2; but the intermediate state (in which neither table contains the item) must not be visible to other threads.

Unless the implementor of the hash table anticipates this need, there is simply no way to satisfy this requirement. [...] In short, operations that are individually correct (insert, delete) cannot be composed into larger correct operations.

With STM, this problem is simple to solve: simply wrapping two operations in a transaction makes the combined operation atomic. The only sticking point is that it's unclear to the caller, who is unaware of the implementation details of the component methods, when they should attempt to re-execute the transaction if it fails. In response, the authors proposed a retry command which uses the transaction log generated by the failed transaction to determine which memory cells it read, and automatically retries the transaction when one of these cells is modified, based on the logic that the transaction will not behave differently until at least one such value is changed.

The authors also proposed a mechanism for composition of *alternatives*, the orElse function. It runs one transaction and, if that transaction does a *retry*, runs a second one. If both retry, it tries them both again as soon as a relevant change is made. This facility, comparable to features such as the POSIX networking *select()* call, allows the caller to wait on any one of a number of events simultaneously. It also simplifies programming interfaces, for example by providing a simple mechanism to convert between blocking and nonblocking operations.

This scheme has been implemented in the Glasgow Haskell Compiler.

Transactional Locking

STM can be implemented as a lock-free algorithm or it can use locking. There are two types of locking schemes: In encounter-time locking (Ennals, Saha, and Harris), memory writes are done by first temporarily acquiring a lock for a given location, writing the value directly, and logging it in the undo log. Commit-time locking locks memory locations only during the commit phase.

A commit-time scheme implemented by Dice, Shalev, and Shavit uses a global version clock. Every transaction starts by reading the current value of the clock and storing it as the read-version. Then, on every read or write, the version of the particular memory location is compared to the read-version; and, if it's greater, the transaction is aborted.

This guarantees that the code is executed on a consistent snapshot of memory. During commit, all write locations are locked, and version numbers of all read and write locations are re-checked. Finally, the global version clock is incremented, new write values from the log are written back to memory and stamped with the new clock version.

Implementation Issues

One problem with implementing software transactional memory with optimistic reading is that it's possible for an incomplete transaction to read inconsistent state (that is, to read a mixture of old and new values written by another transaction). Such a transaction is doomed to abort if it ever tries to commit, so this does not violate the consistency condition enforced by the transactional system, but it's possible for this "temporary" inconsistent state to cause a transaction to trigger a fatal exceptional condition such as a segmentation fault or even enter an endless loop:

Provided $x=y$ initially, neither transaction above alters this invariant, but it's possible transaction A will read x before transaction B updates it but read y after transaction B updates it, causing it to enter an infinite loop. The usual strategy for dealing with this is to intercept any fatal exceptions and abort any transaction that is not valid.

One way to deal with these issues is to detect transactions that execute illegal operations or fail to terminate and abort them cleanly; another approach is the transactional locking scheme.

7

Multiprocessors

Introduction

Even to the casual observer, it is apparent that the time of multicore computing is upon us. In fact, this shift occurred several years in the past. The first general purpose CPU to feature Chip Multi-Processing (CMP) was the IBM POWER4, which debuted in 2001. Today, there is not a high performance processor family without a shipping multicore design. Even our video game consoles are shifting in that direction. The Xbox 360 feature 3-way symmetrical CMP, while the CELL processor uses up to 8 SIMD Processing Elements. With the shift towards multicore systems, it is more important than ever to understand the additional complexities of multi-processor systems over traditional uni-processor machines.

Multicore designs bring almost all the difficulties that previously belonged to high-end MP systems to our desktops, laptops and consoles. Before the shift to CMP, shared memory system design was an esoteric art. Producing high quality MP systems was so difficult that there were multimillion dollar companies, whose sole purpose was to design, build and support large CPU count systems, using commercially available MPUs.

One such example was Sequent (which was bought by IBM in 1999) and their Balance, Symmetry and NUMA-Q systems, but there were many others including Pyramid, Encore and Alliant. These companies and many others devoted their engineering resources to tackling three major problems: memory hierarchy, cache coherency and scalability. This article will cover all three topics in detail, and briefly discuss some additional considerations.

The Cache Coherency Problem

The use of caches in multiprocessor systems presents a bit of a problem. Without special precautions, it is possible for two CPUs to have different values for the same data. An example of this occurring; the ending state (circled in red) shows the problem, where CPU 1 has an old value for X in its cache (note that memory also has an old value, which is fairly common, however, caches must always have the same value).

Instruction Sequence:

CPU 0 – Load X from memory

CPU 1 – Load X from memory

CPU 0 – X = X – 1 (decrement)

CPU 0 – Store X to cache

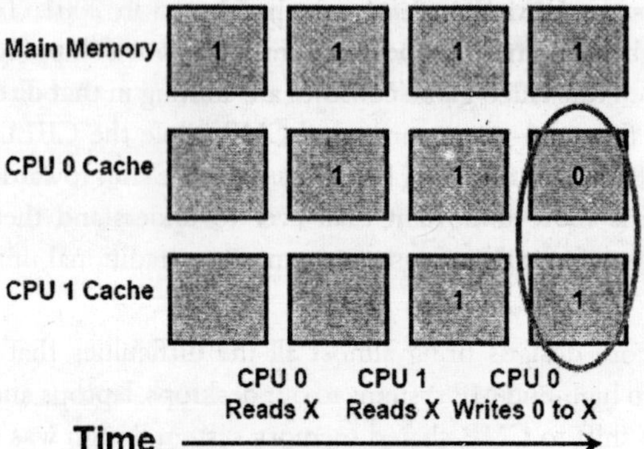

Figure : Cache Coherency

Cache Coherency Protocols, the Solution

A simple way of thinking about cache coherency is that you want to make sure time is flowing in the right direction for all the processors. The *cache coherency problem*, and the heart of the issue is ensuring that each memory address contains the same piece of data from every cache's perspective. This is a slightly informal definition, and the formal one is:

1. A write to an address in memory will eventually propogate to all of the system. This means that every processor will eventually know that changes have been made.

2. Multiple writes to an address in memory are serialized; every processor in the system sees the writes occur in the same order.

A *cache coherency protocol* is just a set of rules that the system designer chooses in order to make sure that both of these properties are observed. All coherency protocols work with cache lines as the basic data structure, and assign each cache line a sharing state which is used to manage the communication between processors. There is a lot of room for variation amongst coherency protocols, but we will try and touch on all the major design differences.

How to Handle Writes

The first and easiest decision for a system designer is how to handle writes to shared data, there are two options: write-update and write-invalidate. Write-invalidate protocols require that when a CPU writes to a cache line, the writing CPU must notify sharing CPUs (i.e. other CPUs with that cache line) that their data for that cache line is now invalid and should not be used. This entails sending out the cache line address, which is relatively short, plus a few bits to indicate that it needs to be invalidated. Under a write-update protocol, the writing CPU updates any sharing CPUs by sending out the new value for the cache line, rather than simply sending out an invalidation message, so the messages are quite a bit larger. For example, in a 4 socket system, sending out a cache line update could take 64-128B, while an invalidate message would likely take around 5-8B. These numbers depend a bit on the virtual addressing capability, cache line size, and message protocol, but a 8-25x difference is still huge. There are currently no shipping high performance server systems that use write update because the bandwidth use is far too high, consequently all further discussions assume write invalidate.

Hops Enough for All

Another key differentiator between coherency protocols is the number of logical hops or stages in a transaction. Most protocols are either two or three hops. In a three hop protocol, the different phases are: request, snoop/forward and response. When a requesting processor misses in its cache, it first sends a query to the home node. Next, the home node snoops the rest of the system and reads the requested cache line from memory. Last, the home node and all processors in the system respond to the request and send data or an acknowledgement back to the original requester. The key to note is that the requesting processor cannot actually use any data until it has received messages from all other processors in the system. In a two hop coherency protocol, the first stage is simply omitted. The requesting processor snoops the entire system and then waits for responses. In general, two hop protocols have lower latency than three hop protocols, but the latter are better suited to directories. The animations, the difference between the two. The top animation is a two hop coherency protocol, while the bottom shows a three hop protocol.

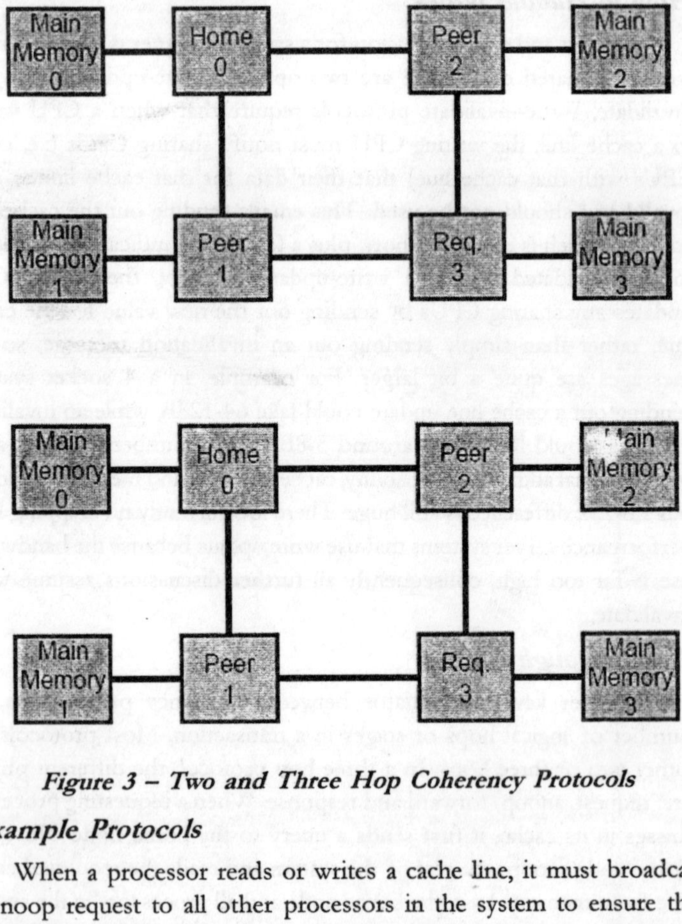

Figure 3 – Two and Three Hop Coherency Protocols

Example Protocols

When a processor reads or writes a cache line, it must broadcast a snoop request to all other processors in the system to ensure that it gets the most recent valid cache line. When a processor wishes to write to a cache line, it must first broadcast an invalidate snoop, which tells other processors to evict that cache line. In both cases, the processor must wait to receive responses from all other processors before proceeding. Since all old copies of the cache line get evicted, there is no risk of a processor mistakenly using incorrect data. The two protocols used for x86 microprocessors are MESI (Intel: x86 and IPF) and MOESI (AMD). MESI is a two hop protocol and every cache line is held in one of four states, which track meta data, such as whether the data is shared or has been modified (i.e. is dirty):

	Clean/Dirty	Write?	Unique?	Forward?	Silent Transition to	Comments
Modified	Dirty	Yes	Yes	Yes	O	Can forward without writeback
Owned	Dirty	No	No	Yes		Must writeback to transition
Exclusive	Clean	Yes	Yes	Yes	MSI	Transitions to M on write
Shared	Either	No	No	No	I	Shared can be dirty or clean
Invalid						Cannot Read

Modified	Dirty	Yes	Yes	Yes		Must writeback to forward
Exclusive	Clean	Yes	Yes	Yes	MSI	Transitions to M on write
Shared	Clean	No	No	Yes	I	Shared implies clean
Invalid						Cannot Read

Chart 1 – MOESI and MESI States

In contrast, MOESI is a three hop protocol with slightly modified states. Under MOESI, a processor can write to a line in the cache, and then put it in the O state and share the data, without writing the cache line back to memory (i.e. it allows for sharing dirty data). This can be advantageous, particularly for multi-core processors that do not share the last level of cache. For the MESI protocol, this would require an additional write back to main memory.

Scalability: Broadcast, Directories and Snoop Filters

While the choice of write update versus write invalidate is relatively straight forward, other design choices are not nearly as simple. In order to maintain correctness, different processors must communicate with each other to ensure that cache remain coherent. The simplest and fastest method is to broadcast all cache coherency messages to all processors.

Unfortunately, this is also the least scalable. Every time a processor has a cache miss, it must broadcast a snoop request and receive all the responses before it can obtain the necessary data. Since each transaction has a single transmission and a single response, broadcasting is relatively low latency. However, the cache coherency traffic is proportional to the square of the number of processors. A modern 3GHz processor might encounter 20M misses/second; which doesn't sound horrible. However, for a system with 8 processors and point to point interconnects, that could be ~240M messages/second per processor. At 32 processors, that could rise to 38,440M messages/sec per processor (in reality, these numbers would be slightly lower depending on system topology, but the scaling difficulties are clear).

Generally, broadcast is ideal for smaller systems, where the scalability isn't needed, but the low latency is beneficial. Broadcast is especially well suited for shared bus designs, since any bus transaction is automatically broadcast. One example of a snoop broadcast system is any 1-4 socket Opteron system, or older Intel based servers based with a single front-side bus.

Directory based cache coherency protocols scale much better, at the cost of slightly higher latency. In a broadcast snooping system, the meta information (sharing and dirty status, etc.) is scattered; there is no single repository for the cache coherency information. As a result, broadcasts are needed to gather all the information. By consolidating all that information into a single logical entity, the amount of bandwidth required can be cut down dramatically. A directory tracks the location and sharing status of the entire physical address space (at the cache line level). Instead of broadcasting coherency messages, the requesting processor will send a request to the directory. The directory determines which other processors have that cache line, and then forward the request only to those processors; this cuts down on coherency messages because processors which do not have the requested cache line are not disturbed. Directory size is determined by the physical address space, cache line size and number of processors. Rather than implement a single directory, which would be a substantial bottleneck, the directory is typically distributed alongside the memory in each node. Consequently, almost all directories use a three hop protocol.

One disadvantage of a directory is that they tend to increase latency. As mentioned before, three hop protocols are higher latency than the simpler two hop protocols. Moreover, in a directory protocol, the home node must look up where to send messages in the directory, which increases the latency further. Another issue is that the directory has a substantially different traffic profile than regular memory. Main memory traffic is dominated by reads; but for every memory transaction, there must be both a read (to find out which CPUs must respond) and a write (to update sharing status) to the directory. The upside is that directory based servers can scale to much larger sizes because they waste less bandwidth: the GS1280 Alpha server, using the EV7, scales up to 128 processors, while SGI's Origin and Altix servers can use 1024 processors. The difference between a coherency transaction in a broadcast (top) and directory (bottom) based system.

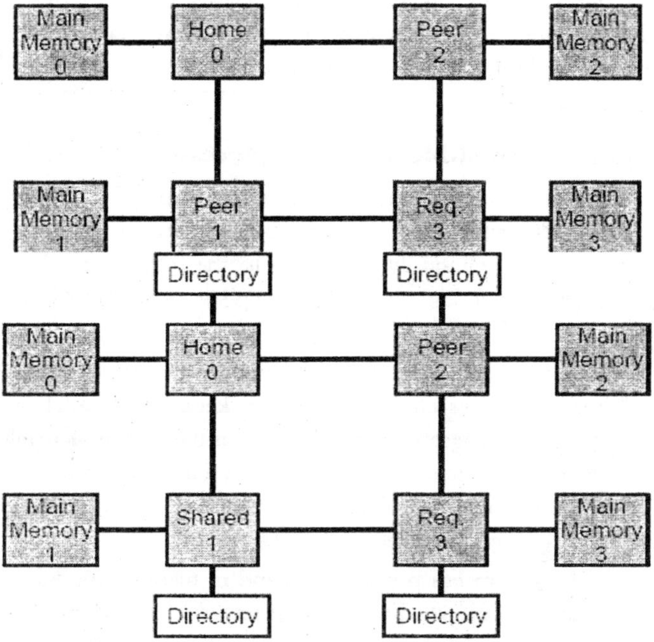

Figure 4 – Broadcast versus Directory Cache Coherency Transaction

In this hypothetical situation, CPU 1 has the cache line requested by CPU 3. The directory can take advantage of this information to avoid disturbing CPU 2 entirely. In the broadcast system, all the processors must be probed and respond to the requester (CPU 3).

There is a middle road between broadcast coherency and directory based coherency, which has become more popular recently: the snoop filter (also referred to as a sparse or partial directory). While the implementation varies, the general idea is to maintain a partial directory. Instead of tracking the entire physical address space, just track all the caches in the system, or all data shared with remote nodes. This lowers the storage requirements substantially and preserves some of the benefits of a directory. Of course, since a hit in the snoop filter isn't guaranteed, and in that case, the system falls back on broadcasting. This can lead to more unpredictable latency and bandwidth for a given transaction. Snoop filters are also slightly more flexible; they can easily be used with both two and three hop coherency protocols. Existing systems that use snoop filters include IBM's X3, the Newisys HORUS, and Intel's Blackford chipset. The Blackford chipset, as an example, contains duplicates of the tags from each processors L2 cache which are used for snoop filtering.

Analysis of Shared Memory Multiprocessors

A shared-memory multiprocessor consists of a number of processors accessing one or more shared memory modules. The processors can be physically connected to the memory modules in a variety of ways, but logically every processor is connected to every module.

We can use any of several metrics to evaluate the performance of a multiprocessor system. In order to keep the model and its implementation manageable, we will focus on the degree of parallelism among the memory modules; that is, we are interested in determining the average number of memory modules that are being accessed simultaneously. The model is as follows:

- The system has p processors and m memory modules. Each processor can send requests for access to any memory module.
- Memory module accesses are synchronized; two modules servicing access requests at the same time start and complete their accesses together. Memory accesses always take one time unit (one memory cycle).
- Processors are infinitely fast. When a processor's access request has been serviced by a memory module, the processor immediately generates a new request.
- Processors send requests with equal probability to each module. The module chosen for a new request is independent of the module chosen for any other request.
- A processor may have only one outstanding request at a time.

- A memory module may service only one request at a time. If more than one request is queued at a memory module at the beginning of a memory cycle, the module selects a request to service at random. All requests not serviced during the cycle remain queued at the module at the beginning of the next cycle.

Let B be the average number of memory modules busy servicing an access request during a memory cycle. Regardless of the number of processors and memory modules, we can implement the model as a discrete-time Markov chain in which the information contained in a state includes the number of memory modules that have requests waiting at the beginning of a memory cycle. Hence, a state also describes the number of modules that will be busy during the next memory cycle. We can find B by solving for the steady state solution of the Markov chain and computing B=Σ(Pr[state i] number of busy modules in state i) We know that the Markov chain has a steady state solution (is ergodic) since the chain will be finite and at least one state will have a self-loop. The chain is finite because the number of ways that processors' access requests can be distributed among the modules is finite. Any state that represents at least one request at each memory module will have a self-loop, since any processor that has its request satisfied during a cycle beginning in that state has a non-zero probability of sending its next access request to the same module.

As usual, we proceed in three steps. We first determine, for a given p and m, the set of all states in the Markov chain. Then, we compute the probabilities for all allowed single step state transitions. Finally, we solve the Markov chain for the steady state probabilities.

It is not possible in general to implement the model using states that only tells us how many modules are going to be busy during the next cycle. Consider, for example, a model for a system with 4 processors and 2 memory modules. A state that only tells us that two modules will be busy during the next cycle does not include enough information to tell us the probabilities of being in the various states at the beginning of the next cycle. This is because two modules will be busy during a cycle that starts with requests distributed among the modules in either of two ways:

- three requests at one module, one request at the other module
- two requests at one module, two requests at the other module.

If we start a cycle with the four requests distributed as in (1), at the end of the cycle we have two requests left at one module, no requests at the other module, and two processors ready to make new requests. The next cycle may start with the four requests distributed as in (1) or (2), or with four requests at a single module. If we start a cycle as in (2), both modules have a request waiting at the end of the cycle. The next cycle cannot begin with all four requests at a single module. We must use a definition of state that allows us to determine how the access requests that must wait during a cycle are distributed among the modules at the end of the cycle, in addition to telling us how many modules will be busy during the cycle. (1) and (2) above illustrate exactly how this is done. Each state specifies how the p requests are distributed among the modules, without regard to which module is which. It is unimportant in (1) to know which module has three requests and which has two, since the modules and processors are identical.

They may all choose to send their new requests to the same module, or each may select a different module from the others, or some may choose the same module while others select different modules. The end result will be some distribution of p requests among the m modules at the beginning of the next cycle, with each possible distribution represented by a different state.

The second part of computing state transition probabilities is to count the number of ways in which processors may choose to make new requests that will result in the same distribution of requests at the beginning of the next cycle (the same next state). Consider the following example with 4 processors and 2 memory modules, as above. Suppose the model begins one cycle with two requests at each module. At the end of the cycle, each module has one request remaining. Two processors will make new requests before the start of the next cycle. If they select the same module, the next state has three requests at one module and one request at the other. There are two ways that this can happen, since there are two modules that they can select and each of these modules has one request remaining from the previous cycle.

To put the two parts together, we compute the single step state transition probability for the transition from state A to state B by multiplying the probability of choosing any set of modules following the cycle beginning in state A by the number of ways we can choose a set of modules that takes us to state B. For the example, the probability of making the transition from the state with two requests at each module to the state with three requests at one module and one at the other is Generally, the process of computing state transition probabilities is more difficult that this example would indicate, even though the process just described always works. The difficulty will always come in the second part-counting the number of ways of choosing where new requests go that take the model to the same next state. For this reason, we recommend that you follow the above procedure to compute all single step transition probabilities for each state. Because the single step transition probabilities for a given state (including a transition back to the same state) must sum to 1, this will provide a useful check on whether or not you counted all the possibilities.

We illustrate the complete procedure with several examples. Let C(n,r) be the number of combinations of n objects taken r at a time, and P(n,r) be the number of permutations of n objects taken r at a time. In the first two examples, we find an expression for the average memory module concurrency as a function of the number of memory modules for a fixed number (2 or 3) of processors.

Symmetric Multiprocessing

In computing, symmetric multiprocessing or SMP involves a multiprocessor computer architecture where two or more identical processors can connect to a single shared main memory. Most common multiprocessor systems today use an SMP architecture. In the case of multi-core processors, the SMP architecture applies to the cores, treating them as separate processors. SMP systems allow any processor to work on any task no matter where the data for that task are located in memory; with proper operating system support, SMP systems can easily move tasks between processors to balance the workload efficiently.

Alternatives

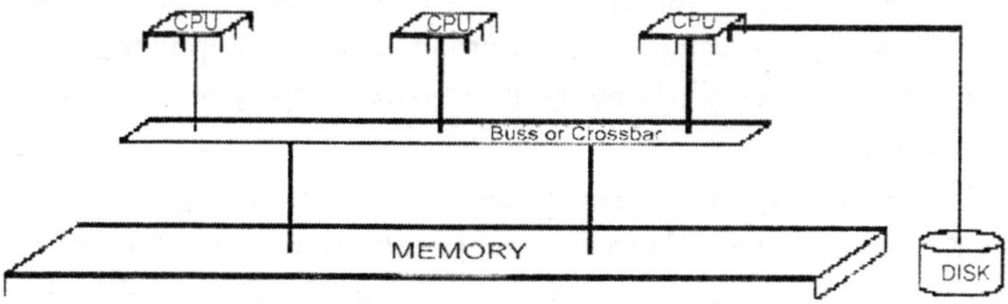

Diagram of a typical SMP system. Three processors are connected to the same memory module through a bus or crossbar switch

SMP represents one of the earliest styles of multiprocessor machine architectures, typically used for building smaller computers with up to 8 processors. Larger computer systems might use newer architectures such as NUMA (Non-Uniform Memory Access), which dedicates different memory banks to different processors. In a NUMA architecture, processors may access local memory quickly and remote memory more slowly. This can dramatically improve memory throughput as long as the data is localized to specific processes (and thus processors). On the downside, NUMA makes the cost of moving data from one processor to another, as in workload balancing, more expensive. The benefits of NUMA are limited to particular workloads, notably on servers where the data is often associated strongly with certain tasks or users.

Other systems include asymmetric multiprocessing (ASMP), which uses separate specialized processors for specific tasks (which increases complexity), and computer clustered multiprocessing (such as Beowulf), in which not all memory is available to all processors.

Examples of ASMP include many media processor chips that are a relatively slow base processor assisted by a number of hardware accelerator cores. High-powered 3D chipsets in modern videocards could be considered a form of asymmetric multiprocessing. Clustering techniques are used fairly extensively to build very large supercomputers. In this discussion a single processor is denoted as a *uni processor* (UN).

Advantages and Disadvantages

SMP has many uses in science, industry, and business which often use custom-programmed software for multithreaded (multitasked) processing. However, most consumer products such as word processors and computer games are written in such a manner that they cannot gain large benefits from concurrent systems. For games this is usually because writing a program to increase performance on SMP systems can produce a performance loss on uniprocessor systems. Recently, however, multi-core chips are becoming more common in new computers, and the balance between installed uni-and multi-core computers may change in the coming years.

The nature of the different programming methods would generally require two separate code-trees to support both uniprocessor and SMP systems with maximum performance. Programs running on SMP systems may experience a performance increase even when they have been written for uniprocessor systems. This is because hardware interrupts that usually suspend program execution while the kernel handles them can execute on an idle processor instead. The effect in most applications (e.g. games) is not so much a performance increase as the appearance that the program is running much more smoothly. In some applications, particularly compilers and some distributed computing projects, one will see an improvement by a factor of (nearly) the number of additional processors. In situations where more than one program executes at the same time, an SMP system will have considerably better performance than a uni-processor because different programs can run on different CPUs simultaneously.

Systems programmers must build support for SMP into the operating system: otherwise, the additional processors remain idle and the system functions as a uniprocessor system. In cases where an SMP environment processes many jobs, administrators often experience a loss of hardware efficiency. Software programs have been developed to schedule jobs so that the processor utilization reaches its maximum potential. Good software packages can achieve this maximum potential by scheduling each CPU separately, as well as being able to integrate multiple SMP machines and clusters.

Access to RAM is serialized; this and cache coherency issues causes performance to lag slightly behind the number of additional processors in the system.

Entry-Level Systems

Before about 2006, entry-level servers and workstations with two processors dominated the SMP market. With the introduction of dual-core devices, SMP is found in most new desktop machines and in many laptop machines. The most popular entry-level SMP systems use the x86 instruction set architecture and are based on Intel's Xeon, Pentium D, Core Duo, and Core 2 Duo based processors or AMD's Athlon64 X2, Quad FX or Opteron 200 and 2000 series processors. Servers use those processors and other readily available non-x86 processor choices including the Sun Microsystems UltraSPARC, Fujitsu SPARC64 III and later, SGI MIPS, Intel Itanium, Hewlett Packard PA-RISC, Hewlett-Packard (merged with Compaq which acquired first Digital Equipment Corporation) DEC Alpha, IBM POWER and Apple Computer PowerPC (specifically G4 and G5 series, as well as earlier PowerPC 604 and 604e series) processors. In all cases, these systems are available in uniprocessor versions as well.

Earlier SMP systems used motherboards that have two or more CPU sockets. More recently, microprocessor manufacturers introduced CPU devices with two or more processors in one device, for example, the POWER, UltraSPARC, Opteron, Athlon, Core 2, and Xeon all have multi-core variants. Athlon and Core 2 Duo multiprocessors are socket-compatible with uniprocessor variants, so an expensive dual socket motherboard is no longer needed to implement an entry-level SMP machine. It should also be noted that dual socket Opteron designs are technically ccNUMA designs, though they can be programmed as SMP for a slight loss in performance..

Mid-Level Systems

The Burroughs B5500 first implemented SMP in 1961. It was implemented later on other mainframes. Mid-level servers, using between four and eight processors, can be found using the Intel Xeon MP, AMD Opteron 800 and 8000 series and the above-mentioned UltraSPARC, SPARC64, MIPS, Itanium, PA-RISC, Alpha and POWER processors. High-end systems, with sixteen or more processors, are also available with all of the above processors.

Sequent Computer Systems built large SMP machines using Intel 80386 (and later 80486) processors. Some smaller 80486 systems existed, but the major x86 SMP market began with the Intel Pentium technology supporting up to two processors. The Intel Pentium Pro expanded SMP support with up to four processors natively. Later, the Intel Pentium II, and Intel Pentium III processors allowed dual CPU systems, except for the respective Celerons. This was followed by the Intel Pentium II Xeon and Intel Pentium III Xeon processors which could be used with up to four processors in a system natively. In 2001 AMD released their Athlon MP, or MultiProcessor CPU, together with the 760MP motherboard chipset as their first offering in the dual processor marketplace. Although several much larger systems were built, they were all limited by the physical memory addressing limitation of 64 GiB. With the introduction of 64-bit memory addressing on the AMD64 Opteron in 2003 and Intel 64 (EM64T) Xeon in 2005, systems are able to address much larger amounts of memory; their addressable limitation of 16 EiB is not expected to be reached in the foreseeable future.

Operating Systems Running on SMP Computers

- BeOS and derivatives
- BSD descendants

- DragonFly BSD
- FreeBSD
- NetBSD
- OpenBSD
- Burroughs (Unisys) MCP (1961-present)
- IBM i5/OS
- INTEGRITY
- LynxOS
- LabVIEW Real-Time Module (version 8.5 or later)
- Linux-based systems
- Mac OS (7.5.5 to 9.2.2) and Mac OS X
- Microsoft Windows NT
- OpenVMS (since VMS 5.0)
- OS/2 (since 2.11)
- OSE real-time operating system (OSE5)
- Plan 9
- QNX real-time operating system (2000-present)
- SkyOS
- Syllable
- Tandem Computers
- Guardian
- NonStop Kernel.
- T/TOS (Tandem Operating System)
- TOPS-10 Operating System for PDP-10 36-bit architecture (True SMP since version 7.01)
- UNIVAC EXEC 8 (1964-present)
- Unix-like systems such as BSD derivatives, Sun Solaris, AIX, HP-UX, IRIX, DYNIX/PTX 4.4.2
- VxWorks
- z/OS
- z/TPF
- z/VM
- z/VSE.

SMP-Capable Processors

- Advanced Micro Devices (AMD)
- Athlon MP
- Athlon 64 X2
- Turion 64 X2
- AMD Opteron
- Phenom
- Phenom II
- Azul Systems
- Vega 1
- Vega 2
- DEC Alpha
- Hewlett-Packard
- HP PA-RISC
- International Business Machines (IBM)
- AIM Apple/IBM/Motorola PowerPC 601, 604, 604e
- IBM POWER
- System z
- Inmos
- INMOS transputers: T400, T800 and T9000
- Intel
- Intel 486/DX
- Intel OverDrive Processor, Socket 7; Intel OverDrive Processor, Socket 8
- Intel Pentium Pro; Intel Pentium II; Intel Pentium III
- Intel Pentium D
- Intel Core; Intel Pentium Dual-Core; Intel Core 2
- Intel Core i7
- Intel Xeon
- Intel Itanium; Intel Itanium 2
- glueless up to four processors (max. 16 in IA-32 compatibility mode)
- Sun Microsystems
- UltraSPARC The Sparkle SPARC Derivative was multi-processor capable in 1991

- SGI/MIPS
- MIPS; MIPS64
- Razamicroelectronic
- XLR
- Tilera
- TILE64
- Cavium Networks
- Octeon-I, II Up to 32 MIPS64 cores Soc.

Multiprocessing

Multiprocessing is the use of two or more central processing units (CPUs) within a single computer system. The term also refers to the ability of a system to support more than one processor and/or the ability to allocate tasks between them. There are many variations on this basic theme, and the definition of multiprocessing can vary with context, mostly as a function of how CPUs are defined (multiple cores on one die, multiple chips in one package, multiple packages in one system unit, etc.).

Multiprocessing: sometimes refers to the execution of multiple concurrent software processes in a system as opposed to a single process at any one instant. However, the terms multitasking or multiprogramming are more appropriate to describe this concept, which is implemented mostly in software, whereas multiprocessing is more appropriate to describe the use of multiple hardware CPUs. A system can be both multiprocessing and multiprogramming, only one of the two, or neither of the two.

Types of Processor Symmetry

In a multiprocessing system, all CPUs may be equal, or some may be reserved for special purposes. A combination of hardware and operating-system software design considerations determine the symmetry (or lack thereof) in a given system. For example, hardware or software considerations may require that only one CPU respond to all hardware interrupts, whereas all other work in the system may be distributed equally among CPUs; or execution of kernel-mode code may be restricted to only one processor (either a specific processor, or only one processor at a time), whereas user-mode code may be executed in any combination of processors. Multiprocessing systems are often easier to design if such restrictions are imposed, but they tend to be less efficient than systems in which all CPUs are utilized. Systems that treat all CPUs equally are called symmetric multiprocessing (SMP) systems. In systems where all CPUs are not equal, system resources may be divided in a number of ways, including asymmetric multiprocessing (ASMP), non-uniform memory access (NUMA) multiprocessing, and clustered multiprocessing (*qq.v.*).

Instruction and data Streams

In multiprocessing, the processors can be used to execute a single sequence of instructions in multiple contexts (single-instruction, multiple-data or SIMD, often used in vector processing), multiple sequences of instructions in a single context (multiple-instruction, single-data or MISD, used for redundancy in fail-safe systems and sometimes applied to describe pipelined processors or hyper-threading), or multiple sequences of instructions in multiple contexts (multiple-instruction, multiple-data or MIMD).

Processor Coupling

Tightly-coupled multiprocessor systems contain multiple CPUs that are connected at the bus level. These CPUs may have access to a central shared memory (SMP or UMA), or may participate in a memory hierarchy with both local and shared memory (NUMA). The IBM p690 Regatta is an example of a high end SMP system. Intel Xeon processors dominated the multiprocessor market for business PCs and were the only x86 option until the release of AMD's Opteron range of processors in 2004. Both ranges of processors had their own onboard cache but provided access to shared memory; the Xeon processors via a common pipe and the Opteron processors via independent pathways to the system RAM. Chip multiprocessors, also known as multi-core computing, involves more than one processor placed on a single chip and can be thought of the most extreme form of tightly-coupled multiprocessing. Mainframe systems with multiple processors are often tightly-coupled.

Loosely-Coupled: multiprocessor systems (often referred to as clusters) are based on multiple standalone single or dual processor commodity computers interconnected via a high speed communication system (Gigabit Ethernet is common). A Linux Beowulf cluster is an example of a loosely-coupled system. Tightly-coupled systems perform better and are physically smaller than loosely-coupled systems, but have historically required greater initial investments and may depreciate rapidly; nodes in a loosely-coupled system are usually inexpensive commodity computers and can be recycled as independent machines upon retirement from the cluster. Power consumption is also a consideration. Tightly-coupled systems tend to be much more energy efficient than clusters. This is because considerable economies can be realized by designing components to work together from the beginning in tightly-coupled systems, whereas loosely-coupled systems use components that were not necessarily intended specifically for use in such systems.

Software Implementation Issues

SISD Multiprocessing

In a single instruction stream, single data stream computer one processor sequentially processes instructions, each instruction processes one data item.

SIMD Multiprocessing

In a single instruction stream, multiple data stream computer one processor handles a stream of instructions, each one of which can perform calculations in parallel on multiple data locations. SIMD multiprocessing is well suited to parallel or vector processing, in which a very large set of data can be divided into parts that are individually subjected to identical but independent operations. A single instruction stream directs the operation of multiple processing units to perform the same manipulations simultaneously on potentially large amounts of data. For certain types of computing applications, this type of architecture can produce enormous increases in performance, in terms of the elapsed time required to complete a given task. However, a drawback to this architecture is that a large part of the system falls idle when programs or system tasks are executed that cannot be divided into units that can be processed in parallel.

Additionally, programs must be carefully and specially written to take maximum advantage of the architecture, and often special optimizing compilers designed to produce code specifically for this environment must be used. Some compilers in this category provide special constructs or extensions to allow programmers to directly specify operations to be performed in parallel (*e.g.*, DO FOR ALL statements in the version of FORTRAN used on the ILLIAC IV, which was a SIMD multiprocessing supercomputer). SIMD multiprocessing finds wide use in certain domains such as computer simulation, but is of little use in general-purpose desktop and business computing environments.

MISD Multiprocessing

MISD multiprocessing offers mainly the advantage of redundancy, since multiple processing units perform the same tasks on the same data, reducing the chances of incorrect results if one of the units fails. MISD architectures may involve comparisons between processing units to detect failures. Apart from the redundant and fail-safe character of this type of multiprocessing, it has few advantages, and it is very expensive. It does not improve performance. It can be implemented in a way that is transparent to software. It is used in array processors and is implemented in fault tolerant machines.

MIMD Multiprocessing

MIMD multiprocessing architecture is suitable for a wide variety of tasks in which completely independent and parallel execution of instructions touching different sets of data can be put to productive use. For this reason, and because it is easy to implement, MIMD predominates in multiprocessing. Processing is divided into multiple threads, each with its own hardware processor state, within a single software-defined process or within multiple processes. Insofar as a system has multiple threads awaiting dispatch (either system or user threads), this architecture makes good use of hardware resources.

MIMD does raise issues of deadlock and resource contention, however, since threads may collide in their access to resources in an unpredictable way that is difficult to manage efficiently. MIMD requires special coding in the operating system of a computer but does not require application changes unless the programs themselves use multiple threads (MIMD is transparent to single-threaded programs under most operating systems, if the programs do not voluntarily relinquish control to the OS). Both system and user software may need to use software constructs such as *semaphores* (also called *locks* or *gates*) to prevent one thread from interfering with another if they should happen to cross paths in referencing the same data. This gating or locking process increases code complexity, lowers performance, and greatly increases the amount of testing required, although not usually enough to negate the advantages of multiprocessing.

Similar conflicts can arise at the hardware level between processors (cache contention and corruption, for example), and must usually be resolved in hardware, or with a combination of software and hardware (*e.g.*, cache-clear instructions).

Bibliography

Aspray, William: *John von Neumann and the Origins of Modern Computing*, Cambridge, MA, The MIT Press, 1990.

Augarten, Stan: *Bit By Bit, An Illustrated History of Computers*, New York, Ticknor & Fields, 1984.

Bass, Thomas A: *The Eudaemonic Pie*, New York, Random House, 1985.

Baran, Paul A.: *The Political Economy of Growth*, New York, Modern Reader Paperbacks, 1975.

Baumann, P. R.: *Computer Assisted Instruction Programs in Geography: Five Climate Programs*, Oneonta, New York, 1970.

Bazilevskii, Y. Y.: *The Theory of Mathematical Machines*, Pergamon Press, Macmillan Co., New York, 1963.

Berezin, I. S.; N. P. Zhidkov: *Computing Methods, Pergamon Press*, Oxford and Addison-Wesley, Reading, Mass., 1965.

Borst, Arno: *The Ordering of Time: From the Ancient Computus to the Modern Computer*, Trans. Andrew Winnard, Chicago, IL, University of Chicago Press, 1993.

Brand, Stewart: *The Media Lab: Inventing the Future at MIT*, New York: Penguin, 1987.

Burke, Colin: *Information and Secrecy, Vannevar Bush, Ultra, and the Other Memex*, Metuchen, NJ, Scarecrow Press, 1994.

Burke, Frank M., *Valuation and Valuation Planning for Closely Held Businesses*, Englewood Cliffs, NJ, Prentice Hall, 1981.

Campbell-Kelly, Martin and William Aspray: *Computer, A History of the Information Machine*, New York, Basic Books, 1996.

Caviglioni O. : *Mapwise: Accelerated Learning Through Visible Thinking*, Network Educational Press, 2000.

Chandler, Alfred D.: *The Visible Hand: The Managerial Revolution in American Business*, Cambridge, MA: The Belknap Press of Harvard University Press, 1977.

Charles R. Morris: *Computer Wars, The Fall of IBM and the Future of Global Technology*, New York, Times Books, 1993.

Copeland, Tom, Tim Koller, and Jack Murrin, *Valuation: Measuring and Managing the Value of Companies,* New York, Wiley, 1994.

Cortada, James W.: *The Computer in the United States: From Laboratory to Market, 1930-1960*, Armonk, NY: M. E. Sharpe, 1993.

Crichton, Michael: *Electronic Life, How to Think About Computers*, New York, Alfred A. Knopf, 1983.

Dasgupta, Subrata: *Creativity in Invention and Design, Computational and Cognitive Explorations of Technological Originality,* New York, Cambridge University Press, 1994.

Dertouzos, Michael L. and Joel Moses: *The Computer Age, A Twenty-Year View.*Cambridge, MA, The MIT Press, 1979.

Desmond, Glenn, and John A, Marcell, *Handbook of Small Business Valuation Formulas and Rules of Thumb,* Valuation Press, 1993.

Edward A.: *Computers and Thought*, New York: McGraw-Hill, 1963.

Edwards, Paul N: *The Closed World: Computers and the Politics of Discourse in Cold War America,* Cambridge, MA, The MIT Press, 1996.

Fishman, Katherine Davis: *The Computer Establishment,* New York: McGraw-Hill, 1981.

G. C. Tootill: *Electronic Computers*, Baltimore: Penguin Books, 1967.

Gavino Morin: *Cyberspace and the Law: Your Rights and Duties in the On-Line World*, Cambridge, MA: The MIT Press, 1994.

Goldstine, Herman H.: *The Computer, From Pascal to von Neumann.* Princeton, NJ, Princeton University Press, 1972.

Gul, F. and Pesendorfer, W.: *The Foundations of Positive and Normative Economics*, New York, Oxford University Press 2008.

Hanson, Dirk: *The New Alchemists,* Boston: Little, Brown, 1982.

Harrigan, K. R.: *Strategies for Declining Businesses.* Lexington, MA: Heath, 1980

Hawkes, Nigel: *The Computer Revolution*, New York: E.P. Dutton, 1972.

Heims, Steve J.: *The Cybernetics Group*, Cambridge, MA, The MIT Press, 1991.

Heller, Robert: *The Fate of IBM,* London, Little Brown, 1994.

Herman H.: *The Computer: From Pascal to von Neumann*, Princeton, Princeton University Press, 1972.

Hollingdale, S. H., and G. C. Tootill: *Electronic Computers*, Baltimore: Penguin Books, 1967.

Holzmann, Gerald J. and Bjorn Pehrson: *The Early History of Data Networks*, Los Alamitos, CA, IEEE Computer Society Press, 1994.

Hsu, Jeffrey: *A Comprehensive Guide to Computer Bible Study. Up-to-Date Information on the Best Software and Techniques*, Dallas: Word, 1993.

James Keller: *Public Access to the Internet*, Cambridge, MA: The MIT Press, 1995.

James R.: *The Control Revolution: Technological and Economic Origins of the Information Society*, Cambridge, MA: Harvard University Press, 1986.

Kasper, Larry J.: *Business Valuations, Advanced Topics*, Westport, CT, Quorum Books, 1997.

Katherine Davis: *The Computer Establishment*, New York: McGraw-Hill, 1981.

Kawasaki, Guy: *The Computer Curmudgeon*, Indianapolis, Hayden Books, 1992.

Kidder, Tracy: *Soul of a New Machine*, New York, Avon, 1981.

Lee, J.A.N.: *Computer Pioneers*, Los Alamitos, CA, IEEE Computer Society Press, 1994.

Levy, Steven: *Hackers, Heroes of the Computer Revolution*, New York, Dell, 1984.

Lewis, Charles: *Premises and Prospects, TCP/IP and the Internet*, B.A. Thesis, New College of the University of South Florida, 1996.

Lukoff, Herman: *From Dits to Bits: A Personal History of the Electronic Computer*, Portland, OR, Robotics Press, 1979.

Malone, Michael S.: *The Microprocessor, A Biography*, Santa Clara, CA, TELOS, 1995.

Marris, R. L., and Wood, A.: *The Corporate Economy*, London: Macmillan, 1971.

Martin and William Aspray: *Computer: A History of the Information Machine*, New York: Basic Books, 1996.

Metropolis, N., J. Howlett, and Gian Carlo Rota: *A History of Computing in the Twentieth Century, A Collection of Essays*, New York, Academic Press, 1980.

Paul N.: *The Closed World: Computers and the Politics of Discourse in Cold War America*, Cambridge, The MIT Press, 1996.

Peirson, G., Bird, R., Brown, R., & Howard, P.: *Business Finance*, Roseville, 1990

Pogue, David and Joseph Schorr: *Macworld Mac & Power Mac SECRETS*, New York, IDG Books, 1994.

Pournelle, Jerry: *The User's Guide to Small Computers*, New York, Baen, 1984.

Ranade, Jay and Alan Nash: *The Best of Bye, Two Decades on the Leading Edge*, New York, McGraw-Hill, 1994.

Robert L.: *Software Creativity*, Prentice Hall PTR, 1995.

Rodgers, William: *Think, A Biography of the Watsons and IBM*, New York, Stein and Day, 1969.

Rose, Frank: *West of Eden, The End of Innocence at Apple Computer*, New York, Penguin, 1989.

Smith, Gordon V., and Russell Parr, *Valuation of Intellectual Property and Intangible Assets*, New York: Wiley, 1994.

Stern, Nancy: *From ENIAC to UNIVAC, An Appraisal of the Eckert-Mauchly Computers*, Bedford, MA, Digital Press, 1981.

Steve J.: *The Cybernetics Group*, Cambridge, MA: The MIT Press, 1991.

Stross, Randall: *The Microsoft Way, The Real Story of How the Company Outsmarts Its Competition*, New York: Addison-Wesley, 1996.

Weibull, J. W.: *Advances in Understanding Strategic Behaviour*, New York, Palgrave, 2004.

West, Thomas L.: and Jeffrey D. Jones: *Handbook of Business Valuation*, New York: Wiley, 1992.

Zachary, G. Pascal: *Showstopper! The Breakneck Race to Creat Windows NT and the Next Generation at Microsoft*, New York, The Free Press, 1994.

R

S

T

V

Index

A

B

C